Tomorrow Will Be
A Good Day

Tomorrow Will Be A Good Day

CAPTAIN SIR TOM MOORE

MICHAEL JOSEPH

an imprint of

PENGUIN BOOKS

MICHAEL JOSEPH

UK | USA | Canada | Ireland | Australia
India | New Zealand | South Africa

Michael Joseph is part of the Penguin Random House group of companies
whose addresses can be found at global.penguinrandomhouse.com

First published 2020
010

Copyright © Captain Sir Tom Moore, 2020

The moral right of the author has been asserted

Set in 13.5/16 pt Garamond MT Std
Typeset by Couper Street Type Co.
Printed in Italy by Grafica Veneta S.p.A.

A CIP catalogue record for this book is available from the British Library

HARDBACK ISBN: 978-0-241-48610-8

www.greenpenguin.co.uk

'Tomorrow will be a good day. Tomorrow you will maybe find everything will be much better than today, even if today was all right. My today was all right and my tomorrow will certainly be better. That's the way I've always looked at life.'

Captain Sir Tom Moore, April 2020

This memoir is based on my own recollection of events, many long past. They may not always be exactly as others recall them. Any mistakes are my own.

Dedicated to all those who serve
on the front line of any battle –
be it military, psychological
or medical. I salute you.

List of Illustrations

Chapter 1
Scene from the 1918–1920 Spanish flu pandemic.

Chapter 2
Arthur Burrows read the first BBC radio news bulletin in 1922.

Chapter 3
In 1927 Charles Lindbergh became the first person to fly solo non-stop across the Atlantic.

Chapter 4
Scottish scientist Professor Alexander Fleming discovered penicillin in 1929.

Chapter 5
The Supermarine Spitfire prototype made its maiden flight in the summer of 1936.

Chapter 6
St Paul's Cathedral survives the attention of the Luftwaffe in the winter of 1940.

Chapter 7
The surprise Japanese attack on Pearl Harbor naval base in December 1941 caused the United States to join the war.

Chapter 8
The Imperial Japanese Army masses on the Burma border in 1942.

Chapter 9
The Allies finally secured victory in North Africa in 1943.

Chapter 10
6 June 1944. D-Day marked the beginning of the end of the war in Europe.

Chapter 11
War leaders Churchill, Roosevelt and Stalin meet at the Yalta Conference in February 1944.

Chapter 12
VE Day in London, May 1945.

Chapter 13
Nagasaki, 9 August 1945. Japan surrendered six days later.

Chapter 14
Minister of Health, Aneurin Bevan, visits a Manchester hospital on 5 July 1948, the day the NHS was founded.

Chapter 15
Britain's first motorway, the M1, was opened in 1959.

Chapter 16
US President John F. Kennedy addresses the crowds in West Berlin in June 1963.

Chapter 17
In 1969 Neil Armstrong and Buzz Aldrin became the first people to walk on the moon.

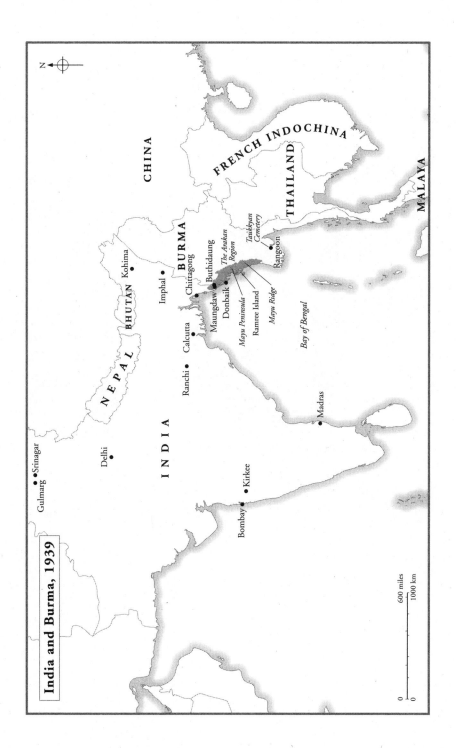

India and Burma, 1939

Prologue

I HEARD THEM LONG BEFORE I saw them, the throaty rumble of their Second World War engines reverberating in my hearing aids as I sat outside on the morning of my 100th birthday. With a blanket draped over my shoulders to protect me from the April chill and my face tilted to the sky, I spotted the valiant Hurricane first as it wheeled in from the west for my birthday fly-past. Then came the Spitfire, that gutsy little plane that captured the hearts of the nation and came to represent the British spirit.

As the aircraft came in low directly overhead, their two young pilots from RAF Coningsby's Battle of Britain Memorial Flight kindly dipped their wings at me before heading home. Raising a clenched fist, I punched the air and cheered along with everyone else, thrilled to bits by this timely reminder of all that helps make this country great. It is this very gumption that I knew would get us through the coronavirus pandemic that held us all in lockdown.

It was eighty years earlier that I saw my first Hawker Hurricane when three of them swooped low over our Yorkshire valley on the day war was declared. I was nineteen years old and I remember thinking to myself, 'So, this is what they mean by war.' I saw more Hurricanes and Spitfires later as a trainee soldier, both bravely fending off German Messerschmitts over Cornwall during the Battle of Britain. And it was Spitfires 5,000 miles away out in Burma that helped us defeat the Japanese as we rolled in to fight them with our tanks.

As the relics of those dark days disappeared behind the clouds and my special birthday fly-past was over, I turned to the film crews back in our garden in force and said, 'I can't believe all this fuss is for me, and only because I went for a little stroll.' In fact, the previous twenty-five days beggared belief, because everything that had happened had sprung from what was started as a family joke when I was recovering from a broken hip. The idea for the fundraising walk that was to change my life first came to me a few weeks after I'd returned from another routine check-up at the local doctor's surgery and – as usual – had taken the staff some chocolates to keep them going.

'You're such an inspiration, Tom,' said Clare, one of my favourite nurses, after I told her I was considering ordering a treadmill. 'I can't think of many ninety-nine-year-olds who'd be thinking about buying a running machine!'

'It's you lot who are the inspirational ones,' I countered. 'For all the patience and kindness you've shown me over the last eighteen months, for the doctors who saved the life of my son-in-law, and for those who cared so wonderfully for my late wife Pamela. I only wish I could do more.'

Clare's parting advice to keep mobile was what sparked my mini challenge two weeks later, by which time we were all under lockdown. It was Sunday, 5 April 2020, the first really sunny day of the year, and my daughter Hannah and her family, with whom I live in Bedfordshire, decided to have a barbecue. Instead of doing my exercises in my room that day, I decided to take my walker outside for the first time and try a few laps of our 25-metre driveway. In what was a typical, fun conversation, my family began to tease me.

'Keep going, Granddad,' Benjie, sixteen, called as he flipped the burgers. Georgia, eleven, laid the table and Hannah said casually, 'Let's see how many you can manage.' Her husband Colin added, 'We'll give you £1 per lap, so see if you can do a hundred by your hundredth birthday.'

I thought they were joking because I hadn't walked that far since I came out of hospital eighteen months earlier, but as I kept walking, step after step, I began to think about what they'd said. What if I did raise a bit of money and gave it to the nurses and other healthcare workers who'd looked after us over the years? Even £100 would be a nice gesture. And how much might I raise if I could manage enough laps before my 100th birthday to help them combat Covid-19? Maybe if Hannah could persuade enough people to donate then we might be able to make a small contribution towards our brave army of frontline carers to whom I owed so much. But first I had to manage one whole lap.

Two years earlier I'd have managed 1,000 laps or more, but after a silly fall in my kitchen I'd fractured my hip, broken a rib and punctured a lung, which almost did for me. I have to admit that my subsequent loss of mobility knocked my confidence and badly affected my independence. Before that I'd been fit and well – driving, mowing the lawn and managing much of the gardening myself, even using the chainsaw. In my nineties I'd travelled to India and Nepal on my own because I wanted to see Mount Everest. I flew over the summit and sent some postcards home, then came back. Life is to be lived and I've always believed that age is no barrier to living it.

Once I'd finished the first lap that Sunday and earned myself a pound, I turned my walker carefully and attempted lap number two. 'That's it,' Hannah encouraged, laughing. 'You might even make a fiver!' Secretly, I wondered if I could, but with the family egging me on, there was no way I was going to stop. They knew me well enough to accept that I'd do my best. A Yorkshireman's word is his bond. Before I knew it, though, they'd set up a fundraising page for me with a £1,000 target, contacted the local media to help drum up support for what they called my 'Walk with Tom', and left me to do the rest.

I find the events that followed hard to fathom, even now. All I did was go for a walk, but it seemed to touch a nerve. As I ticked off my laps slowly and steadily, step by step, ten each day, my modest little fundraiser went viral and my target was surpassed within twenty-four hours. Before I knew it there were journalists at the gate, TV crews in the garden, and

I was on breakfast television. As the money kept flooding in, so I kept walking. The entire adventure was so surreal and exciting that it really put a spring back in my step and I thoroughly enjoyed every second. Never in my almost 100 years on this Earth could I have imagined just how much we would go on to raise.

I am still so humbled and grateful for the love and gratitude I have received from far and wide. I'm in awe of the generosity and kindness of all those marvellous people who contributed to what started out as one old man's attempt to do his bit. It has gone far beyond my wildest expectations. I want to thank everyone from the bottom of my heart, not just for the amount we've been able to give to the NHS but for the wonderful boost you have given me and my family.

Before all this happened, I was a quiet little soul living out my days peacefully and reflecting back on my life with its long and happy marriage, two lovely daughters and four terrific grandchildren. I was preparing to mark VE Day and then VJ Day to commemorate seventy-five years since the end of World War Two, a conflict in which I'd served in India and Burma as part of what has become a largely forgotten campaign. And, of course, I was looking forward to marking my 100th birthday at a nice little party with friends and family before returning to peaceful obscurity.

After my walk, though, it seemed that everyone not only knew my name but also wanted to know much more about me. I'm now known around the world as simply 'Captain Tom'. I am thrilled that I inspired so many people to undertake their own fundraising efforts, especially the younger generation, because they are the future. Everyone keeps saying that what I did was remarkable, when it was actually what everyone did for me and for the whole country that was remarkable. It has certainly filled me with a renewed sense of purpose.

Astonishingly at my age, with the offer to write this memoir I have also been given the chance to raise even more money for the charitable foundation now established in my name. Its goals are those closest to my heart, with a mission to combat loneliness, support hospices and help those facing bereavement – all in the wake of the unprecedented crisis we found ourselves in. I am so deeply honoured to be given yet another opportunity to serve the country of which I am so very proud.

This, then, is my story.

Tom

I.

'It is wonderful what great strides can be made when there is a resolute purpose behind them.'

Winston Churchill (1874–1965)

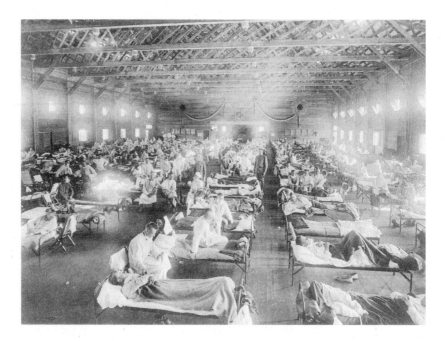

Scene from the 1918–1920 Spanish flu pandemic.

'DON'T WORRY ABOUT OUR TOM,' my eighty-one-year-old grandmother told my mother when I went off to war at the age of twenty. 'I'll be looking after him from Heaven.' True to her word, Granny Fanny was dead within a year and I like to believe that she's been looking after me ever since.

I almost gave up believing in Heaven, mind, when as a lad I watched agog while a huge hot-air balloon disappeared into the clouds above my hometown at the Annual Keighley Gala. Staring up at the summer sky, I saw the brave parachutists who'd hurled themselves from the gondola basket appear as if by magic and come floating down to earth. My delight turned to disappointment when the aeronauts were unable to report that they'd found the Heaven that I'd always been told was just 'up there'. It was the first time in my young life that I questioned my parents and realized that sometimes children are spun a pack of lies.

Aside from that unexpected revelation, however, I had an extremely happy childhood growing up on the southern slopes of Rombalds Moor, West Yorkshire, in an area widely – but usually incorrectly – known as Ilkley Moor. Also renowned as 'Brontë Country', it was a place tourists flocked to by steam train and charabanc in their thousands to see where the three Brontë sisters had lived in nearby Haworth.

Sadly, none of those talented young writers lived to see forty due to complications from tuberculosis, and their mother also died young, of cancer. In Yorkshire and probably elsewhere, people used to say the secret to old age is to choose your grandparents and then your parents, and if that's the case then I did all right.

Granny Fanny Burton was one of eight children who'd been born and raised in Keighley. At the age of twenty-six, she'd married barber John Hird and in short order they had four children, of which my mother Isabella, born in 1886, was the eldest. Grandfather John, who died of cancer at the age of fifty-two, six years before I was born, worked in the family hairdressing and shaving saloon known as W. N. Hird's in Church Street. This was a grand double-fronted establishment, and an advertising flyer from the period lists it as a hairdresser, bookseller, newsagent and general dealer, selling everything from stationery and umbrellas, to cigars and slates for schoolchildren to write on. As a young girl helping out her father in the store, my mother used to lather up the faces of customers needing a shave.

My father Wilfred Moore was born in 1885, the youngest of four children – two boys and two girls. His father Thomas, who'd been born on a sheep farm in Hawes, Wharfedale, and couldn't read or write, incorrectly registered him at birth as Wilson. When Thomas arrived at the registry office, Wilson was the only name he could remember. Thomas had fallen in love with my grandmother Hannah Whitaker, the elegant daughter of a besom maker. For those who don't know, a besom is an outdoor broom fashioned from twigs. Hannah worked happily as a maid in service at a house called Club Nook Farm near Skipton, but resided with her family in a village called Hubberholme. With no other means of transport, Thomas would walk or ride his horse ten miles there and ten miles back at weekends just to woo her.

Once they were married in Hubberholme parish church, the couple moved to Keighley where my grandfather, who'd trained as a mason in Bradford when he saw no prospect in farming, took up building work. One of his first jobs was to build a wall around the 300 acres of Cliffe Castle, a grand private home that later became a museum. This job took him four years and he was paid sixpence an hour. When it was finished the local quarry owner commissioned him to build four houses in the Parkwood area in order to use up his excess wall stones, and this eventually led to the creation of an entire residential district. Thomas's reputation and business grew and then he was approached by local baronet Sir Prince Prince-Smith who asked him to construct several shops in Cavendish Street. From this they went on to build some of the most prominent landmarks in the district, including several mills, the Town Hall, the Jubilee Tower, Strong Close Works, additions to historic Whinburn Hall, a block of stables, three schools, the Star Hotel and properties in Bradford.

Keighley was heavily involved in the manufacture of woollen textiles, with large firms concentrating on every aspect of the industry, from sorting and spinning wool to textiles, manufacturing washing machines and allied contraptions. Alongside this was a massive engineering industry with huge concerns of up to 6,000 employees creating, building and installing the complex machinery, such as the tools, looms and lathes with which to make cloth.

Thanks to my grandfather's success the family had means, so Wilfred and his three siblings received the education that he had been denied, although they were what was known as 'half-timers', with half their day spent at school and the other half in some form of employment. Having left school at fourteen, my father joined the family firm where his older brother William, known as Billy, was already employed. Thomas Moore & Sons was by then operating out of premises in Alice Street, from which shire horses pulled the heavy carts. Wanting a home that reflected his success in the town, my grandfather built a large detached house at 90 Banks Lane, Riddlesden, which was then a village on the outskirts of the town. Thomas named his new home 'Club Nook' after the farm where he'd first met my grandmother Hannah. When it was complete, the family moved from their previous home, a house called Hazelroyd on the Skipton Road. They never looked back.

With a partly castellated exterior and a small turret that carried a flagpole, Club Nook was a fine stone property that had several unusual decorative features, such as stained-glass windows, stone lintels and oak doors, all salvaged from other, grander properties that Grandfather had dismantled over the years. He'd always loved horses and owned a horse and cart for many years, until the advent of cars. It was Grandfather who'd purchased the finest shire horses for the firm's wagons and insisted they were looked after royally in an immaculately maintained stable. Such was their beauty that they were lent out to the town for the gala and other events. At Club Nook the garage for Grandfather's beloved De Dion-Bouton automobile was designed as carefully as his stables and he even had stained-glass windows installed. People said that he treated that fancy French vehicle much like he treated his horses. It was polished to within an inch of its life and was never allowed out in the rain. The family joke was that fresh water and hay had to be prepared for it each morning and at night it was bedded down in straw.

Once settled into Club Nook, Thomas built four more houses alongside it, the first next door for Uncle Billy and his wife Edith (known as Elsie), which they called Westville, and the next one along for my Aunt Jane and her husband. The others were sold and my father Wilfred, who was still single and living at home, was told that he would inherit Club Nook one day. The fourth sibling, his sister Maggie, received nothing, as she was the black sheep of the family who'd disgraced herself by eloping with a man against my grandfather's wishes and then asking for money to emigrate to America with him. Furious, Grandfather said he would pay her fare there but not back. This he did, but Maggie later returned – alone – and was never given a house. Instead she married a local joiner and was excluded from the family forever.

My father, who was always quite small in stature and an innately artistic person, loved animals, flowers and nature, history and craftsmanship. Despite being just over five feet tall he took up photography at an early age, using a heavy and cumbersome camera to take pictures of the town and its people, and – later – his prized hens and dahlias (for which he won all kinds of trophies). He had hopes of becoming a professional photographer one day, but at the age of twenty-one he caught a mystery virus that left him deaf in both ears. In an era when medicine was far less advanced than it is today, he was never told what exactly had caused his disability, only that nothing could be done about it. This news would have been bad enough, but he then realized that his debilitating condition would make a photographic career – in fact, any career – impossible, so he had no choice but to remain in the family building trade, constantly deferring to his relatives who could hear.

In his unexpectedly silent world, my father developed some skill as a lip reader, but this was entirely self-taught and very rudimentary, as there were no national associations for the deaf and very little help from the medical sector. Deaf people in the early 1900s were often seen as 'defective' or inferior, outcasts from normal society. There were even suggestions that they should never marry for fear they'd pass it on. Without any access to sign language, which wasn't widely taught or even encouraged, he was only able to understand if someone shouted into one ear. This rendered all normal conversation impossible, denied him access to music or bird-song, and must have left him feeling very isolated.

The saving grace of Father's disability was that it protected him from the horrors of the Great War, which he would otherwise have been expected to endure. The 1914–18 conflict with Germany that started when he was twenty-nine sparked a mass wave of patriotism across the land and thousands volunteered for Lord Kitchener's 'battalions of pals' in which friends, neighbours and relatives were encouraged to serve together so that they could support each other on the battlefield. Joining in groups became especially popular in the northern towns, where entire streets signed up, most of the men dying together in the brutal four-year conflict that claimed the lives of 10 million soldiers.

Whole neighbourhoods were wiped out, leaving streets full of widows. Almost all of the 2,000 'Bradford Pals' and 750 of the 900 'Leeds Pals' – part of the West Yorkshire Regiment – died in a single hour on the Somme as they walked together into a hail of German bullets. Two hundred and sixty-nine young men from Keighley were lost in one year alone, and all 900 who were dead by the war's end were commemorated on the imposing stone memorial that my grandfather's company built and which still dominates Town Hall Square.

The other men in the Moore family were also spared the trenches, my grandfather Thomas for being over the age limit at sixty-three, and Uncle Billy, then thirty-three, for reasons I never knew. My mother Isabella would have been very relieved that Father was safe, as were her three brothers, Arthur, Thomas and Harry, who worked in munitions, two of them on airships in Cumbria and at Cardington in Bedfordshire and the third at the Woolwich Arsenal.

A headmistress at a little local school, Isabella Hird was even shorter than my father, standing at less than five feet, but she'd set her cap at my father early on and was determined to make him her own. They made a good match physically and had courted a little but then had a falling-out. Knowing his route home from work, she waited for him on the corner of High Street and Low Street, peering through the glass in a shop window so that she could step out and surprise him, as if by chance. Her ploy worked and they were married on 26 April 1916, in a church in Oakworth. At thirty, she was an age that many in those days would have considered made her an 'old maid', but I always thought it was brave of her to marry a deaf man, and she was right to pursue him, for they were very happy throughout their forty-nine-year marriage.

The newlyweds moved to 14 Cark Road, Keighley, a two-up two-down terraced house with a third bedroom in the attic and a good-sized cellar. The front was quite smart but the back sloped down to Flasby Street via a *ginnel*, a northern word for an alley between buildings. Next to the back door was a round hole through which the coal was delivered and poured. My sister Freda was born at home in 1917 shortly before the global Spanish flu pandemic that killed millions, including more than 220,000 in Britain. The deadliest pandemic in history came in four separate waves – two in 1918, one in 1919, and the final one in the spring of 1920. As a baby, Freda would have been especially vulnerable throughout that period and, towards the end, my mother was pregnant with me.

Fortunately, none of my family was directly affected, but the horror of it was impossible to avoid. At Raikeswood Prisoner of War Camp nine miles away in Skipton, where almost 700 German soldiers were held after the Great War, the virus quickly took hold. Several guards died and hundreds of prisoners were infected. In 1919 ninety of them were brought to the Fever Hospital at Morton Banks in Riddlesden where forty-seven died. They were buried with full military honours in Morton cemetery.

I came along on 30 April 1920, a few months after the virus burned itself out. It was a year and a half since the war ended and the very day the British government under Prime Minister David Lloyd George ended military conscription. Like Freda, I was also born at home and Granny Fanny would have assisted, as midwives cost money, were few and far between, and had only recently been officially certified. Fortunately for everyone concerned, mine was not a troublesome birth and I caused my mother very little bother. In the year of my birth George V was on the throne, Winston Churchill was War Secretary, Rupert Bear was born in a cartoon featured in the broadsheet *Daily Express*, and the suffragette Sylvia Pankhurst was jailed for six months for campaigning for women's right to vote – something that wouldn't happen for another eight years. My arrival in the world was just one among 1.1 million live births in the country that year, the highest number since records began. It was also an important year for the Duke of

York who met Elizabeth Bowes-Lyon, a lady who was to become our country's beloved Queen Mother.

I lived in Cark Road with my parents and Freda for the first eleven years of my life and was very happy there. There was no electricity but we had candles and some lighting by gas, the smoky smell of which can still take me straight back to my youth. In my small bedroom at the back of the house and below Freda's attic room there was a gas bracket with a naked flame, while downstairs in the kitchen – the main room of the house – we had incandescent mantles, which were unusual for the time.

Our house was relatively modern compared to many in town. It had a kitchen-cum-living room with a large built-in coal-fired range and a separate gas oven at the top of the cellar stairs. The washing was done down in the cellar in the 'set pot' or furnace pan. This heavy iron bowl was proudly made by The Rustless Iron Company (Trico) of Keighley, who sold them in their millions around the world. The range heated all the water for the house via a back boiler and this could be drawn off through taps in our bathroom, which had a proper bath for our weekly hot wash on a Friday night. Every house on our street also had an inside flush toilet, which was quite unusual as a lot of the poorer properties near the gas works still had blocks of shared outside privies. The tenants there used to wear heavy clothes to bed so that they wouldn't get too cold when they had to go out to use the lav at night.

Like most women of the era, my mother operated to a strict regime and Monday was washday, which was always a nuisance if it was raining and the washing couldn't dry. Mrs Maskell, our home help, would arrive first thing to fill the set pot with water and light the gas fire underneath. Then she and Mother – sometimes helped by Freda and Aunt Jane – would get to the washing. Once it was done one of them would scoop the dirty water out of the set pot with the 'ladle' – a wooden tankard with a handle. The washing would then be hung out to dry if the weather was fine, or draped over a clothes rack made of long wooden poles hauled to the ceiling by a rope and pulley system. There was a mangle with wooden rollers to squeeze the water out of the clean washing and one day when I wasn't home Freda caught the forefinger of her right hand in it, which had the effect of crushing it. By all accounts, she screamed and screamed, and it must have been extremely painful. As a largely unsympathetic little brother, however, I was more fascinated by the fact that it left her finger hooked like a little parrot's beak for the rest of her life.

Tuesday was ironing day, Wednesday was market day (my favourite), Thursday was baking, and Friday cleaning. Like all good Yorkshire housewives, Mother's front step was scrupulously scrubbed as this indicated that she was a good, clean woman. When I was five, my mother's weekly routine was upended for a while because she became pregnant, and one day she went into hospital to have the baby. Sadly, she came home empty-handed. It was never talked about other than that my infant sister's name was Wendy and she'd been christened. I didn't realize the significance of her absence or how sad my parents must have been until a lot later.

Not long afterwards it was my turn to go into hospital when I developed a high temperature. Our GP, Dr Chalmers, diagnosed scarlet fever and I was taken to the Fever Hospital at Morton Banks where the German POWs had died of Spanish flu after the Great War. My father was a kind man but we weren't allowed to be ill and he wasn't impressed. Generally speaking, if we were struck down with anything, then a bottle of medicine was bought from the chemist or doctor. When it was finished, we were better – no arguments. If we had a cold we were given a wine glass full of the bitter and clear Fennings Fever Mixture – 'The Family Medicine' and it was so foul that we'd decide to recover quickly, which I expect was the point.

Scarlet fever, a virulent bacterial infection, was a bit more complicated than anything Fennings could cure. It was also highly contagious and there were several other children on my ward suffering from it. When my parents came to visit they could only wave at me through a window. I'll never forget my dear mother's brave smile of encouragement. She needn't have worried as I was well looked after by the nurses, but I wasn't allowed home until my skin was dry and the scabs on my rash had cleared up.

Scarlet fever sometimes killed people, but it didn't affect me long-term and I was soon back home and running around as usual. Mrs Maskell used to say to my mother, '*Yr Tom tows a sel wi lakin*', which was Yorkshire/Irish for, 'Your Tom tires himself out with playing.' And play I did, although I rarely remember being tired. I was active then and active all my life, and it would clearly take more than a little fever to carry me off.

2.

'*I avoid looking forward or backward,
and try to keep looking upward.*'

Charlotte Brontë (1816–55)

Arthur Burrows read the first
BBC radio news bulletin in 1922.

IN THE SUMMER OF 1925 I witnessed something of a momentous event – my father bought his first car, a maroon Rover 8. It was a four-seater, eight-horsepower vehicle, built in Birmingham, with just one door and a hood. The cost was around £130, equivalent to many thousands of pounds now, but to me it was priceless.

The door was on the passenger side because of the spare wheel, and the windscreen wiper had to be operated by hand. There were no windows in the back, but my sister and I had little curtains to pull across if it became too windy. My parents had raised me never to gloat but I was secretly a little bit proud of the fact that ours was the first car in our road, although the man next door had a motorbike with a double sidecar for his wife and daughter.

Unusually, my father taught Mother how to drive when the general feeling was that women shouldn't. She proved to be a better driver than he was, but if we were caught out during the terrible winter fogs, when the coal smoke from the factories made it impossible to see your hand in front of your face, it would still be Mother who'd get out and walk slowly in front of the car. In fairness to my father, it was a considerable advantage that she could hear another vehicle approaching. Once Father had that car our lives changed for the better, because instead of remaining relatively local, or as far as we could walk or cycle, we travelled further afield. There were day trips up on to the moors, visits to Haworth and Bolton Abbey and, most Sundays, we went to Whitby on the east coast – a journey of about ninety miles each way in a vehicle with a maximum speed of 40 mph.

At the beginning of each trip Father gave me the map and asked me to navigate, which was nerve-wracking until I got the hang of it. He or Mother would only go where I told them (yelling into his ear if he was driving) and he'd constantly ask me and Freda questions along the way like, 'What river are we crossing now? What's the name of that mountain?' If I didn't know the answer I was in trouble. He wanted to make sure that I was competent with a map because navigational prowess wasn't common at all. Not many people travelled far from home and even fewer had cars. It was a skill that I never lost and one that proved vital to me later.

We'd usually stop halfway for a picnic lunch at Sutton Bank, part of the Hambleton Hills, which offered spectacular views over the Vale of York all the way across to the White Horse at Kilburn, a huge figure cut into the sandstone by a schoolmaster and a team of volunteers in the 1850s. At a gradient of about 1:4, Sutton Bank was so steep that many cars weren't able to make it or could only go up in reverse. Sometimes my mother, sister and I would have to get out and walk, but it was always worth the climb. Once we reached the coast we'd make our way to the beach at Sandsend where Father would hire deck chairs for the day and he and Mother would settle down with a Thermos flask of tea and a rug over their knees.

Freda and I would put on our knitted swimsuits to swim and *lake* or play all afternoon. A word to the wise, woollen swimwear sags woefully once wet. If it was very hot, Father would roll up his trousers to paddle and – in an act of great ceremony – unbutton his stiff white collar, something he only ever did on holiday. Mother, too, would paddle, but the pair would never swim. Instead, they'd watch us playing happily and treat us to ice creams. Freda and I loved it there. If we weren't swimming we would hunt for crabs or little fishes in the shallows left in the sand. But our greatest delight was to search for pieces of the local black gemstone called lignite, and better known as jet, to take home and polish. Those were innocent, happy days indeed.

All thoughts of beaches and swimming and jet had to be forgotten when I went to school because, from the age of five, I attended the fee-paying Drake and Tonson junior school in Temple Street, Keighley, cycling the one and a half miles to and fro to take my place behind a little wooden desk.

A good little boy who learned to read and write well enough – using sharpened HB pencils and paper and not slates, like my predecessors – I never misbehaved or was sent to see the Scottish headmistress, Mrs Kirk. Instead, I did as I was told in my class of about twenty, chiefly because of our very kind teacher Miss Ruth Moffitt who was in her twenties and wore 'kiss curls' in her hair. There are a couple of photographs of me in school pageants beating a drum and blowing a trumpet and, although I look a bit miserable, I remember it as a happy time.

Freda attended the same school but was in a class above me along with a lad called Denis Healey, who'd moved to the area with his family and later became Chancellor of the Exchequer and then a lord. He was pleasant enough and his father was principal of the local technical college, but his mother was one of the nicest ladies you could ever meet. She was what we would have called 'a treasure' and she often invited Mother and us for afternoon tea at her house, which was unusual. Everybody loved Mrs Healey for her kind and open disposition.

School was fine but the lunches weren't a patch on my mother's fare, so I usually came home for them. She was a very good cook and an excellent baker, and the one who taught me all I know in the kitchen. Her Victoria sponge was outstanding and her moist ginger parkin the best I ever tasted. Even later, during periods of rationing once war broke out, we never starved. Although my father was progressive for the era and of the belief that women should get a fair deal, Mother was still expected to provide three meals a day. I never had the sense that she resented her role, though, or missed being a headmistress. Having married late, she'd found the perfect mate with never a cross word between them – mainly because she knew to keep her mouth shut. And she looked after us all very well indeed.

For breakfast (pronounced *brake-fust*) we had porridge and bread, then there was a meal of meat and potatoes at 'dinner time' – twelve o'clock sharp – that had to be on the table ready for when my father walked home for lunch. There was a hot supper in the evening, and a roast of beef or lamb every weekend. Granny Fanny, who'd always seemed old to me, usually joined us for that. Oftentimes, Mother would take us the mile to my grandmother's house in Queen's Road, Ingrow, by tram (which we called a 'tracker'). I didn't mind the noisy, rattling carriages that offered a special reduced rate before 8 a.m. for factory workers, but what fascinated me most was the conductor, in his peaked cap and uniform, a leather bag for tickets and change strapped across his body. At the end of the line he would step out and, using a very long pole with a hook, he'd unhitch the tram wheel from the overhead cable and connect it to the opposite one so that the tram could return to Keighley. It was a delicate operation but, with all the passengers watching, he never missed it once.

Granny Fanny's house was little more than a one-up one-down – a tiny property periodically shared with my mother's favourite brother, Arthur. It had no garden and an outside privy. I loved going there because Granny Fanny was such a kind, sweet woman who saw the good in everybody, no matter how badly they might treat her. She was the most Christian person I had ever met and a devout churchgoer at what was known as a 'Primitive' Methodist church, just as her late husband John had been. Although she didn't have any sweets, she used to feed me sugar lumps, something that would be frowned upon today. She was also a wonderful cook – not the kind who used weighing scales, mind. She made the best rice pudding and always in a large enamel dish, the same one she used for her traditional Yorkshire pudding.

Fanny wrote all her recipes beautifully by hand into a little book which my mother inherited and which I still possess. Aside from my favourite, her oatmeal biscuits*, which I became quite proficient at with her guidance, the book includes dishes

---

*   **Oatmeal biscuits**

   Cook in the oven at 180°C for 15 minutes. You can use butter instead of lard.

6 oz of oatmeal	2 teaspoons baking powder
6 oz of flour	1 egg
4 oz of sugar	¼ teaspoon carbonated soda
3 oz of lard	a pinch of salt

Mix ingredients into paste. Roll out very thin. Cut into shape and bake.

like roast ox tongue and boiled tripe, jugged hare or rabbit pie. In the days when people ate every part of the animal, including the 'lights' (lungs), brains, liver, kidneys and heart, there was one recipe for something called French soup that involved boiling an entire sheep's head. We never had that but I'm not sure I'd like it, as I've never been one for offal. The book also explained how to make every kind of lotion and potion for ailments from lumbago (lower back pain) to gout, because people were minded to take care of their own health. Free healthcare to the masses was a long way off and if you went to see a doctor or called one out then you had to pay.

I remember once being on my bicycle in Bingley when my wheels got caught in the tramlines. I fell off and cut my cheek quite badly and someone helped me back on my bike, whereupon I cycled the four miles home, dripping blood. My mother took me to Dr Chalmers who stitched up the wound. I can't recall how much it cost but it was probably £1. I was lucky that we could afford it as many people couldn't and would either have to patch themselves up or find a poorhouse somewhere run by an ex-nurse.

If I wasn't at school or it was the holidays then my favourite day of the week was always market day. Keighley had an open-air market in the High Street every Wednesday morning and Freda and I would happily go with Mother to help her with the shopping. The market was always buzzing with noise as people arrived from far and wide, on foot, by bike or in a pony and trap. The stallholders called out the prices for their wares, which were laid out on trestles resting on barrels, and the women of Keighley, all in hats, would parade up and down beneath the awnings, deciding which fruiterer to patronize or which cheesemonger to buy from, as they chatted to friends and neighbours. All the while, around the fringes of the market there would often be the poorer children of the town, watching and waiting hollow-eyed for a stray apple or a dropped loaf.

I have always adored butter, and this was kept in round, insulated tubs two foot high. There was a choice of several different types so samples would be handed out on the end of a wooden lollypop stick – salted, unsalted, farm butter or 'foreign'. Once Mother had chosen the one she wanted, the woman at the stall would scoop it out and then pat it into a little square with special wooden butter pats before wrapping it in greaseproof paper to go in Mother's basket. Flour, sugar and every kind of dried bean and pea were kept in big sacks and scooped up into paper carriers whose bottoms fell out if they got wet when we carried them home (Freda would be the first to laugh if the bottom fell out of mine). The brown peas Mother used in stews came in a more durable cardboard tube so I was always happy to carry those. There was also sago and tapioca, duck and hens' eggs and plenty of fresh vegetables, but only ever local and in season. We'd never heard of things like bananas or pasta, and meat and fish would only be bought from the butcher's and the fishmonger's and never a stall, as there was no refrigeration. My favourite store was called Home and Colonial, which sold tea and general groceries and was a bit like a modern-day department store. And I also liked the hardware store Gott & Butterfield where one could buy anything from a fireplace to a box of matches.

On special occasions and only ever on a Saturday, Mother would put on her best hat and take us to Lingard's on the corner of Kirkgate and Westgate in Bradford, the grandest store I had ever seen. The feature that fascinated me most there was the overhead cash transport system whereby the petty cashier – who sat in a central booth – would screw money into a canister and then pull on a cord that would zip it along the ceiling via a series of pulleys. It was received by somebody high up, physically and figuratively, who'd count the money and send back the change. Other shops had a vacuum-type system that worked in a similar fashion, and as all things mechanical fascinated me I could have played with these little cash railways all day.

From the age of about eight, most of my playtime at home involved a dog, the first of which was Pat, a young Golden Cocker that nobody else wanted because he had a deformed paw and walked with a limp. Father's brother, my Uncle Billy, heard about this little runt and brought him to me as a gift, telling me, 'Every boy should have a dog.' Pat was still tiny and too small to do much with when Freda took him out one day and he darted out in front of a lorry at the bottom of Barr Lane and was crushed. She was even more upset than I was and blamed herself for killing 'our Tom's dog'.

When Uncle Billy heard what had happened he brought me an older Cocker from the same breeder; another spare nobody wanted. I named him Billy and he was a super dog who slept in the kitchen and would come out on the moors with me for hours on end, rain or shine. I'd leave after my bowl of porridge and be home in time for my tea and no one would even worry. On a normal hike I wouldn't see anyone aside from a few hardy souls, so Billy and I would walk and walk on our own, exploring every beck and crag, peering into every barn and rummaging around every ruined farmhouse. He'd sit patiently while I collected sticklebacks or frogspawn in a jam jar with a piece of string tied around it for a handle.

I can't say Mother was always pleased with what we brought home but she put up with it.

The rolling, sheep-dotted countryside that had inspired novels like *Wuthering Heights* and *The Tenant of Wildfell Hall* was endlessly entertaining to a boy and his dog, not least because it constantly changed with the seasons. There was thick ice and deep snow in the winter, when the Rivers Tarn or Aire would freeze over, whereupon I'd strap on wooden ice skates and take a spin (and usually a tumble) along with Freda and dozens of others. Spring in the Dales brought a mass of wildflowers like primroses, bluebells, cowslips, buttercups and daffodils. I'd always pick bluebells to take home to Mother, and Freda and I would go picking basketfuls of daffodils with her to fill every vase in our house with their unique scent. Then in summer there would be blazes of heather and gorse and there'd be rowboats on the river or we'd swim in the canal. In autumn there would be a rich carpet of fallen leaves, bracken and lichen before winter set in again, with its blizzards and thick fogs that killed hundreds from bronchitis.

I knew my way around well enough so I never once got lost or into any trouble. Since childhood, I'd learned how to read the landscape, assess the weather and note the landmarks. As a country boy, I only ever needed to go somewhere once and I'd remember it forever. That innate skill remained with me my whole life and was so natural to me that I could never understand people who didn't possess it. I could tell north at night by finding the Pole Star, and in the daytime I'd look to see which side of the trees the moss grew on, knowing that south would be smooth. I could smell rain and snow on the air and knew from a change in the wind direction if it was headed my way. I often carried a pair of binoculars and would look for curlews and other wild creatures. Even in driving wind and rain, Billy and I would carry on and I never seemed to catch a cold. Poor weather was no deterrent at all. He didn't care any more than I did – he was just happy in my company.

He only had one fault – he'd snarl at everyone, even me, once you gave him his bowl of food. Nobody could take that off him and he'd lift his lip if anyone came near. Despite that trait, he was my best friend and I never felt I needed anybody other than him and my family. Perhaps thinking I was too self-contained, Mother insisted that I join the choir at St Peter's Church in Halifax Road because the choirmaster was teaching Freda the piano and suggested I should take up singing. This was my parents' Church of England place of worship, while Granny Fanny was devoted to the Alice Street Methodist Chapel. To please everyone, I went to both churches and enjoyed a bit of everything. The choirmaster at St Peter's informed me that I could sing for him until my voice broke, which it eventually did, but I can't have been terrible because I sang a few solos and he entered me for a singing contest – even though I didn't get a mention.

My sister Freda and I got along all right most of the time, but she had her own friends and dolls to play with and I was probably the annoying younger brother who got in the way. We were always much better out of doors or on holidays together, playing by the river or with animals, with never a cross word spoken. There's one happy photograph my father took of us feeding a tethered goat in the summer of 1926 up at Coxwold near Thirsk, with his lovely old Rover car in the background. I'm in a straw hat and she's in her school boater and summer uniform with her initials embroidered on her pale dress. That was the best of us. It was different once we were confined to the house, where she teased me rotten and often made me do chores and the like. This usually meant carrying heavy things for her or Mother, shelling peas, cleaning out the grate, bringing in the coal or laying the fire – all things I didn't want to do.

The one fire we had in the house was in the parlour, which was only used for visitors. This room had the best furniture with white antimacassars draped over the backs of the chairs to protect the upholstery from the Macassar oil used universally as a 'pomade' on men's hair. Nobody knows what that is these days, and Brylcreem largely replaced it. At Christmas we would decorate the parlour with a small tree and paper chains and Father would play the piano as everyone stood around and sang. Even though he couldn't hear the music and could only feel the vibrations, I was amazed how good a 'plonker' he was on the keys, reading the score as he'd been taught as a child and playing his favourite song, 'In the Garden with Angeline'. It was when the music stopped that he found it more difficult, because normal socializing wasn't possible and one of us would always have to sit by his side to translate. This would often be me as Mother was being the hostess and Freda was busy pretending to be a lady or needling me about something.

Whenever I complained to my mother about Freda, her reply was, 'Never mind. Your time will come,' making it perfectly clear – with a smile – that there was no help coming my way. She and Freda were very close, the way mothers and daughters often are, and because they did most of the domestic chores together. I was also close to my mother, who was a kind and lovely lady and someone I could talk to quite easily. My relationship with my father was quite different, however. I loved him dearly and he was a great guy and always a good friend to me, but because he was so deaf I was never able to have the kinds of conversations most boys had with their fathers. I used to see other sons chatting away to their fathers and think, 'You are so lucky.' The fact that I never could saddens me still. It was frustrating and tiring that he could only understand me if I shouted in his ear, which meant all conversations were kept to the bare minimum, plus he wouldn't say much in return if it meant that I'd have to respond. My mother, who was as bright as a button, would chatter away to Father all the time as if he could hear every word, although I think he mostly nodded and smiled in response like he did at family gatherings.

His deafness precluded them from going to most normal social engagements together, although they always went to watch her brother, my Uncle Arthur, in one of his many local Gilbert and Sullivan productions, which my father enjoyed for the spectacle. In spite of all these difficulties, he and Mother had a lovely relationship and he was very lucky to have her as a wife and the mother to his children. They both loved gardening and spent a lot of time outside together, teasing each other a fair bit. One of the things he used to say about her – repeatedly – and which always made him chuckle was that she was so small that she'd have made a good jockey.

Although he was working full-time, my father involved me whenever he could in the company and always took me to be his ears at the auction sales he attended to buy parts and vehicles. I'd listen to the bidding and place his for him when he was ready. As a treat, he'd take me – never Freda – to the picture house with him, so it was something that was special just for us. I loved being there with him and would have watched anything at all just to be in his company and I believe he felt the same, but I also knew that the silent movies were a godsend for him because they had subtitles. He wasn't at all happy when talking pictures came in and I didn't like them either, as the sound was often scratchy and muffled to begin with. A few of the stars I'd always imagined with deep, masculine voices spoke very differently with high, girlish tones or with unexpected accents and not at all as I'd thought. 'Talkies' were the death knell for many actors for exactly that reason.

There were five cinemas in Keighley and we sometimes went to the Picture House or the Regent, but the Cosy Corner was the one we liked best. We could walk there and rarely took the tram. The cinema was quite a low-grade theatre with wooden benches at the front, known as the penny seats. As soon as the doors opened, people would race to get to them and that stampede became known as 'the tuppenny rush'. Father and I sat in proper seats a bit further back but it was still very basic. Our favourite films were the Westerns with heroic cowboys played by actors like Buck Jones and Tom Mix, battling it out with the Red Indians as an enthusiastic lady pianist at the front plonked away, playing rousing music for all the fight scenes – something my father was often lucky enough not to have to endure.

Just when things looked desperate for the hero, the film would stop and the words we hated to see would flash up . . . *To be continued next week!* That was agonizing, as we had to wait what seemed like ages to find out if the baddie had won. There was never anything to eat or drink in the picture house, not even ice cream in those days. If we wanted ice cream we'd buy it in town from an Italian with a two-wheeled handcart, although there was only ever one flavour – vanilla – served in a wafer sandwich or a cone for twopence or fourpence, depending on the size, and once the vendor sold out he would have to go home and make some more.

Whenever I was out with Father and people saw me shouting into his ear to translate what others were saying, the majority were sympathetic and patient or, better still, showed no reaction at all. There were, however, a few lowborn types who used to snigger or call out, 'Deaf old fool.' This always made me very sad and I resented their comments deeply to begin with. After a time, I realized that my Father never heard them and that if I responded in any way, then he would find out what had been said. It didn't happen frequently but, whenever it did after that, I bit my tongue and pretended that I, too, hadn't heard their insults.

Granny Fanny often used to cite the old adage, '*Sticks and stones may break my bones, but words will never hurt me*,' and I tried to remember that in those moments. I'd been raised to be kind and compassionate to all so, after a time, I trained myself to feel only pity for the poor souls who had nothing better to do than tease the afflicted.

3.

'If life were predictable it would cease
to be life, and be without flavor.'

Eleanor Roosevelt (1884–1962)

In 1927 Charles Lindbergh became the first person
to fly solo non-stop across the Atlantic.

I DON'T THINK I WAS A spoiled child in the material sense, but I was spoiled with love from every member of my family, apart perhaps from my cold and aloof Grandmother Hannah, and even she probably loved me in her own strange way.

I knew that my father was delighted to have a son and, although he was a man of his era with rules to be upheld, he treated me very nicely and every week he gave me six-pence for pocket money to spend on whatever I liked. Usually, this would be squandered in the sweet shop on liq-uorice dips in sherbet and gobstoppers with the aniseed ball in the middle. Or I might buy a roast potato from Spud Mick who sold them off the back of a cart in town. He was one of the so-called 'characters' of Keighley, often described locally as 'simpletons' or 'not right up top'. Others like him included 'Emily Matchbox' who sold matches, and 'Freddie Gramophone' who had a wind-up gramophone that he played in the street. These people largely had to fend for themselves and the lack of care or consideration shown to them seems shocking now.

Anyone with a hint of a mental health issue would be threatened with a trip to the local asylum at Menston near Guiseley in Wharfedale. All someone had to say was, 'Do you want to go to Menston?' and that would be enough to put the fear of God into them. Menston was our bogeyman, one of those large Gothic establishments built in the late 1880s designed to lock up the mentally ill and keep them away from the public. Initially called the West Riding Pauper Lunatic Asylum, it was entirely self-sufficient with its own agricultural land, gardens, water supply and even its own dedicated railway. In the years before mental illness was considered treatable, poorly inmates would be given electric shock therapy, often without anaesthetic, and there were later reports that some were restrained and locked in their rooms until they died. Needless to say, it was somewhere I never ventured near.

Father's own sanity in the face of his social isolation was, I believe, saved by his love of plants and of animals. Before I was born he and my Uncle Billy were known around the world as 'Messrs Moore Brothers', breeders of rare hens such as prize-winning Partridge Wyandottes and Plymouth Rocks, as well as Cochins and Buff Orpingtons, some of which fetched as much as £30 each – the price of a horse.

Poultry breeding, rearing and showing was a major sport in the north of England during the early years of the twentieth century leading up to the Great War. There were many local societies and the *Keighley News* ran a weekly Poultry Breeding column for years, in which my father and uncle regularly featured. The largest one-day show in our region was at Bingley, where they usually walked away with the cup, much to the delight of Grandfather Thomas, who was also a keen poultry 'fancier'.

They also travelled to shows all over the country to show their birds and in a 1904 edition of *Poultry* magazine their twenty-acre poultry farm in Lawkholme Lane was described as 'a famous exhibition farm'. The four-page article added:

*Messrs Moore Brothers were little known in the Fancy three years ago,
yet today their name is famous and highly respected wherever fanciers do
congregate in these islands, in America, in the Colonies or on the Continent. Will and Wilfred Moore are the sons of Mr Thomas Moore, a
well-known and much-respected citizen of Keighley and the brothers are
ever ready to admit that their father's advice and encouragement have
done much to account for their success, for Mr Moore Senior has been a
lover of poultry all his life and takes a very keen interest in the stock
[. . .] as vice-president of the Partridge Wyandotte club, a variety to
which he is sincerely attached.*

By 1909, however, the brothers appear to have given up
breeding hens altogether and no longer attended any of the
shows. Both had married by then and war was on the horizon,
so business pressures may have brought about a change of
direction. My father hung on to one corner of the old poultry
farm and planted an orchard there with apple, pear and plum
trees. He also grew his prize-winning dahlias but never a
single vegetable, even during the Second World War when
places like Victoria Park were dug over for potatoes as part
of the nationwide 'Dig for Victory' campaign. I'd sometimes
go with him to his beloved plot but I wasn't a patient gardener
and plants never grew fast enough for me.

The secret to his dahlias was good manure. When I was a
lad, Thomas Moore & Sons had a pair of magnificent shire
horses called Prince and Duke, and Father used to take me to
their stables at the yard to feed them at the weekends, while
he collected up a sack full of their droppings. On my grandfather's orders the stables were still kept in immaculate
condition with plenty of clean hay and straw, and the horses
had the finest feed. Prince was dark brown and Duke was a
mix of black and brown, and they were enormous as they

41

towered above me over the half-open stable door, often knocking off my cap in their eagerness to be fed handfuls of oats. I was very sad when the company upgraded and bought first a Model T Ford and then a Leyland tipping truck to carry men and materials.

The well-trained horses, who were put out to grass in happy retirement, seemed a lot less trouble to me as all anyone had to do was twitch their reins. With the trucks the workmen had to crank a handle to start the engine and – in the days before hydraulics – wind the tipper up and down themselves. It was another era ended.

Every manufacturing town had one week's holiday a year known as a *wake* so that the various mills and factories could operate all year on a rolling basis. Ours was the last week in July, known as Keighley Feast Week – the seven days of the year Freda and I anticipated the most.

Father and Mother would pack up the car with all that we'd need and we'd set off excitedly to Whitby for five whole days, staying in a little boarding house overlooking the shunting yard for steam engines, which felt like my very own mechanical paradise and one that few others appreciated. It was in Whitby that I caught my first ever fish off the end of the pier using a line on a hand-held wooden frame. It was about eight inches long and of unknown variety, but I took it back to our boarding house and asked the landlady to fry it for my breakfast, declaring it the most delicious fish I had ever tasted.

We sometimes went to Bridlington or Morecambe for a change and on one memorable trip to Southport Sands my mother paid five shillings for me to take a pleasure ride, sitting behind the pilot of a Great War biplane and flying up over the bay. That was absolutely thrilling and I couldn't believe my luck. I'd watched the plane go up and down with paying passengers several times over so I knew there was nothing to be afraid of, but once I was strapped in behind the pilot, my hands gripped the sides tightly. There was an incredible noise when the engine started and then we took off across the sands and lifted up into the air, flying high up over the bay which suddenly looked like a model town with tiny people waving. That was quite a moment for me as it was the first time I'd ever been in an aeroplane. I wish I could recall what it was – it may well have been a Sopwith, but that particular name has slipped down the cracks. The only sadness for me was that the flight was over all too soon. A part of me secretly wished Mother had paid the extra two shillings and sixpence to go even higher and further. When we finally rolled to a halt the plane tipped over on to one wing whereupon a man came running out to tip us back so that we could safely clamber out. I ran back to my parents pink-cheeked, windswept and wild-eyed and grateful.

At Christmas we always went to the Theatre Royal in Leeds or the Alhambra in Bradford to see the festive pantomime, which Father enjoyed even though he couldn't hear the calls of: '*Oh, no it isn't!*' that we all cried out with glee. And at Whitsuntide weekend, which fell on the seventh Sunday after Easter, we went as a family to Blackpool Tower Circus, the most amazing spectacle of my young life with wild animals, acrobats and clowns. The things I liked most were the beautiful white horses with large feather plumes attached to their headgear, ridden by pretty girls in skimpy costumes who bravely jumped on and off as the horses galloped around the ring. Even at a young age I was especially taken with the girls, and the heady smell of their perfume mingled with a mixture of greasepaint and horse sweat lingers in my memory still.

Some of the same girls would appear later walking a high wire or dangling precariously from a trapeze as we all gasped when one nearly fell (something she *nearly* did every year). There was a contortionist and a troupe of little people, known then as 'midgets', who performed hilarious routines. One of the most dramatic acts featured elephants and lions and tigers performing tricks, something that's quite rightly banned these days as it isn't natural or fair to make an elephant stand on one leg or have a tiger jump through a burning hoop while a 'tamer' cracks a whip. In those innocent days we all thought it was spectacular and – as committed animal lovers – were pleased to see that the animals seemed sleek and well fed.

There was even a swimming pool that appeared as if by magic beneath the circus ring in which the same showgirls would perform synchronized routines in even skimpier bathing costumes, and one would 'disappear' down an outlet while everyone feared she had drowned. Then there'd be sea lions balancing balls on their whiskery noses and splashing the crowd with their flippers as a strong smell of fish pervaded the air. It was magical, entrancing and utterly bewitching to a young lad from Keighley.

Sitting eating vanilla ice cream in little tubs with wooden spoons, I think we all loved the circus equally, but the person who seemed to enjoy it the most was my father who especially loved the clowns. Grandfather Thomas had taken Father to the same circus as a boy – when he could still hear – so he knew all the routines with buckets of water and the ones filled with scraps of paper thrown at the squealing audience. He also knew the punch lines and the calling out of 'Behind you!' as the clowns hid behind the grumpy Ringmaster. Father would start to laugh before the clowns even got to the end of their routines because he knew exactly what would happen and what they were about to say. His favourite clown of all, by far, was Doodles, a Scotsman in a top hat who stood at just four feet ten inches and was the longest serving performer in Blackpool at thirty years. We all loved him the best, and when he died and his son stepped into his oversized shoes, it just wasn't the same.

The biggest excitement of Feast Week came on the last weekend when the Keighley Gala would be held – pronounced *'gayler'* in Yorkshire. Crowds of up to 30,000 would turn out for the major social event in the local calendar. It always began with a grand mile-long procession of pageantry, quadrille bands and decorated floats weaving their way through the town to Victoria Park. There, every kind of entertainment could be found including fairground attractions, sporting events, music and dancing by people dressed up in exotic national costumes from around the world. There was the famous 'Flying Pigs' carousel, with pigs instead of horses, and the spectacular balloon ascents that proved to me that Heaven didn't exist.

These balloons, made locally and sponsored by Yorkshire companies, were often filled by burning town gas that was cheekily obtained by tapping into a convenient gas lamp. It was a potentially lethal process that took all day. Once filled, the plain balloons covered in netting would lift a 'gondola' or basket carrying the aeronaut and at least one parachutist who would throw themselves out at heights of between 2,000 to 3,000 feet. One of these fearless men and women was local motorcycling celebrity Alec Jackson who ran a motorcycle shop in East Parade, Keighley. Alec had been a Royal Flying Corps pilot, and competed at the legendary 'TT' or Tourist Trophy races in the Isle of Man. I watched breathlessly as this man I already thought of as a hero floated safely to earth.

Watching all this with me would be Walter Mitchell, my closest friend and a lad who lived across the road and two doors down from us. Walter and I went everywhere together, on foot or by bike, and played football on the playing field. Our favourite game was 'kick can', which involved putting an old can in the middle of the road and kicking it. We each had to run to where it landed and whoever got there first would kick it again. It was a game that could be played quite safely on the roads back then because – apart from the odd lorry – most deliveries were by horse-drawn wagons, and the biggest hazard was the manure that littered the streets until it was collected for gardens or by the local yardsman whose job it was to sweep the streets and clear the snow in winter.

My sister Freda also had a friend in our road and she had a pretty younger sister called Nancy Barraclough. Pretty girls attracted me all my life. Nancy was my first crush and we played together in each other's gardens, although we were too young to do anything but tear around and throw marbles which we called 'glass Ollies'. Her toys were all dolls and mine were wooden, the best of which was a wooden tip-up lorry into which I'd put things like oats or flour before pouring them out. When I was quite small my father gave me a piece of wood, some nails and a hammer, so I used to bang the nails into the wood – tap-tapping away – and soon learned that if I hit my thumb it hurt so not to do it again. Later I played with jigsaws and made lorries or something with wheels using my Meccano construction kit. I also collected cigarette cards for a while, trading them with friends, and then stamps from a mail order company called Stanley Gibbons. In the end I gave them all away as I never received the ones I really wanted from faraway countries with interesting pictures of birds and mountains – the kinds of places I hoped to see for myself one day.

As a child who rarely left my hometown, I was largely ignorant of the world and its politics, although I was aware that we seemed to have a new prime minister almost every year (five changes between 1920 and 1929 alone). I also knew about the Great War because the grand war memorial built by Grandfather Thomas and his men was unveiled in front of 25,000 people when I was very small. In the years immediately following that war we would still see men walking around in their military greatcoats and, sometimes, parents walking shell-shocked sons who were gibbering wrecks after the trenches. I remember one veteran with a leg that was a round wooden peg, and there was another who had no legs at all and wheeled himself round in a little trolley.

My grandfather employed several men who'd been affected by mustard gas in the trenches and all had hacking coughs because of it. He was known as an excellent employer and when it came to pay day – every Saturday lunchtime – he insisted that the wives come to the works too so that they'd receive some of the money or the men might drink it all away. One thing the men did do with their hard-earned cash was to rush to Uncle Chadwick's pawnshop and collect the 'Sunday suits' they needed to wear to church and step out in at weekends. This they did after their weekly wash in the slipper baths provided at the Keighley Public Baths and Wash Houses in Albert Street. The Sunday suits were pawned again the following week to raise a bit extra – no doubt to be spent in one of the town's hundred or so pubs and clubs or in its sixty off-licences.

None of the men in my family drank much and they didn't smoke either. My parents might enjoy a small sherry each at Christmas or my father would have a 'tipple' with a customer, and then it didn't take much to turn him into a happy little soul with a fixed grin on his face. The Moore men weren't big fans of conventional sports like football either, and Father only ever took me to watch rugby matches because one of his young labourers was a scrum half in the Keighley team. Something he did follow was cricket, but Father couldn't listen to it on the wireless so he'd travel to Headingley in Leeds to watch it live. His hero was the late great W. G. Grace, the legendary cricketer with the big bushy beard who'd played in twenty-two test matches and died five years before I was born. Grandfather Thomas had also been a big fan and used to take his sons to see 'W. G.' play.

I don't recall much about my grandfather other than that I respected him. He was the kind of man everyone respected even though he couldn't read or write. Best of all, he was kind to me and always gave me a gold sovereign at Christmas, which was quite a lot of money and worth about £50 in today's terms. I'd put it with the half a crown my father gave me each birthday and save it for something special; I never squandered money on unnecessary things. My grandfather and his wife Hannah had both come from the bottom of the pile and the one thing they had in common was that they were both always very 'tidy', but then I was brought up in a tidy family. My father was tidy and Uncle Billy was tidy. It was expected. Grandmother Hannah was especially tidy, always immaculately dressed and smelling of lavender. She wore high-collared blouses and had her white hair piled up high on her head like Queen Mary, who I think she must have modelled herself on.

While my grandfather never forgot his roots, mingling easily with the men and enjoying every visit to Blackpool to walk 'the Golden Mile', my grandmother went once and refused to go again. She snobbishly declared, 'Blackpool is awful. It smells of fish and chips and sweaty feet.' She might have been right, but none of us minded. After that, she never did return, which was a pity because she missed out on some very happy family days out. I sometimes wondered how she could have forgotten where she came from and become so pointedly upper middle-class, but I think now that maybe it was precisely because of her lowly background that she had vowed to rise above it. She suffered from bronchitis all her life due to childhood poverty and was often confined to the house, but whenever she emerged from her chamber she went by the Victorian maxim that children should be seen but not heard. She died of her chest when I was nine, and I couldn't feel sorrow for someone I didn't know, who'd never showed any real interest in us, or gathered us to her bosom like dear Granny Fanny.

One relative who did take an interest, however, was my mother's brother Uncle Arthur, of whom Mother was especially fond. He was the one who'd worked at the Short Brothers airship works making rigid observational airships for the Admiralty during the Great War, in direct response to the threat of German Zeppelins and U-boats. After that he moved to Birkenhead near Liverpool where he was employed in the shipyards in between treading the boards as a leading light in the New Ferry and Birkenhead Operatic Societies. When he moved back to Keighley in 1923 he became first the manager and then the master pastry chef at a fashionable confectioner's called John Hammond & Co. in North Street, which had a popular tearoom upstairs. Arthur was known for his fine fancies and wedding cakes and always made us a beautifully decorated chocolate yule log every Christmas.

He never married or had children and in 1936 was presented with a long service medal from the Keighley Amateur Operatic and Dramatic Association where he was known for his love of Gilbert and Sullivan works. He was also made a life member of the Keighley Theatre Group. His only holidays were taken with the much older John Hammond who owned the confectioner's, and it was only later in life that I realized that they were probably gay. This would have mattered nowt to me, as I loved him all the same. When John Hammond died, the business changed hands and Arthur found work as a clerk at the local council, a job he remained in until retirement.

I can't imagine him being very happy in a boring office job because I think of him as such a lively character and one who was determined to enjoy life. When I was eleven years old, he took Mother and me to London for the first time. We stayed in the Strand Palace Hotel and, although everything seemed vast and the numbers of trams and people were over-whelming to this Yorkshire lad, I enjoyed the visit hugely. We walked everywhere and went to all the usual tourist spots like Madame Tussaud's, Buckingham Palace and Big Ben. I think we might even have gone on the Underground. Arthur spoiled us rotten. Even though I never saw as much of him as I would have liked, he was one of my first male role models.

Within a year of that happy trip, however, family life changed forever when my eighty-one-year-old grandfather Thomas died at home in August 1931, two years after my grandmother. I was sad about that, for he had always been kind to me and I knew that he was a good and decent man who had pulled himself up by his boot strings. Although he'd been tough on his errant daughter Maggie, he'd been generous to his other children and very supportive of my father. His men adored him and the townspeople held him in high regard. Not surprisingly, his funeral was well attended and an extensive obituary in the *Keighley News* described him as the town's 'oldest builder' and a man who had played a large part in its development. 'He was in business on his own account for something like 54 years . . . and always had a high reputation as a builder,' it went on. 'Keighley has numerous examples of his excellent work. His death removes an interesting personality.'

Upon my grandfather's death my father inherited Club Nook, as promised, so in 1932 we left the home I'd always known and moved to the much grander property in the village of Riddlesden that I only knew from family visits. Our new home was undoubtedly an improvement and I even had a bigger bedroom, but I wasn't so impressed by its electricity and telephone, garage, garden and separate wash house. What thrilled me most was the fact that my lovely Uncle Billy lived next door and that there was a huge field behind the house with a gate and a direct path to the moors by Silsden, Rivock and beyond. For this young lad and his dog it was the dawn of a whole new age.

4.

'The world was never more unsafe
for democracy than it is today.'

Prime Minister Stanley Baldwin
(1867–1947)

Scottish scientist Professor Alexander Fleming
discovered penicillin in 1929.

BILLY MOORE WAS PROBABLY the person who influenced me most in my childhood and beyond. A hill-climbing motor-bike trials rider when he wasn't helping to run the building company, it was Billy who nurtured my love of motorcycles and taught me all I needed to know about engineering and mechanics – skills that were to serve me well throughout my life.

He kept his collection of bikes and spare parts in a base-ment beneath his house next door to ours and as soon as his day's work was done he could be found there, tinkering away, much to the annoyance of his wife Elsie. She was badly crip-pled because of a congenital hip problem and I remember her as a crooked little figure. Her condition meant that she couldn't have children, so she wasn't a particularly happy person to be around. She refused to come to any family parties, even at Christmas, which meant that Billy couldn't come either. I think that's why he found release in sport. Famous riders like Alec Jackson (who'd parachuted out of the balloon) used to come to see him because Billy also organized motorbike trials and was an expert on the respected Scott motorcycles made in Shipley. These had iconic names like Super Squirrels and Flying Squirrels, referred to fondly as 'the Flyers'.

Happily for me, during those early years in Riddlesden I found in Billy a father figure I could have all the meaningful conversations I'd never been able to have with my own father, and without shouting. Billy's cluttered basement under the living room of the main house was like an Aladdin's cave, and each time I hurried down the little outside steps to see him I could smell the petrol and hear the metallic clanking of his tools as he stripped down yet another engine. It was the messiest place I had ever been in, littered with every kind of motorbike part along with half-assembled vehicles strewn haphazardly on a floor permanently sticky with oil. I loved it. Billy kept the engines of his vintage trials bikes scrupulously maintained, but he never bothered to scrape off the mud they'd accumulated en route and it fell to the floor to add a grittiness underfoot.

He also kept a succession of wonderful and interesting cars in his garage including an M-type MG sports car and – for a while – a beautiful blue Bugatti 35, which would be worth a great deal of money today. I remember him taking me for a ride in that and turning the heads of all those we passed. Perhaps not surprisingly, to an impressionable young boy like me, Billy felt like a man to worship. As I already had my own complete set of tools, given to me over the years by Father, I was more than happy to tinker along with Billy and watch as he took an engine apart, piece by piece, stripped everything down and then put it all back together again, chatting all the while. It was Billy who surprised me by revealing that Father also used to take part in hill trials but that he sold his bike when he met my mother, 'because he didn't dare take her where he'd been'. The suggestion was that my old dad had been a bit of a ladies' man, which I can quite believe is true as he always lit up in the company of women.

And it was Billy who encouraged my father to drive me to Manchester to watch the relatively new 'dirt track motorbike racing' (now known as speedway) at the Belle Vue circuit, which we both enjoyed enormously. Belle Vue was a Victorian wonderland once known as the 'Showground of the World' with up to 2 million visitors a year. It boasted a zoo, a circus, a fun fair and a concert venue called The Kings Hall. The stadium next door was used alternately for greyhound and motorbike racing and became home to the celebrated Belle Vue Aces speedway team. One of them was a chap I got to know called Oliver Langton, who raced JAP bikes (for J. A. Prestwich of London), had a motorbike shop in Skipton, and was a fearless rider. Father and I would take our places in the grandstand and hold our collective breath as the riders diced with death on the dirt track below at speeds of up to 50 mph. There were a lot of choking exhaust fumes and the noise was so incredible that sometimes I would cover my ears as Father laughed, impervious to the screaming engines.

Every week Uncle Billy had *The Motor Cycle* and *Motor Cycling* magazines delivered, which he'd hand on to me once he'd finished them. I was so impatient for them, I used to wait and wait, then read them from cover to cover before starting over again. All my old comics like *The Wizard*, *Boy's Own* and *The Rover* were soon forgotten. This was the only reading I required. I also lost interest in my hobbies such as cooking oatmeal biscuits and rug making, which we did each night when we sat together as a family listening to the wireless – everyone but Father, of course, who read his newspaper or a book instead.

Our wireless was a Philco from its 'cathedral' range, which came in a wooden dome-shaped case with a cloth-covered grill and all sorts of switches and dials. It was the best of its type with five valves. Mother liked listening to dance music played by the famous big bands broadcasting from London hotels led by the likes of Henry Hall or Jack Payne. Freda and I were 'Ovaltineys', members of a children's radio club sponsored by the Ovaltine malted milk drink company that broadcast on long wave on Radio Luxembourg on Sunday evenings. Laughing at the comedian and singing along to the songs, we'd work away at our rugs made from kits sent to us on mail order by the Readicut Rug Company from Wakefield. These had pre-cut lengths of wool instead of the previous tiresome skeins, bespoke canvases, and a little tool each to hook the wool through. It was an addictive new fad that provided several nice rugs for the house. Freda and Mother would chatter idly away while they hooked and I dreamed of one day riding my own motorbike. I didn't for one moment imagine that my dream was about to come true.

It happened on a day when I was out exploring an old barn on the edge of the village with Billy the dog and my friend Walter. In a dark corner of the ramshackle building, half hidden under a tarpaulin covered in dust, I discovered something really rather wonderful. It was a 1921 Royal Enfield two-stroke, two-speed motorcycle – quite a find. The eleven-year-old motorbike with two flat tyres looked like it hadn't been run in years. My heart pounding with excitement, I knew it was exactly what I was looking for. I was only twelve but I boldly approached the owners, who were friendly enough, and they sold it to me for one of my precious half-crowns. I walked the motorbike the half-mile home and rolled it into my father's immaculate garage, with its neat shelves and inspection pit, a place that was a stark contrast to Billy's grubby basement. I don't recall even telling my parents about my find at first, but if I had they wouldn't have been surprised. In fact, they'd have smiled and said, 'We're surprised it's taken you this long, Tom.'

Nor were there any offers to help or interfere. This was my project and it was up to me to either get the thing going again, or give it to Billy for parts. I must have been quite a practical little boy because I took that mucky, seized-up old bike to pieces, put it back together again and got it running. Nobody helped me; I'd watched Billy and read enough magazines so I knew what I had to do, which included cleaning out all the old fuel and oil that had gummed up the works. The biggest problem came when I had to put all the pieces back in reverse order, but I was mechanically minded so I got over that.

Until I gained my driving licence at seventeen I could only drive my bike over the back fields, which I did all the time. This joyous experience served me well the following year when a friend of mine called John Driver decided to play a trick on me. His uncle owned a farm in the Dales that kept horses and, although I'd loved Prince and Duke, I'd never been on one in my life. 'Why don't you give it a go?' John suggested, before helping me on to an animal that I later discovered was an ex-steeplechaser. No sooner was I seated than he whacked its hindquarters hard and the horse took off at breakneck speed across the moors. I could easily have died, but I stayed on only because I was accustomed to riding a motorbike. Once I'd survived the first few minutes I actually quite enjoyed the experience – and especially the speed – but it wasn't something I cared to repeat.

Thanks to my adored motorbike magazines, I knew exactly where I wanted to go at great speed – the Isle of Man TT races that Keighley's fearless Alec Jackson had competed in successfully during the early 1920s (when he wasn't throwing himself out of balloons). The TT had started in 1904 as a 52-mile time trial for drivers of touring automobiles who wanted to go faster than the 20 mph speed limit imposed on the mainland. The following year a trial for motorcycles was introduced. The TT's Snaefell Mountain Course had categories for 250cc, 350cc, 500cc and sidecars and was run over a week on 37 miles of closed public roads that varied in height and terrain from sea level to 1,300 feet. As I leafed through the articles in Uncle Billy's magazines, my new hero soon became Stanley Woods, an Irish rider who raced Norton motorcycles with enormous success, and first entered the race on a Cotton motorbike when he was just eighteen. He had twenty-nine international Grand Prix wins and took the TT cup ten times, later switching to Moto Guzzi and then Velocette motorcycles. The TT was considered to be the most dangerous racing event in the world because of the exceptionally high speeds of 80 mph around the course's tight corners. Since it began twenty-five years earlier in 1907 there had been some thirteen deaths. A further three riders died in 1934 alone but that, perhaps, was the thrill. It certainly excited me and was all I could talk about.

Once my parents realized how much motorcycling meant to me, they often drove me and Freda to watch Billy take part in his reliability trials. These happened once a month or so and always at the weekends, so they became a regular family day out that was always exhilarating. The courses were sometimes as long as a hundred miles and chosen for their natural hazards, such as impossibly steep gradients, muddy water splashes, perilous hairpin bends, loose shale and incredibly rough ground with large boulders and deep potholes. Riders lost points if they wobbled, zigzagged, put their feet down, were 'footslogging' or walked their bikes up the steepest inclines.

The sport was so popular that it was covered in all the papers and in 1926 the *Yorkshire Post* bought what was considered to be an unclimbable 400-foot hill near the market town of Pudsey and renamed it 'Post Hill'. They then donated it to Leeds Motor Club just so that they could use it for trials and call it the 'steepest hill climb in the world'. That was one of my favourite legs of the events and we would watch Billy and the other riders at perilous angles as they struggled to keep on their bikes. Each major trial was covered in *The Motor Cycle* magazine with action photographs of the many riders who raced for a Challenge Cup in teams. Sidecars and three-wheelers were also allowed and there were several famous lady riders who took part.

Making a day of it with sandwiches and a Thermos flask of hot tea, we would drive out and I'd pick one of the best spots for some action, such as a really steep hill or a particularly muddy water splash. Then we'd settle down and wait for the sound of the riders' engines. My excitement would mount as they drew closer and closer and then I'd watch, utterly enthralled, as they came through one by one to tackle that particular hazard, trying hard not to get splattered or wet. Whenever Billy loomed into view, usually caked in mud and hardly able to see through his visor, we'd take a special interest and be sure to try to congratulate him at the end – if we could even find him in the scrum of sweaty, dirty men patting each other on their backs outside some local inn.

Father usually carried his camera with him, a pastime I was soon to adopt, and when I was seven years old he took a cracking photo of me standing atop a stone gateway during one trial in my shorts, wellington boots, coat and flat cap, watching with high excitement as one of the lady riders raced past in her leather coat and helmet. That picture just about sums up my happy childhood.

Compared to such excitements, school seemed deadly dull and I only went because I had to. I also made sure to walk the ten minutes home for lunch every day after pushing away in disgust a plate of my first – and last – school dinner on day one.

My parents were determined that Freda and I should have a proper education so she was sent to Keighley Girls' Grammar School, where my mother was on the board, and I attended the Boys' Grammar School, a privilege my father also paid for. At the age of fifteen Freda left school and was apprenticed as a seamstress to two spinster sisters called the Wrights who lived in one of the Dales. I was also to be apprenticed somewhere if I did well enough in my studies, which I doubted. I was grateful at school for the company of my friend Walter, who I didn't see quite so much of since we moved house, and who had been usurped in my affections by a new friend called Charlie Dinsdale, who lived three doors down from Club Nook and whose family owned William Laycock & Co., Tanners and Leather Workers.

There were three streams in my school – A, B and C – depending on ability. 'A' was for the bright boys who were taught Latin and Greek in preparation for university. 'B' was for middling boys who learned German, and in 'C' you learned French and manual crafts, which was important for those who wanted a future in the town. I was in 'C' stream, but I didn't mind this at all because it was exactly what I needed, plus I had a crush on my French teacher, whom we knew only as 'Mademoiselle'. If I'd been put in the 'A' stream it would have been death because I wasn't the brightest boy. I became brighter as I got older, mind.

A solitary child of the moors, I was never a team player and only played rugby and cricket because I was told to. My preferred sport was cross-country running, especially alongside the River Aire, a route I often took with my dog. I also enjoyed geology and studying different rock samples, many of which I already knew. What I hated most was maths and algebra, not least because our maths master walked around with a yard-long wooden ruler that he whacked down hard across your spine if he thought you were idling. Nobody could ever tell me the benefit of learning calculus, so I never did, because I couldn't think what good it was going to do me. Although I enjoyed geography and especially learning about the British Empire as far afield as Canada, South Africa, India and Australia – in the days when maps had our colonial possessions coloured in pink – I wasn't cut out for academics and only ever liked the practical stuff.

Fortunately, we dumb 'C' stream boys were given wood-working, textiles and engineering to study with a marvellous teacher called Will Midgley. Working in metal and wood was right up my street. With Mr Midgley's encouragement, at the age of twelve I made a solid wooden box with a padded seat that I still have. It was so useful to have these practical skills and, having been prepared by my father and uncle, I was good at them from the start.

Despite learning skills that could have been useful at Thomas Moore & Sons, it was never automatically expected that I'd join the family firm when I was old enough, as my father and uncle had. My mother especially wanted me to make a better go of it and get a management job. I remember her telling me, 'Never settle for a £10 a week job,' and it was she who pushed me. When I left grammar school in 1935 aged fifteen, I was articled to the water engineer of Keighley for three years; a job I loved because I was given so much freedom. My boss was a man called J. Noel Wood who'd served as a captain in the Royal Field Artillery during the Great War. In 1927 he'd married my favourite primary school teacher, Miss Moffitt, and because of that I think he was especially kind to me.

My work involved learning about surveying so there was a lot of drawing involved, and I had to take notes of any works going on in town if water pipes were being replaced, as well as testing for leaks. It was an interesting time. Thanks to him, I'd be allowed to drive the waterworks van on my own up on to the moors behind Haworth and the Brontë family home, take samples from streams, test for their pH values, or measure the quantities and flow for the town supply. It was just like when I'd been a child, roaming about desolate areas on my own with Billy the dog for company. Only now I was being paid a little something to take off on my own adventures up into the Dales, charting wild and beautiful unknown territory in places where few people went. It was the perfect job for me and in the days before mass tourism I had places to myself like the great rock outcrop of Robin Hood's Stone, or I could visit the pagan Cowper's Cross. There was also the famed Swastika Stone at Woodhouse Crag, probably hand-carved by Roman legions with the ancient tribal symbol of divinity and luck that was later hijacked by the Nazis.

Once I was in gainful employment, my parents decided to leave me at home when they next went on holiday, to Scarborough. They suggested I invite a school friend for company, which I did. He came to stay and was surprised to discover that my mother and Granny Fanny had taught me how to cook because, in his family, that was considered women's work. A man of his time, that was also my father's view and as a consequence he was quite hopeless in the kitchen. He could just about boil an egg or heat some gravy for a pie. 'He'll have to die at least one day before me,' Mother always said, 'for, without me, he'd starve.' She'd brought me up not to be helpless and to have a 'can do' spirit. I was encouraged from an early age to help out in the kitchen and make food for the house, like my oatmeal biscuits. I was also her 'whipper' who whipped up the butter for her prized sponges, a process that took a good twenty minutes and left me with an aching arm. I may have been a strange little boy but I used to watch how Father was completely dependent on my mother and I thought to myself, 'Tom Moore, you will never be dependent on any-one else for your food.' I wasn't and I've not been long since.

I also started to take more of an interest in girls, which was easier for me than for Charlie Dinsdale who'd left school to work in his father's tanning company in Queen Street, where they made hides belts called picking bands used on looms in the mills. Tanning was a smelly business that involved steeping hides in fermenting oak bark, which in turn seeped into the pores of every worker and their clothing – an odour Charlie quickly discovered put off most girls. Smelling of fresh air, rivers and moss, I didn't have that problem, however, and when we both took up Sunday school lessons chiefly because we fancied the young girl teaching it, I was certain I'd have a better chance. In the end neither of us got her.

My first girlfriend was a Keighley lass called Ethel Whitaker who worked in a shoe shop in town so I was never short of shoes. I must have been about fourteen when we first started dating, but all that meant was walking around the town together, having an ice cream, or going to the Regent cinema which had upholstered twin seats in the back row. It was all very innocent. I broke up with her after a while as I was easily bored and wanted to focus on my apprenticeship and riding my motorbike. I'd also become interested in rambling and rock-climbing, tackling the sheer Cow and Calf rock formation at Ilkley, which – according to legend – was created when the giant Rombald stamped on the rock as he was fleeing an enemy, separating the cow from her calf. This I would free-climb to a height of about forty feet wearing my regular clothes and shoes with thick rubber soles. Even though people fell and hurt themselves, helmets weren't suggested for activities like this until many years later.

I also joined the newly formed Youth Hostels Association, staying cheaply in brand-new and comfortable boys-only hostels all over the county. And I became a member of the Skipton Potholing Club, potholing in the hills above Skipton and Grassington, where we explored the water holes eroded into the limestone. For that I'd wear a trilby hat to protect my head, good stout lace-up shoes, and a tighter-fitting tweed jacket than usual so that it didn't get snagged on anything sharp. And after Father gave me my own little folding camera, I'd taken up photography like him and became a member of the Keighley & District Photographic Society where he developed his photographic plates. He was a patient teacher but was always pushing me to be better, with comments like, 'Is that the best you can do?' Mostly, I took pictures of motorbike trials, while he continued to catalogue scenes in and around Keighley that he knew would have some historical significance later. These included the laying of the first tram tracks in the town, the construction or demolition of buildings, visits by dignitaries, various galas and the last tram returning to the depot before the trolley buses replaced them.

When I was fifteen, I saved up for a coach trip organized by *The Motor Cycle* magazine to the Isle of Man to watch the TT race and take photographs. Father kindly lent me his half-plate camera, which was about as modern as you could get (although ten times the size of the more fashionable Box Brownie). It was the first of two summer visits I made to the island on my own via the Liverpool to Douglas steamship ferry that seemed to turn everyone else green but me. For that first trip in June 1935 I had done my research and as soon as I got there I set myself up at Creg-Ny-Baa, an important corner where I hoped I'd get some good shots of my hero Stanley Woods. It also had a café where I bought myself a sandwich and a cup of tea with money Father had given me.

An announcer told us what was happening on a tannoy system and there was great excitement when the race began. On the first of the eight laps, the riders came by at such a speed that all we could hear was the roar of the bikes and smell the waft of their exhaust fumes as they sped past in a blur. It was hard to tell which rider was which, although I did spot Stanley Woods from behind. Listening to the commentator, I was pleased to learn that he was in the lead. As we waited for the next lap, my fellow spectators seemed far more interested in what I was doing with my camera than with the latest developments in the race. Without a tripod, I had to hold it steady and level and turn quickly from right to left to capture images of the bikes as they sped past at speeds of up to 84 mph. If I moved too quickly or there was camera shake the images would be blurred. Fortunately, I not only managed to get a few shots but I also captured my hero, who went on to win that day. The following year he'd retire from racing, so I was glad that I'd seen him in action and I was able to tell Father and Uncle Billy all about it when I got home.

Billy was kind enough to show an interest in my trip but the TT was too fast and dangerous for his taste – two riders were killed that summer, although not on the day I was there. He was really only interested in his vintage bikes and the arduous time trials that took skill, stamina and an understanding of the terrain. As speeds increased, however, even these became more dangerous and riders were often injured. In fact, there were so many accidents that the RAC and AA decreed that they could no longer be run on any public roads. The danger was soon to make itself felt far closer to home, because not long after I'd returned from the Isle of Man, Billy had a serious accident on a narrow road near Guiseley, colliding head-on with a car. He suffered a serious head injury from which he never fully recovered. He spent some time in Keighley General Hospital and when he came out he suffered from terrible headaches and couldn't ride again, which was a great pity. I know he missed it sorely.

One night a year later, in June 1936, we were woken as a family by the sound of Elsie screaming in the small hours. Father and I put on our dressing gowns and slippers and ran next door to find her distraught and pointing at the garage. She'd been on a Chamber of Trade excursion to Edinburgh for the day and arrived home very late to discover that Billy wasn't in bed. When she went looking for him she heard the sound of an engine running in the garage, from which was emanating the smell of exhaust fumes that left what she later described as 'a peculiar taste' in her mouth. That's when she found Billy in the driver's seat of his saloon car. The garage was separate to the house and only a few feet away from my bedroom, but I hadn't heard a thing.

Father and a passer-by went in first and turned off the engine and then I followed behind, before we all fell back coughing, as Elsie wailed. Dear Uncle Billy was slumped across the front seat and very obviously dead. He was fifty-five years old. We will never know for sure, but the family was convinced that he had committed suicide by going to his sealed garage while Elsie was away, sitting in his car and starting the engine. Father asked Mother to attend to Elsie and take her into the house, and then he and I had to carry his body inside. I was sixteen years old and I will never forget lifting his feet and shuffling backwards with the dead weight of my beloved uncle resting in my hands.

After Billy's death Father discovered that his older brother had some serious financial problems and, as he'd largely been running the building company, this had later repercussions for us as well. It was such a sad ending for a man I had so admired and I would have loved to have known more, so that maybe I could have better understood. Sadly, however, we never spoke of it again and nor did any of us put on the black armbands of mourning that were normal for those times. The message was clear – Billy's death was something we were all very sorry about but the Moore family wouldn't be making a fuss.

The *Yorkshire Post*, the *Leeds Mercury* and the *Keighley News* published many warm tributes to Billy's long motorbiking career, before reporting on the public inquest that had, by law, to be held. I didn't attend but I saw the reports in which the pathologist and the police were quoted in full. My father was spared the need to give evidence, I suspect because of his deafness. After a few other witness statements from Elsie and the passer-by who was first on the scene after her, the pathologist estimated that he had been dead for more than three hours when Elsie found him. Having listened to all the evidence and in the absence of a note, the Coroner kindly returned a verdict of accidental death from carbon monoxide poisoning. He said that Billy must have been carrying out a repair to his car at the time of his death and hadn't realized that he might die from the exhaust fumes in an enclosed space. We were grateful for the verdict but we all knew the truth. Billy was no fool.

Elsie never recovered from the tragedy. She shut the door on us and the world and, a year later, she sold the house and moved, first to a much smaller property a few streets away, and then – after a couple of years – somewhere further afield. I can't recall ever seeing her again. Nor was I ever given the opportunity to have anything of Billy's as a keepsake, or to go through his basement for spare parts – something I'm sure he would have wanted. I couldn't even keep his motor-cycling magazines as Elsie had someone in to clear away the lot. It was as if Billy had never existed. But not to me. He has always lived on in my heart.

5.

'*Nothing in life is to be feared, it is only to be understood. Now is the time to understand more, so that we may fear less.*'

Marie Curie (1867–1934)

The Supermarine Spitfire prototype made its
maiden flight in the summer of 1936.

NOT LONG AFTER BILLY'S DEATH my parents suggested I take a holiday to a boys-only camp on the Isle of Man with a couple of friends from school. I think they must have thought it would raise my spirits, as I was sorely missing my uncle. Off I went with a camera and a suitcase and stayed in a wooden hut for a week with two lads, one of whom was Stanley Shackleton and the other was known to me only as Pickles.

We had a pleasant enough time and travelled all over the island where I took lots of photographs I later developed with my father, including one I'm especially proud of. It showed the famous Laxey Wheel, the largest working waterwheel in the world, originally designed in 1854 to pump water from a mine that excavated lead, copper, zinc and silver. Travelling anywhere always opened my eyes to the world beyond my own and it was during those years that I realized how fortunate I was to be fit and well, have a loving family, a roof over my head and food on the table.

I didn't have to go far to know that this was the time of the global 'Great Depression' with mass unemployment in a post-war slump made worse by the stock market crash of 1929. There was a great deal of poverty in Keighley and if the mills were affected then the workers were too. Some ran off to Spain to join 4,000 British volunteers fighting 'the virus of fascism' in a bitter three-year civil war they may have had little understanding of. A few may have been tempted into it by the offer of a small wage. In Britain there were several hunger marches – many of them from the north of England – in which men and women walked from areas of high unemployment to protest outside Parliament. There were also riots in London and huge rallies that often turned into pitched battles as Prime Minister Ramsay MacDonald ordered an urgent review of the government's policies on unemployment. In the United States Franklin D. Roosevelt enjoyed a landslide victory over former president Herbert Hoover with a promise of a 'new deal', including unemployment insurance for the disenfranchised. And in Germany Adolf Hitler of the National Socialist Party became Chancellor of the Reich with similar promises to restore his country's beleaguered fortunes after the Great War.

I knew that people were worried about Hitler and fearful of the rise of nationalism in Germany, but that all seemed a long way away until my first encounter with Germans much closer to home. It was in May 1936 when the famed *Hindenburg* airship suddenly appeared in the skies over Keighley one sunny evening and hovered there. We all came out of our houses to stare at the giant silver cigar-shaped balloon, and my father captured a rare photograph of it from his bedroom window. At 800 feet long, the LZ 129 *Hindenburg* launched in March of that year was the world's largest commercial Zeppelin. It regularly flew approximately 100 passengers and crew to and from America and Brazil. On its way from Germany to the US on one of those epic three-day voyages, the airship, with swastikas on its tail, diverted to Keighley specifically so that a missionary on-board could drop a parcel and flowers in honour of his brother Franz, who'd died of the Spanish flu contracted in the Skipton POW camp seventeen years earlier.

Two local boy scouts, stunned by the sight of the huge balloon hovering over them like a spacecraft, picked up the package near the Devonshire Arms Inn and ran home to tell their families. Aside from the spray of carnations, there was a small cross made of jet and a letter that read:

To the finder of this letter please deposit the flowers and cards on the grave of my dear brother, Lieutenant Franz Schulte, 1 Garde Regt, zu Fuss, POW in [a] cemetery in Keighley near Leeds. Thanks for your kindness. John P. Schulte, the first flying priest, Aachen, Germany. PS Please accept the stamps and the pictures as a small souvenir from me. God bless you! I said the first holy mass on the Hindenburg, 9 May 1936.

The boys did as they were asked and the remembrance from the sky attracted national interest. They even made it on to the British Movietone News and people flocked to the German grave. It was discovered that Lieutenant Schulte, twenty-six, was in the German Army Flying Corps and had dropped bombs on London before being shot down in Kent. Questions about the visit were asked in the Houses of Parliament and, with the political situation in Europe a cause for concern, there were fears that the parcel drop had been a ruse to take strategic photographs of the area in preparation for possible future bombing raids. No one could have suspected that a year later the hydrogen-filled *Hindenburg* would burst into flames as it came in to land at a naval airfield in New Jersey, America. Thirty-six people would be killed, but the 'flying priest' would not be among their number.

Another thing that focused our attention on Germany that summer was the Olympic Games held in Berlin, and the first to be televised. I can remember watching some of the events on the newsreels at the picture house and applauding the success of the American track and field athlete Jesse Owens. He won no less than four gold medals, much to the fury of the racist Hitler who'd put his best athletes forward and refused to shake Owens' hand.

Like most teenagers, however, and even though my parents were both members of the local Conservative Association, I was ignorant of what Hitler's politics meant for the world or how much the Depression that facilitated his rise was also leading to widespread social change. I do remember the Jarrow Crusade in the October where some 200 men marched from Tyneside to London after the closure of their shipyard, a former hive of industry that had manufactured over a thousand ships. These dour-faced men in dark suits and flat caps didn't pass through Keighley but went from Jarrow to Ripon to Leeds via Harrogate then Wakefield, Barnsley and Sheffield before heading south, a march that took them a month. It was reported in the cinema that the marchers gathered a lot of support with people feeding and housing them along their route. There was a great deal of sympathy locally too for those who were out of work, but equally there were those who weren't so sympathetic. Ironically, despite their grand effort, in the end it was the next war that intervened on the Jarrow men's behalf and not the government.

Grateful to be in full-time employment during such difficult times and still on my upward trajectory towards a management job, I passed my driving test which meant that I would finally be able to take my motorbike on the road. Unfortunately, I'd sold my Royal Enfield to raise a bit of cash and it was a while before I got my next one.

When I finished my articles with Mr Wood he kindly presented me with a beautiful sixteen-piece engineers' drawing set complete with compasses and protractors in a box lined with blue velvet, a prized possession I still have. Almost immediately I started at Bradford Technical College on a three-year civil engineers' course and became a student member of the Institute of Civil Engineers – not bad for a boy who hated calculus. My dream was to become a civil engineer constructing bridges or roads, but first I had to get qualified. As Bradford was ten miles away I cycled there and back on my Raleigh bicycle until my father bought me my second motorbike – a 1936 BSA 600cc side valve. I rode it to college day after day and it was a lovely journey through the Yorkshire countryside.

I also had a new girlfriend, Marjorie Butterfield, whose mother ran the Black Bull pub in Haworth. Marjorie was another pretty girl and petite with a skirt to match as, happily, skirts had graduated from ankle-length to flared just below the knee. I brought her home to meet my parents and they seemed to like her. As long as it didn't look as if I was getting too serious with anyone, I never had any trouble from them about any of my girlfriends, not least because my father liked pretty girls too.

I wasn't a natural dancer but at sixteen I took lessons in the waltz, foxtrot and quickstep. I did this chiefly to get girls because there were dances in Keighley every week and I needed to get by. The public dances were held at the Keighley Baths in the winter, and the better private ones you had to be invited to. Whether I went alone or took Marjorie, I had to be well turned out and look tidy in a dark suit – never woollen work clothes. We'd dance to ballroom music from London led by people like Joe Loss and his band. These were either broadcast live on the radio or played on a record via a loud-speaker. I don't recall my sister Freda ever coming to our dances, which is a shame because she missed out. She'd only ever had one boyfriend, a lad my father didn't approve of because he 'didn't look right', and that was that. She never had another, in deference to him I think, which was a pity because she would have made a marvellous mother.

Despite the normality of my carefree teenage years with college and dances and family, I knew that beyond my own limited horizons there was a growing sense that we were under threat because we couldn't avoid the feeling that another war was possible. The latest news from Europe was constantly on the wireless or screened at the picture house, and the latest from Germany filled the pages of the *Daily Mail* that my father read every day along with the *Keighley News* every Saturday.

In a strange sort of way, I think this gradual build-up numbed us to the possibility of conflict, as it was expected for so long. We were never a family who worried openly so I don't recall much talk between us about what was happen-ing, although I now appreciate how terrifying the thought of my being sent to war would have been to my parents. This would have especially affected my father who only ever wanted us to all stay together, safe and well. My mother must also have feared I'd be conscripted but she would never have confided that in me. I'm sure I get my optimistic nature from her. In fact, both parents generally looked on the bright side and approached life in the same spirit as I do – try not to worry too much about tomorrow. Tomorrow will be a good day.

I was probably too busy reading my motorbike magazines and having fun with girls to follow developments and, even then, I naively regarded war as something of an adventure. Besides, there had been plenty of events closer to home to focus on in recent years. Back in 1935 the nation had come together for the Silver Jubilee of King George V – for which my parents bought a commemorative china mug to add to their collection of royal memorabilia. A celebration at Riddlesden Hall had been organized by the council with cups of tea, cake and lots of bunting. Not long after, in January 1936, the King had died at the age of seventy. I remember his passing but not the funeral other than that I got the day off work so I went out on the moors with Billy. By the end of the year it was all change again, as Edward VIII abdicated the throne, for the love of an American divorcee, Wallis Simpson. This was not at all popular and there was a lot of discussion about that and no sympathy for him. The feeling was that he was being selfish and disloyal. He should have stayed and done his duty. But, as with most things, it all worked out beautifully in the end because Edward turned out not to be terribly suitable and already had leanings towards the Nazis, who were gaining considerable power. Edward's stammering younger brother was a delightful person but he didn't want to be king. He did well, however, with the help of a good wife, and if it weren't for the abdication we wouldn't have had Queen Elizabeth II, the best monarch our country has ever had.

Even though the news was getting worse from Germany and in 1938 its troops marched into Austria in what was known as the Anschluss, not long afterwards my Uncle Arthur took me on my first foreign holiday – to Switzerland – only a few hundred miles away from the Nazis in Salzburg. Everyone was uneasy about the Germans making inroads into Europe but nobody suggested that we should cancel our trip, which is an indication of how much we underestimated the danger. Arthur and I travelled by boat and train to the medieval city of Lucerne and then crossed Lake Lucerne to see the monument to the Swiss national folk hero William Tell at Altdorf. We visited a tunnel carved through the ice under the Rhône Glacier and walked the Aare Gorge with its spectacular mountain passes. That holiday really opened my eyes to the world beyond Britain and was very special. And I always loved spending time with Arthur who was unfailingly kind. It never once occurred to me that we might come to any harm in Europe but when we finally got back to Riddlesden, I heard Arthur confess to my mother, 'I was worried the whole time.' And, from the look on her face, she had felt the same.

With war looming, the government realized it had a massive shortage of soldiers so the Emergency Powers (Defence) Act called up all military reservists and volunteers for mobilization, while the Military Training Act required all fit and able men aged twenty and twenty-one to register for national service. I still had a year to serve at Bradford Technical College, which I knew my family would expect me to finish and I hoped I'd be able to.

Although war was half expected and we'd heard the disembodied rantings of Hitler and the German propagandist 'Lord Haw-Haw' blasting out of our wireless, everyone had been clinging to the hope that it could be avoided. This was especially true after Prime Minister Neville Chamberlain (my eighth government in nineteen years) returned from Germany waving a piece of paper signed by Hitler and declaring, 'Peace for our time.' So when hostilities were finally declared at 11 a.m. on 3 September 1939, two days after Germany invaded Poland, it came as a shock.

Father, Mother, Freda and I sat in silence around the Philco at Club Nook and listened to Chamberlain declare those now legendary words:

'I am speaking to you from the Cabinet Room at 10 Downing Street. This morning the British ambassador in Berlin handed the German government a final note stating that unless we heard from them by eleven o'clock that they were prepared at once to withdraw their troops from Poland, a state of war would exist between us. I have to tell you now that no such undertaking has been received and that consequently this country is at war with Germany.'

The four of us looked at each other blankly for a moment and then Mother told Father everything that had been said. His eyes glistening, he shook his head and left the room with her, while Freda and I sat in silence, wondering what it would all mean. I think when you are young you aren't especially upset by anything, so I wasn't perhaps as shaken by it as the older generation. More than the declaration of hostilities, it was the sight of three Hawker Hurricanes flying over our valley that shook me. I remember looking up at them and thinking, 'So this is really war.'

Because Britain still had fewer than a million soldiers trained – compared to France's 5 million – everything then changed for my generation. Men weren't volunteering as they had in the previous war because they knew what had happened to the millions who never came back. If there hadn't been conscription in the Second World War then I think many people wouldn't have gone.

Something needed to be done, so the National Service (Armed Forces) Act enforced conscription of all fit males aged eighteen to forty-one. Those engaged in vital industries or performing civilian work of national importance like farming were exempted, but I didn't qualify for either. My cousins were all girls, so I was the only one in the family to be called up. I still took it lightly and used to tell people jokingly, 'Well, the King sent me a little note saying that he was a bit pushed for people and we'd got some trouble in Germany and would I mind joining. I didn't, so I registered.' The harsh reality was that being called up set in motion the long and drawn-out process of selection that sifted out the medically exempt, the mentally unstable and the conscientious objectors, who had to contribute in some other ways as ambulance drivers or stretcher bearers. The hourglass had turned.

I wasn't afraid of fighting for freedom and democracy and never once questioned that I, too, might have to face up to our common enemy. The Germans started it and I felt it was my duty to defend our country. Two of my friends had already been called up – Charlie Dinsdale, who'd joined the Territorial Army in 1938 while at university and was enlisted into the 1st Battalion of the Duke of Wellington's Regiment (West Riding), and another pal called Brian Booth from Bradford Tech who'd joined the RAF and would be a German POW for four years. He came from a nice family who lived in a big house in Burley in Wharfedale over the moor. His father owned a limestone quarry outside Skipton, which, although I didn't know it at the time, would prove to be a lifeline to me later on.

For the first few months after war was declared, however, nothing really happened and life went on much as before. This period became known as the 'Phoney War', with no large-scale military strikes and the government focusing on economic tactics and naval blockades. The biggest shock was the sinking of the battleship HMS *Royal Oak*, torpedoed by a German

U-boat with the loss of more than 800 lives in October 1939, soon after war was declared.

In the district of Keighley, as in the rest of the country, we quickly adapted to the new rules and regulations of war that included the rationing of food, petrol and clothing, pulling little hoods like cowls over car headlights, and the obligatory issuing of gas masks in cardboard boxes. I helped my parents fit blackout curtains to be drawn every night and we became accustomed to seeing municipal buildings heavily protected by sandbags. As we were in a valley and weren't felt to be a primary industrial target, there were no public air raid shelters in Riddlesden that I was aware of, but a new air raid siren was installed at the Coney Lane electricity works in Keighley and one group of Riddlesden families dug themselves a seven-foot-deep, seventy-yard-long trench, into which they were planning to huddle. As yet another indication of my parents' stoic attitude to war, no such trench was dug in our garden and we never even took delivery of one of the corrugated Anderson shelters that many others installed in a panic.

The town had an early influx of child evacuees from Bradford, which seemed more likely to be bombed because of its heavy industry. More than a thousand children came in special trains and fleets of buses that brought them to reception centres before they were distributed to homes. Mother took two into Club Nook some time later and local schools had to adopt double shifts for classes. In time, the Keighley workhouse for the poor that had only closed in 1930 reopened its doors to take in more than a hundred elderly people from London. Great play was made of the fact that the oldest was ninety-six. Poor old thing.

In preparation for an expected all-out German attack by land, air and sea, civil defence plans were immediately put into effect. The Secretary of State for War Anthony Eden made a broadcast calling for men between the ages of seventeen and sixty-five to enrol in a new force, the Local Defence Volunteers (LDV), later changed to the Home Guard and better known these days as 'Dad's Army'. I volunteered immediately, as did many others. Within months almost 1.5 million men had enrolled in what was dubbed the 'ragtag militia', including my Uncle Arthur, who drove lorries and ambulances throughout the war. There is very little said about the LDV and some people didn't know it even existed, but it played an important role in allaying fears that Germany would drop spies by parachute into Britain who'd live and work amongst us unseen, reporting on any military information or ways to lower morale. Posters appeared everywhere with warnings like: '*Loose Lips Sink Ships*', and '*Be Like Dad – Keep Mum*'. The reasoning behind blackouts and the removal of all road signs was that not only would Luftwaffe pilots be unable to identify towns and cities but the spies they dropped wouldn't be able to find their way around.

We in the Riddlesden LDV had no uniforms or weapons to begin with but were placed under the command of a former Great War major in the Royal Engineers named William Moore (no relation), one of the most senior figures in our village. An excellent commander, he was an architect in Bradford but he lived in a house near the church. We had a rather loose arrangement to meet each night at dusk at Upwood House, which was on the road to Rombalds Moor. I was the youngest in our little group of nine and we only patrolled at night because I was at college during the day and the others were working. From Upwood we went out in groups of three, each armed with a First World War Ross rifle and about twenty-five rounds of ammunition that we weren't supposed to use. Oh, and we had khaki armbands with the letters LDV on them – for all the good that would do. I still have mine.

Some of the men had served in the previous war and knew how to handle a weapon, but although I'd been out rabbiting a couple of times to earn fourpence per rabbit, I had never used a rifle. We were taken up to a firing range just above Oxenhope, shown a round target like a dartboard with a bull's-eye and we were each handed a rifle and five rounds of ammunition. I loaded my weapon, fired the heavy old rifle and hit the target with my first two rounds. As ammunition was short I wasn't allowed to fire any more, which was a shame. I never got to find out if those first two were just a fluke.

Our orders were to patrol all night with the utmost vigilance then report back in the morning and return our weapon. We worked in shifts and the owner of Upwood, Mr Driver – who owned the local grocery shop and was the uncle to my friend with the steeplechaser – gave us one of his outbuildings equipped with a little stove and a kettle where we could take a break. Although the area wasn't as industrial as Bradford, Keighley did have a railway station with goods yards, several textile mills, a foundry, at least two engineering works, warehouses, the tannery, and the water and gas works. Most of the women in the weaving sheds were making vital cloth for the Army, and Dean, Smith and Grace, one of the bigger employers, made what was known as 'the Rolls-Royce of lathes'. During the war, they provided a hundred lathes a month as part of the munitions effort, mainly used aboard 'repair ships'. (The son of Smith, whose name was Duke, incidentally, was a keen motorcyclist and the first person I ever knew who had a prized Vincent HRD 1,000cc bike.)

With all these potential targets for the Luftwaffe, the main role of the LDV was to remain vigilant, especially after dark. I'd never been walking about in the dead of night before, least of all staring up at the stars hoping not to see a black silhouette or a white dot, so that in itself was new. It was cold but there was no snow and we were Yorkshire folk from the moors so we were accustomed to the climate. Fortunately the spies never came (or, if they did, we missed them) and I don't know what we'd have done with them if they had. We did have one bit of excitement, though, on a night when we were on the hill and one of the men spotted what looked like somebody sending signals from the town. There were repeatedly flashing lights, which seemed to be sending a message, and this created a great deal of panic. We hurried to report what we'd seen to Major Moore and men were sent with rifles to hunt down the secret signaller. In the end it turned out to be a blind that had come loose and was flapping in the wind.

The LDV and later the Home Guard did a very important job during the war and are rather unsung as volunteers, I feel. Throughout the hostilities, more than 1,200 of them died, when they could easily just have stayed at home. I wasn't the only one in my family doing my bit because, even though she was only five feet tall, Freda, who was twenty-three, volunteered for the women's Auxiliary Territorial Service, or ATS, as soon as she was eligible, and Mother joined the Women's Voluntary Service. Once again, Father couldn't contribute anything because of his impaired hearing, which must have been another frustration for him.

6.

'Life is either a daring adventure, or nothing.'

Helen Keller (1880–1968)

St Paul's Cathedral survives the attention
of the Luftwaffe in the winter of 1940.

IT WAS IN EARLY APRIL 1940 that I received my letter from the War Ministry telling me that when I reached the age of twenty I'd be called up for conscription into the 8th Battalion of the 'Dukes', the Duke of Wellington's Regiment (West Riding). This had formerly been a WWI service battalion of Kitchener's Army and its motto was *Virtutis Fortuna Comes* – Fortune Favours the Brave.

I'd already accepted that this was how it would be, but seeing it written down in black and white was quite a defining moment. In truth, I was rather looking forward to the idea of being in uniform, travelling and having different kinds of experiences. And I was right to think that, as being conscripted didn't do me any harm at all. I imagine that my parents weren't very pleased about the news but I don't recall any tears being shed, and if they were they weren't in my presence. Talking of tears, I decided to end it with my girlfriend Marjorie before I left, as I didn't want to go to war with any responsibilities or emotional ties and I didn't think it would be fair on her either. She took it well enough, good lass that she was, and I think we both knew that we weren't right for each other.

In May 1940 the Germans invaded France, the Netherlands and the Low Countries, which felt far too close to home and made war seem even more real. My mobilization papers came through, giving me a week or so to prepare myself and pack only bare essentials. I was instructed to bring a suitcase in which to put my civilian clothes once I was issued with my uniform. On 25 June I had to report to the Infantry Training Centre (ITC) at Weston Park near Otley, a large country estate where the regiment was mustering as infantry.

The first man from the Moore family ever to go to war, I bade farewell to my family that glorious summer's day and fondly ruffled Billy's fur. Once again my mother's eyes remained resolutely dry and, in any case – of the two of them – it was more likely to have been Father whose lip would have trembled.

Granny Fanny was there but very old and rather worn out as she sat knitting socks for the armed forces. I bent to kiss her on the cheek and said, 'Goodbye, Granny,' but she gripped my hand, looked up into my eyes and replied firmly, 'No, Tom. It's goodnight.' I squeezed her hand even tighter and gave her another quick peck, unable to speak and hoping that I'd misunderstood her meaning.

That was the last time I ever saw my lovely Granny Fanny, and it was only after I came back from the war that Mother told me that she'd promised to look after me from Heaven.

Setting off for basic training felt a bit like going on holiday. I strapped my suitcase to the back of my bike, waved cheerio to my family and drove the eleven miles to Otley on a warm summer's day. When I arrived at Weston Park in my civilian clothes and cap, I discovered it was little more than an open field dotted with about 500 bell tents – one of which was my new quarters. I leaned my bike up against a wall and went to find out what they wanted of me.

The weather remained glorious and it was a delightful place to have an introduction to the British Army, but from the moment we arrived we found ourselves having orders barked at us while we were quickly divided into alphabetical groups. As civilian soldiers, none of us knew what we were doing – we couldn't even march in a straight line – and the NCOs must have despaired. Nevertheless, once we reported in, we were processed, given a quick medical check – where my weight was noted as 'spare' – and sworn in. I was given an ill-fitting uniform, an Army pay book, an identity disc and a form on which to write a short will – I appointed Uncle Arthur as my executor because I wasn't planning on dying any time soon and assumed that he'd outlive my parents. And I left everything I owned to my sister Freda.

There was a mess tin and 'eating irons' and something called a 'housewife', which was a small cloth bag full of things for mending and polishing, including a strip of fabric to put around your buttons to protect your uniform from polish. I was handed a pair of underpants and a vest, some trousers, a shirt and battledress, webbing and a pair of size 11 boots. The tallest in my family by several inches, Private T. Moore 193763 was five feet ten inches in his stocking feet and ten stone four pounds, the same weight I've been all my adult life.

Laden with kit, we were each assigned a tent to share with five others, which meant hardly any space at all. Our 'beds' were thin mattresses on the ground without sheets – just coarse wool blankets smelling of the gentian violet they'd been soaked in to prevent contagious skin conditions. To begin with we just nodded at each other, because it was all so new and nobody knew anyone else. We were aged between twenty and thirty-five, from every occupation and recruited across a huge catchment area. Some were from cities like

Huddersfield and Hull, but the majority were farm labourers from agricultural or smaller towns. The thinking behind having Yorkshiremen all together was partly logistical but also so that we'd understand each other better and, I suppose, support one another. It wasn't quite the Pals battalions (a mistake if ever there was one), but the principle was the same.

With no mirrors in our tent I had no idea what I looked like in uniform but the cloth was rough, the boots pinched and the quarters were cramped. We learned very quickly how to lay out our uniforms for inspection and how to polish our shoes to the point that we could see our own reflections in the caps of the toes. Our first meal together comprised a square of processed meat, some bread and tea, and I've no complaints. We did well enough for food in the Army generally but it was never as good as Mother's. As soon as we had eaten we were set to work learning how to become soldiers. It was clear we had to take orders straight away, no questions asked, and that is exactly what I was prepared to do.

On day one at Weston Park I made an important decision. I looked at my fellow soldiers and I looked at the officers and I knew that was where my ambition lay. From that moment on, it was my intention to get a commission. After all, fortune favours the brave, or so the motto claimed. As an officer I could see that I'd have a better life with a better uniform – brown boots instead of black. They had a better Mess, better food and better conditions, and I looked forward to having more responsibility. This was my determined decision and the only person who gave me any advice about it was me. At twenty years old, I was 100 per cent committed to being the best soldier I could be and by doing so earning a commission.

With this in mind and after attending an initiation talk presided over by my first ever officer, a second lieutenant called George Savile (whose full name I discovered was Lord George Halifax Lumley-Savile), I walked up to him and asked, 'Sir, can you tell me how I set about getting a commission?'

This lord of the realm was only a year older than me but looked aghast. 'You cannot speak to me directly, Private Moore. If you want to speak to me, you must do it through the sergeant.'

I wanted to say, 'Stuff you,' but I kept my mouth shut and thought to myself: 'I'll set about this in my own way then.'

In many respects Army life didn't feel that different to home, as I'd always been an early riser, polished my own shoes, made my own bed, and done various duties. I took to basic training with little complaint. More men arrived until we were just under a thousand and, separated into platoons, we learned how to do endless drills or 'square-bashing', march in unison and perform guard duties. We were taught how to clean, dismantle, reassemble and fire rifles, and then a not very bright NCO from Keighley taught us how to use a Bren gun. We also did bayonet training by charging at straw men depicting the 'Hun', before stabbing them and twisting the blade.

There was a lot of marching along unforgiving roads and climbing up steep hills day and night to begin with, but the weather stayed fine and I'd been used to walking on the moors all my life. What was different, was marching in time to the unofficial regimental song, 'The Dukes are Coming up the Hill, Boys'. Keeping my eyes and ears open from the start, I quickly learned that the regimental sergeant major was some-one worth keeping in with, so when he asked if he could borrow my motorbike to visit his ladylove, I immediately agreed. After that, I never had to do another route march again because – if ever there was one – he made me second dispatch rider instead. Taking my bike to camp had served me well and that simple act followed me, for good or ill, for the next five years.

I soon made other friends in the Army too, the kinds you are in service with. They were perhaps comrades more than friends and not necessarily the type I'd take home for tea. If we presented ourselves tidily enough to pass inspection we were allowed out on leave for a few hours or even home occasionally, which was especially important to the men who were married or in a relationship. Once again, I was grateful that I was free. But the effects of the war were already making themselves felt when I went into a café on one of my leave days and ordered scrambled eggs. When it arrived I couldn't eat it as it was made with powdered egg and looked and tasted awful. I said to the waitress, 'You can't possibly call this scrambled eggs!' and I suspect she agreed.

On my first weekend off that August I rode home on my motorbike to formally introduce 'Private T. Moore' to the family – the ex-grammar schoolboy who'd been transformed into a soldier. Mother let out a little sigh when she saw me but Freda said I looked 'very tidy'. The reaction I remember most of all, though, was my dog Billy who hated to see me dressed in uniform. It was as if he didn't know me and he snarled and growled and couldn't be soothed.

Keighley was much the same, but on the Saturday night I went out with two chums from Bradford Technical College, Brian Booth and 'Snowball' Rogers (so called because of his white hair). We went to a pub and had a drink or two of Timothy Taylor's (although I could only ever manage half a pint), and then had something to eat. Spurning my uniform that night, I swapped the flat cap that had been glued to my head as a nipper for the trilby that I thought made me look a bit posh. We also wore 'plus fours', which were tweed or cloth knickerbockers and the most ridiculous item of clothing, but that was the 'in' thing at the time and we were young and stupid.

It was a good evening, but as we were heading home we heard the distinctive wail of the air raid siren followed by the throbbing of aeroplane engines and then bombs dropping over Bradford way. This was happening across Britain with frightening regularity as the Germans started bombing our island home whenever it suited them. As the sky lit up in the distance we wondered what devastation was being caused, and we soon found out. In the course of that night more than 160 bombs fell on Bradford, killing one woman and injuring hundreds of people. An estimated 10,000 windows were shattered and Lingard's – my favourite childhood store – took a direct hit, leaving only its grand facade. The Luftwaffe also bombed the Odeon Cinema in Manchester Road (formerly the Paramount), which – with 2,930 seats – was the largest in England. Incredibly, no one was killed as the film, starring Walter Pidgeon and Deanna Durbin (who had a lovely singing voice), had finished just ten minutes earlier.

With the war getting closer and closer, I was still determined to be the best Private Moore ever at Weston Park, a ploy that served me well. After a few months I was made up to Lance Corporal with a pay rise of ninepence per day, still under the command of Lieutenant Savile. A few days later we were doing a battalion exercise on a hill where we had to pretend to engage with the enemy. By early afternoon and the finish of the first stage it just so happened that I ended up being the leading person on top of the hill, in charge of a couple of hundred men. I received a message informing me that we had suffered some 'casualties', and asking what I was going to do about it. Me being me, I sent a straightforward message back to Lieutenant Savile, saying simply, 'I have lost some men, sir. Can I have some more?'

I didn't receive a reply and the day continued all right, and when it was getting towards teatime we all just wanted to go home. The colonel in charge came to me and said, 'You've been pinned down by the enemy, Moore. What's your plan?' I looked at the lie of the land and saw where the enemy was and said, 'Well, sir, I'll come back down and take my men round that way.' My manoeuvre was such a success that it put a stop to the entire exercise and we all went home for tea. I thought the officers would be as happy with me as the men seemed to be, but instead I was brought in front of Lieutenant Savile for a dressing-down.

'Lance corporals do not send messages back asking for reinforcements, Private Moore,' he told me crisply. 'That is up to the officer concerned.' I was well and truly ticked off, as I didn't understand about the protocol or the strict chains of command. I think Lord Savile must have secretly admired my spirit, however, because from then on he and I were fine and my nerve sowed the seeds of a longstanding friendship. In time, and despite our unpromising first encounters, I came to think of him as the embodiment of how an officer and a gentleman should be.

After a while, rumours began to circulate that we were to be moved on somewhere else to complete our basic training. Soon after that we were given ration packs of sandwiches and loaded on to a train bound for Newquay in Cornwall. Our destination was another tented camp in a field not far from Wadebridge, which we reached by bus. Even though we were largely untrained – an entire battalion spread out in companies – our task aside from furthering our knowledge of all things military was to patrol the northwest coast because it was still anticipated that Germany might imminently invade.

During the evacuation of Dunkirk in June 1940, more than 300,000 British troops stranded in France had been rescued by the Royal Navy and a courageous flotilla of 'little ships' manned by civilians. The fear now was that the Luftwaffe would come after them. As in Bradford and elsewhere, the Germans continued to carry out multiple bombing raids on Britain to harry us as often as they could. Shipping, convoys and ports were systematically targeted along with RAF bases. And with France fallen, there was also a separate threat of invasion by sea. Then, for three months starting in July 1940, the nation held its collective breath during the Battle of Britain when the Royal Air Force did such a valiant job. While we watched helplessly from a distance, German bombers flew in to bomb the dockyards at Devonport in Plymouth and the city of Truro. We also witnessed several dogfights overhead with Spitfires on patrol, marvelling at the turn of speed and the way they outran the heavier Messerschmitts.

Against enormous odds, the brave young British and Allied pilots, many of them only in their twenties and with a life expectancy of something like three weeks, defended us against an enemy that was attempting to blockade us by air and sea. They gave what Churchill called 'their finest hour' in shooting down German bombers faster than they could be replaced. Thanks to them, and having failed to gain control of the air, Hitler would eventually call off his planned invasion of Britain and turn his attention to Russia instead.

As Winston Churchill would say of our pilots later that year, 'Never in the field of human conflict was so much owed by so many to so few.'

Our small role in the general British defence plan of Cornwall was to guard what I only recently discovered was a decoy airfield designed to confuse the German pilots. Our orders were to 'stand to' in readiness to protect the Bristol Bulldog fighter biplanes that were a throwback from just after the Great War. Not appreciating the subterfuge, we were shocked at how limited the British air capacity seemed to be. Little did we know that it was all part of a scheme to protect the main aerodrome at St Eval, a Fighter Command sector headquarters during the Battle of Britain that had helped save the nation from a full-scale German invasion.

We were given a single Maxim machine gun to fire at enemy aircraft, a weapon that was even older than the planes, and with a canvas rather than a metal belt. We just about managed to assemble it but never dared fire it. We also had a Lewis gun that fired one round and jammed, so we didn't do much with that either. All the local beaches had to be off-limits and impenetrable, so another of our tasks was to lay rolls and rolls of barbed wire and tubular scaffolding along the coast to prevent enemy landings. Then at night, in groups of no more than three, we were instructed to patrol the cliffs and watch out for a German invasion.

It was like the Riddlesden LDV all over again and I have no idea what we could have done against a fierce, well-equipped enemy. In the face of a troop of Wehrmacht invaders I suppose we'd have fixed our bayonets, tried to look as if we meant business and shouted, 'Stop! Who goes there?' If Hitler had only known who was guarding the Cornish coastline at the time, he could have sent a couple of lads across in a boat and they would have won the war. Fortunately, we got away with it.

We spent several months in North Cornwall doing route marches with mock air attacks and continuing our weapons training using dummy bullets. On days off we went into Padstow and drank scrumpy cider, which was too potent for my liking. Of course we were always on the lookout for girls, but there didn't seem to be too many around. I expect their fathers locked them away the minute we hit town. Although I was a hardy moorsman, I've never been as cold as I was that winter. I had a bottle of ink in my kitbag that froze solid. Not that I used it much, mind. I was never a good correspondent to my parents for all the years of the war. I just wasn't a letter writer and, although I knew they would have been worried and would have loved to hear from me, we were very limited by what we could say anyway because of censorship. That was just an excuse, though, as I rarely put pen to paper and if I did my letters were brief.

I did receive a few from them and learned that Freda had been made up to a corporal in the ATS. It wasn't until later that I found out she was an RAF plotter and administrative NCO on an airfield in Wales along with her closest friend Daisy, whom she'd known since school. My father – who'd always considered himself Freda's guardian – would have been especially worried for her. With both of us away, life must have been very different at Club Nook for my middle-aged parents, but they did have two young evacuees to look after by then so I hoped that was a distraction.

I, meanwhile, was still determined to show my mettle as a soldier whenever I could. As Orderly Lance Corporal I was placed on main guard duty one night, which meant policing anyone coming in or out of the camp. As I was patrolling I came across a chap I knew trying to sneak out illegally. Without hesitating, I barred his way and told him that he couldn't leave. He insisted he had to, so I put him on a charge. If I hadn't I might have been demoted and I couldn't let that happen. This action alone marked me out to my superiors as somebody who was prepared to take on authority, as I think they'd been waiting to see if I could. It probably didn't make me very popular, but the lad concerned did come to see me afterwards to apologize and said he'd been desperate to see a girl that night. He assured me he had no ill feeling.

Shortly after that I received another stripe and became full corporal and then, in March 1941, I was recommended for the OCTU or Officer Cadet Training Unit. Before I was admitted I needed a reference and Major Moore from my LDV days kindly provided me with one, confirming that he had known me for ten years and could account for my 'good moral character'. The subsequent recommendation form for officer training described me as aged twenty years and seven months, in medical category '*A1*', and my military character as '*very good*'. My technical qualifications were listed as: '*Three years practical. Two years theory in civil engineering.*' Under the heading Power of Leadership, the interviewing board wrote: '*Good. Little more confidence required*', although another CO said I was, '*Quick-witted with sound common sense*', and would make a '*useful officer*'. They designated me '*suitable*' for OCTU and, with their stamp of approval, I achieved my career ambition in less than six months.

7.

*'Believe me that every man you see in
a military uniform is not a hero.'*

The Duke of Wellington (1769–1852)

The surprise Japanese attack on Pearl Harbor
naval base in December 1941 caused the
United States to join the war.

By the spring of 1941 Britain was under almost constant bombardment from the Germans in what became known as the Blitz. Major cities such as London, Coventry, Belfast, Portsmouth, Plymouth, Bristol, Glasgow, Liverpool and Newcastle were especially badly hit and British morale took quite a dip.

Blackouts were by then the norm, as were taped-up windows to protect human flesh from shattering glass. There were sandbags everywhere along with near constant sirens, when people fled to underground shelters. Air raid precaution wardens, police officers and firefighters did sterling work, and with everyone busy in the war effort, there was a thriving black market trading in clothing, petrol, food and luxury items at a time of ever stricter rationing. In Africa, Rommel was starting to square up against British forces in the Western Desert, and Italy and Germany were being bombarded in retaliation. Yugoslavia and Greece fell, and 100,000 British women were summoned to the factories to do war work. By June the Nazis had broken their pact with the Soviets and invaded Russia.

While the world burned, I arrived at the OCTU at Droitwich near Worcester for an expected six months. As was the custom, I was immediately stripped of my hard-won rank and had to wear the white cap band and tapes on my shoulder that singled me out as a cadet. From there we were moved to Heysham Head near Morecambe to finish our training, and I spent my twenty-first birthday there that April with my sister Freda, who came to visit and bring a few small gifts from the family. I hadn't told anyone in the battalion about my birthday and wasn't planning on marking it in any way, but when Freda wrote and said she was coming, I asked for a few hours off and took her to a Lyons Corner House for a brew. I have a photo of us that day, with me in uniform.

My fear at the OCTU the whole time was that I might fail in some way and be RTU'd or 'returned to unit', but once I arrived I realized that I wasn't there to learn about manoeuvres or battle tactics at all; I was there so that they could decide if I was suitable to be a 'gentleman and an officer'. It wasn't a particularly snobbish environment because we were all Yorkshiremen together, but it did feel a bit like being in school and applying to become a prefect. I must have done all right because the course ended with me being commissioned into the 9th Battalion as a second lieutenant that August. There was no big fanfare; I merely received a notification from my commanding officer. Simple as that.

By then it was a certainty that we'd be sent overseas soon and I wondered where to – North Africa, perhaps, where every man was needed after Rommel and his Afrika Korps entered Tripoli, or into Europe where the Germans had invaded Yugoslavia and Greece? Maybe further afield to protect the furthermost reaches of Empire? First, though, it was to the Regimental Depot at Halifax to be kitted out and prepared for a draft to whichever unit I'd be assigned to. It was there that I made a very good friend by the name of Philip Thornton from Monmouthshire, who was a year younger than me and far better educated. His father had fought in the Great War and Philip had been to public school at Marlborough and was due to read classics at Cambridge. He had a passion for music and birds – of the feathered variety. He also spoke as warmly of his parents as I spoke of mine. He'd first joined the 'Buffs' Young Soldiers Battalion (Royal East Kent Regiment), was transferred to the Royal Warwickshire Regiment and then commissioned into the Dukes. We hit it off from the start and he was the first of my comrades that I'd have taken home for tea.

Three of us were told to present ourselves to the adjutant shortly after arrival and, being polite, when we were sent in to see him we removed our hats. For this crime we were immediately blasted with, 'Who the devil told you to take your hats off? You do not take your hats off. You only take your hat off when you're on a charge.' Thus was my introduction to being an officer.

To my dismay, Halifax turned out to be another field encampment, but whilst I may have been disappointed by the accommodation, it did have one major point in its favour – an unusual motorcycle combination of a motorbike with a side-car that had drive on both wheels, rather like a four-wheel drive car. It was designed to tackle the kinds of hills Uncle Billy and my childhood heroes once struggled with. Showing an interest helped me because I was drafted to Winchcombe, Gloucestershire, where the 9th Battalion had been re-roled as an armoured unit in the Royal Armoured Corps to bolster the existing cavalry and Tank Corps regiments. Looking back, I realize that I probably wasn't chosen for this draft because of my brilliance; it was just that the Army was so short of men they had to rely on reserves and grammar-school-educated men like me, especially any who knew their way around an engine. I was nevertheless delighted, as I knew that I'd thrive in an environment where I was dealing with all things mechanical and could use my pre-war technical experience.

In the heart of the Cotswolds I met a big London lad called John Billham, who rose through the ranks with me to Captain and remained an acquaintance for many years. I also got along with a chap called Jim Stockley, who served alongside me for the rest of the war.

After receiving some quick basic training in AFVs or Armoured Fighting Vehicles, we were finally told where we were to be drafted next – India. I can honestly say that I wasn't nervous at the news, although I had never expected to travel so far. With the war heating up in the Far East, the expectation was that we'd be fighting the Japanese who'd already invaded Manchuria, China and, more recently, Indochina (Vietnam) in the autumn of 1940. With imperial ambitions of its own, Japan was at loggerheads with the Americans and it seemed likely that it also had designs on the British Empire. British and Commonwealth soldiers were already defending the mountains of the tribal North-West Frontier of India where it was feared the Germans might try to invade from the Middle East, so the more easterly areas were earmarked for us.

Naively, I liked the sound of combat in India. This was what I'd been trained for the previous nine months, after all, and as a young man who'd long been interested in maps and the more exotic places I'd seen on stamps, I regarded it as one long adventure. War was still just a word.

Late that August I travelled with Philip and several other officers to Liverpool where we found a vast armada of vessels at anchor in the harbour. We reported in and boarded our ship, the *Duchess of York*, a 20,000-ton ocean liner owned by the Canadian Pacific Steamship Company. She was one of the many requisitioned cruise liners that plied back and forth between Britain and the colonies throughout the first half of the century.

We were embarking for India on one of what were known as 'the WS Convoys' (for Winston's Special), travelling in a flotilla of about ten ships initially. Our convoy comprised merchant vessels carrying vital cargo, many of which were armed with mines, anti-aircraft guns, torpedo netting and anti-submarine guns; our 'troopers'; plus a few Royal Navy vessels whose names we were never told as part of the security policy to keep us in general ignorance. One of these escorts was known to many, however – the WWI battle cruiser HMS *Repulse* on what proved to be one of her final voyages.

After pulling away from port, our eight-week journey would take us north to the Clyde to meet up with more vessels, then around the top of Britain, not far from Scapa Flow where HMS *Royal Oak* had been torpedoed two years earlier. We'd then make the long journey south past the Rock of Gibraltar towards Africa. Aside from the gales and the high seas, these were some of the most treacherous waters in the world thanks to German warships, aeroplanes, French coastal batteries and the feared U-boats that prowled the depths. In what Winston Churchill called 'the Battle for the Atlantic', Britain organized hundreds of escorted convoys to supply troops, food, raw materials and equipment to battlefields and besieged countries during this period and yet thousands of ships were sunk by air attack or torpedo as the Germans set out to destroy every-thing that moved. It was not a comforting thought.

There had been a collective sense of relief in May of 1941 when the *Bismarck*, a battleship Germany had claimed was unsinkable, was successfully attacked. Around a hundred

British naval vessels took part in the chase and the *Bismarck* was finally sunk in the mid-Atlantic with the loss of over 2000 lives. It didn't stop the Germans, however, and the almost daily Allied sinkings continued. In late May the *Colonial*, bound for Cape Town from Liverpool, was lost to three torpedoes and the crew saved by a British battleship. In September 1941, while we were at sea, a vessel called the *Cingalese Prince* making the return trip from Bombay to Liverpool was torpedoed and sunk by a U-boat south of the Cape Verde islands. Fifty-seven died and naval vessels had to rescue the remainder. And while we were at sea, a German torpedo off Gibraltar sank the *Ark Royal*.

On-board the *Duchess of York* there wasn't much point in dwelling on the dangers, and little opportunity. Conditions were extremely cramped as every space was packed with men and equipment. I shared a comfortable enough cabin with John Billham and was never more grateful that I'd been commissioned, as the regular men were packed into the airless hold in hammocks and only ever came up on deck for some fresh air for a brief period once a day. This would have been unpleasant at the best of times, but especially when the going was rough.

The men were good at entertaining themselves, however, and there were lots of PT exercises and a ship's boxing championship as well as other activities including films and lectures on the care of weaponry in India. We also had concert parties with men dressed up as women and doing little sketches. It passed the time. For us officers there were various courses to run between meals, the last of which was inexplicably referred to as 'dinner', which had been at noon for all of my life.

Having proved to my commanding officers in the previous nine months that I was capable with mechanics, I was given the task of instructing the men on the workings of a petrol engine. This was all but hopeless without an actual engine because I was trying to teach people who'd never even seen the inside of a car the finer points of a carburettor with the use of a skimpy one-line paper drawing. There was no model to show them, and most of them didn't even know where a carburettor went or what it did anyway. It wasn't easy, but I had no shortage of volunteers because my classes allowed them up on deck for an hour or so. I couldn't blame them, especially as we approached Africa and the weather became increasingly tropical.

In mid-September we stopped briefly outside Freetown, Sierra Leone, where one of the ships in our convoy needed assistance, but there was no shore leave as the harbour was too small to accommodate such large vessels. Then we headed south again and travelled around the Cape of Good Hope to Cape Town. It was early morning when we arrived at the end of September and I was up on deck early as usual, so I saw the city and Table Mountain in the sunrise and was so impressed. I had rarely seen anything quite so beautiful and I imagined the top to be as smooth as a tennis court, and somewhere I would like to visit.

We rested there for four days so that the crew could refuel the ships and restock supplies, and I have to say we were treated fantastically well by the locals. This is where being an officer really came into play – especially after four weeks at sea – because we were welcomed with open arms into what was effectively a peacetime environment. This meant invitations to one cocktail party or dinner after another, and being shown the city. Best of all, we were driven around in a brand-new Studebaker Champion, a beautiful American car that boasted the first column change gear lever on the steering wheel that I had ever seen. I was even more impressed and, for those four days, it didn't feel like there was a war on at all.

Once we returned to the *Duchess of York*, our convoy set sail again, making a rendezvous with other vessels at Durban, and then onwards to India. We finally berthed in the harbour at Front Bay in Bombay, known as 'The Gateway to India', on 22 October 1941. Granny Fanny must have been looking out for me because for the whole of our journey we managed to avoid the attentions of the enemy.

The *Duchess of York* wasn't so lucky, however, because in July 1943 she was so badly damaged by German air attacks during a similar convoy to ours sailing 300 miles off Spain that the Royal Navy rescued those it could from her burning wreckage and sank her to avoid drawing the attention of U-boats. Now that I was in India, the guardian angel I didn't even know I had yet would have her work cut out for her.

From the moment we arrived in India we were assaulted on all sides by clamour and chaos and colour. It was a country that immediately struck me as unbelievably strange and hot and foreign. It was an entirely different world and nothing during my life in Yorkshire had ever prepared me for this. I loved it.

As we disembarked in an orderly fashion, everyone pressed in around us in an extremely disorderly fashion, trying to sell us things or carry our luggage. We each had our kitbags but officers were also allowed personal luggage as well, so I had a big leather suitcase with my best suit, some casual clothes and other personal stuff including a camera. The quarter-master was shouting at us not to allow strangers to take our bags; there were bearers employed by the Army especially for that. I relinquished my suitcase to one of the latter and that was the last I saw of it. It was put into storage in Bombay with all the rest, but we later heard that a ship had been bombed in the harbour and exploded, causing a huge fire that burned down the warehouse. I lost everything, and the only compensation was a small insurance payout.

The temperatures in India were something none of us had ever experienced before. Having survived the hustle and bustle of the Bombay quayside we were taken to the railway station – another experience in itself – teeming with crowds of people, birds and animals; sights and sounds and smells we could hardly credit. We were given some Indian currency and put on a train to Poona, a distance of about a hundred miles in packed carriages that crawled along painfully slowly. Our 'air-conditioning' consisted of a galvanized container with a big lump of ice in it around which we could sit and fan ourselves. That was all they had and it was quite necessary, as it did get a bit hot.

In Poona we were driven southeast to our new quarters at the Kirkee Royal Artillery barracks about five miles out of town and quickly settled in. There were 500 in our battalion. Mercifully, we officers were given not tents but airy bungalows around a central courtyard that housed the Officers' Mess. The buildings were designed to combat the heat, which meant that we were finally a bit more comfortable. I was in a room with three other officers, including Philip Thornton, and we each had an Indian servant or bearer. It felt quite luxurious.

The food was good too, as there was a proper cookhouse with Army cooks so there was meat, potatoes and vegetables and no upset tummies – yet. Eating has never been a priority for me and even as a boy I could go a day without food when I was on the moors with Billy. I'd be fine as long as I had my porridge for breakfast, a routine I maintained in India after I taught the cooks how to make it right, with plenty of hot creamy milk and lots of sugar. 'I don't want a slice of porridge,' I'd warn them. The rice pudding out there was disappointing, however, and nothing like Granny Fanny's – just a stodgy mess with a smear of something that called itself jam. It wouldn't do at all. But I was happily introduced to curry for the first time and many of the Anglo-Indian dishes that were popular at the time, such as kedgeree. There were other novelties for me too.

I'd never been much of a one for alcohol and could only ever manage a small beer, but in Kirkee I was introduced to a 'sundowner' favoured by the Raj that I became quite partial to. It was called a John Collins (precursor to the better known Tom Collins), and was really just a gin lemonade made with fresh lemon juice and sugar syrup. It was extremely refreshing and we thought we were all being a bit posh drinking it. Even now, I enjoy one if someone is kind enough to make one for me.

Our seemingly endless supply of gin came from an unlikely source. It was provided by Philip Lloyd, our Cambridge-educated Army padre, who was also the Bishop of Nashik and appeared to have a secret supply. I liked him very much and he must have been a very compelling person because he persuaded me to be confirmed at his church in Nashik, something I'd avoided up to that point despite my teenage devotion to the Sunday school tutor in Keighley. The Bishop and I got on very well and when we were talking one day he suggested I should do it sooner rather than later, so I said yes. There was only me, and I think it felt right to be doing it in a time of war somehow. My family had been chapel or churchgoers all their lives so I considered myself a Christian and always had a quiet kind of faith.

In the first few weeks in Kirkee we were issued with *topees*, which were WWI pith helmets with a lip or little curtain at the back to protect the back of the neck from the sun. They were heavy and hot so we switched them for Australian-style hats with a brim. They weren't much use either so we went back to our regimental black berets but these were the worst of all, as black doesn't reflect the sun and just made us even hotter. Incidentally, we had all been issued with new Royal Armoured Corps badges for our berets and ordered to wear them instead of our Duke of Wellington's Regiment ones, but in a quiet mutiny we all switched back to our original badges, insisting that we were still proud 'Dukes'.

In the event it hardly mattered because as the temperatures rose there were very few caps worn and many of the men wandered around in shorts and boots, only to discover that the mosquitoes would gorge on their bare skin so shirts went back on. On orders from above, mosquito cream had to be applied, sleeves rolled down at sunset, and trousers worn at night. Some of the men also suffered from prickly heat and were covered in a terrible rash but most of us adapted quite well to the climate and had few problems aside from sunburn. It was long before the invention of sunblock and there were no 'factors' to consider other than what time the sun would set.

Once settled, our battalion – as 146 Regiment Royal Armoured Corps – became part of the 50th Indian Tank Brigade. This had a number of units of tank regiments and an infantry battalion that included the 25th Dragoons, the 19th King George's Own Lancers, the 45th Cavalry Regiment and the 2nd Battalion, the 4th Bombay Grenadiers. Brigadier Schreiber, our GOC or General Officer Commanding, was a man no one much liked. In fact, he was the kind of commander who made people tremble in their boots. Everyone thought he was mean, but I just thought he was in a hurry and under enormous pressure to get people trained up. Thankfully, our daily dealings were mainly with Lieutenant Colonel Pat Woods, who was as nice a person as you could hope to meet. He only had one eye, having lost the other playing squash, but he was a good officer who had the loyalty of his men.

The plan was to train us up for tank warfare as quickly as possible because there was a new urgency. On 7 December 1941, six weeks after we'd arrived in India, the Japanese bombed Pearl Harbor in Hawaii to cripple the US Pacific Fleet. There had been simultaneous attacks on Singapore, Hong Kong and other key ports as part of the Japanese plan to seize control of the Dutch East Indies oil fields and expand their empire into South East Asia. Three days later HMS *Prince of Wales* and HMS *Repulse* (which had escorted our convoy) were both sunk in the South China Sea by a swarm of Japanese torpedo planes, with the loss of almost a thousand men. The attack on Pearl Harbor finally brought the United States into the war and made Japan an enemy of all the Allies. As loyal cogs in His Majesty's war machine, we were tasked with defending the dominion from her new enemy.

This prospect wasn't something that was taken lightly because the Japanese were feared, chiefly because they didn't mind if they died. Known for their devotion to duty based on the Samurai code of *bushido* – the sacrifice of the individual for the sake of honour – they were also known to treat their opponents atrociously. Those men were completely without morals, torturing and starving people to death. Failure was not an option and any member of the Imperial Army who was defeated or taken prisoner of war was expected to kill themselves in a ritualistic suicide known as *hari kari*. Only this would appease their ancestors, honour their divine Emperor, and atone for their disgrace.

Anyone they captured or defeated was also considered disgraced, only to be treated with contempt. Hence the survivors of the ships they attacked were strafed in the water and those poor souls captured in Singapore were forced to build the impossible Burma Death Railway in unspeakable circumstances. It was a good job we didn't know much about that to begin with, but the one thing we did know was that we were completely unprepared to face them yet, and so were many of those in charge.

8.

'Live as if you were to die tomorrow.
Learn as if you were to live forever.'

Mahatma Gandhi (1869–1948)

The Imperial Japanese Army masses
on the Burmese border in 1942.

WE REMAINED IN KIRKEE for several months and it was quite a pleasant place to be. The town of Poona had a selection of shops and, from one of them, I bought myself a Kodak Autographic camera to replace the one I'd lost. It also had an excellent Chinese restaurant, a place I visited often with my friend Philip Thornton and other fellow officers like John Billham. Aside from curry, this was my first introduction to Asian food, which was about as far removed from roast beef and Yorkshire pudding as you could get. Always open to new experiences, I loved it.

The first time I went into town, I borrowed a bicycle and was given directions, but I made a mistake. When I reached a crossroads there was a signpost that said 'City' in one direction and 'Cantonment' the other. I had no idea what cantonment meant but I knew what city meant so I went that way. This was my introduction to the extreme poverty of India, because the 'City' was where all the poorest people lived cheek by jowl in little more than hovels by the side of the road. As I cycled slowly through, I wondered if I was in danger because I had never seen anything like it in my life. The men and women, in turn, stared back at me – the rare sight of a skinny young British officer in khaki shirt, shorts and pith helmet in their midst. Of course, despite my nervousness, no one did anything or harmed me in any way. I'm sure they assumed I was just another member of the Raj, who generally treated them with contempt, a fact that came to sadden me. As I was to discover, however, the Indians were a peaceful and gentle people and I never had anything to fear. Nevertheless, I didn't make the mistake of cycling into the City again.

There were a few eligible daughters of the Raj living in the posher areas of Poona, and of course some chaps did their best to woo them. To their surprise, the girls were extremely old-fashioned and rather snobbish, just like their parents. If approached in a flirtatious way, these young ladies would look the men up and down and say, 'I can't possibly talk to you until you have given your card to Daddy.' In the face of such resistance they were quickly forgotten and the men got down to the serious business of drinking cocktails, playing sport and enjoying the camaraderie of the camp.

Before too long, we were moved out towards the Deccan Plateau and a place called Dhond, situated between two mountain ranges, the Western and Eastern Ghats. This sparsely populated area with no nearby towns and no chance of respite was where we were to start proper training with the tanks. Here we found a vast area peppered with lakes and flat farmland formed of dark sticky clay or 'cotton soil'. For a lot of the men in India this mud was a real problem and they lived knee-deep in the stuff for months on end during the monsoon season, but, fortunately for us, when you have tanks you have to keep out of wet ground so we had tarpaulins and found hardstanding wherever we could. The only way we got wet was through constant perspiration, for which we were supposed to take salt tablets.

Nevertheless, at Dhond began the start of real hardship that didn't let up until the end. In the dry season our tented encampments were open spaces plagued by mosquitoes, dust, biting ants and almost unbearable humidity and heat. There was no insecticide and the flies were everywhere, swarming around food and people. India also had an alarming array of poisonous snakes and I have to say that encountering spiders the size of your hand takes a bit of getting used to. One night in bed I woke up screaming because I thought a snake was crawling across me only to find it was nothing more than a river of sweat pouring off my chest.

The latrines were just two stinking holes in the ground surrounded by a couple of narrow strips of canvas slung on poles. There might occasionally be a bit of netting to keep the worst of the flies off and you had to hold your breath to use them. We had no bathing facilities to speak of and frequently had to douse ourselves in cold water from a bowser to wash away the worst of the sweat and the grime. Small canvas baths were provided but they only held a few inches of tepid water so it was hardly worth it. The local rivers might have offered some relief but we were warned not to swim or wash in them for fear of leeches. While in monsoon season the water was too filthy and muddy because of the run-off to even contemplate wading in.

All I wanted to do was to be put to work, so I was pleased when I received my latest orders. Because it was known that I understood how to operate most vehicles, I was put in charge of training men in tank warfare, even though I'd hardly ever been in one. Within a short time I had to acquaint myself with the British-made Valentine, designed by Vickers. This tank had acquitted itself fairly well in the North Africa Campaign and earned a reputation for reliability, but it was one of those vehicles the clever boys in the Ministry of

Defence hadn't really thought through because, although it was meant to be an infantry support tank, its only gun was a little two-pounder (40 mm) which was quite useless against the German Tiger tanks with 75–105 mm guns. Men on the front lines said that when a Valentine shell hit the side of one of those it didn't even penetrate, it just glowed.

The Army upgraded to bigger American tanks in the desert and sent their leftovers to us, even though they were never really suitable for the Far East. The Valentines had a maximum speed of 15 mph and the driver had to rely utterly on the commander for directions and warnings about obstacles. The trouble was, the commander's vision was almost non-existent once inside a sealed tank and if the turret was facing the flank. When I first crawled inside one I knew immediately that if it were hit then the three-man crew would be trapped and at the mercy of the enemy.

Putting those thoughts aside, I focused on the training. The good news was that the Valentines were pleasant enough to learn on mechanically and better than the lightly armoured Stuarts, also used throughout the campaign. Best of all, the driving system was simple enough to teach someone who had a basic knowledge of engines. There was no steering wheel and the accelerator was the only thing it shared with a car, so you pulled two levers back to brake, pushed them forward to go forward, and engaged them one at a time to go right or left. It seemed easy enough to me and some took to it like ducks to water, but many never did, including the worst driver of all – known to all by the nickname 'Crasher' White.

Nicknames are common in the Army, so anyone with the surname Miller became known as 'Dusty' (because millers are dusty), and anyone called Hudson was 'Soapy' (because of the Hudson brand of soap). I became known to one and all as 'Tommy' Moore. This wasn't something they'd say to my face, but I didn't mind because it was always spoken with affection as well as being a reference to being a 'tommy' or soldier. It could have been a lot worse. There was one chap from Yorkshire called Arthur Robinson who was known as 'Connor' Robinson because '*khana*' was Urdu for food and he was always first in line for some grub. And that was one of the kinder nicknames. *Khana* wasn't the only useful bit of Urdu, as we also picked up '*paani*' for water, '*chapati*' or '*roti*' for bread, and '*doodh*' for milk. But perhaps the most important word for any British soldier based in India was '*chaa*' for tea, although you had to be careful that the tea wasn't made with goat's milk and didn't come overly sweet, although as I've always taken at least two sugars in tea and coffee it was fine for me.

My fellow officers were among my students and all survived the course before being given their own tank to command. One of those was Philip Thornton, an excellent officer and my good friend. The hope and expectation was that I too would be given command of a tank with which to fight the Japanese in British-run Burma, which is where we knew we'd be heading after the Imperial Army captured the capital Rangoon in March 1942, cutting off Burma from the outside world. After three months of training men every day, I did finally get my own tank to command, along with a crew of my choice. And I would be the commander of not one but three tanks, the others commanded by sergeants or NCOs. A Valentine tank has a crew of three – a driver, a gunner and a tank commander – each a specialist in his own field. They also have to have a basic knowledge of the other two roles to cover all eventualities, and be familiar with the tank's first-aid kit.

The choice of individuals for compatibility and temperament is very important in such a confined space. They should be people you can rely on and get along with.

I picked two skilled and personable men who I felt I could trust and then I had to christen my tank. Tradition dictates that each tank is given a name by its commander, which is then painted on the side. More often than not, it is the name of the commander's wife. As I didn't have one of those, I was slightly at a loss. Then John Billham, my friend and fellow second lieutenant from Winchcombe, told me about two mythical giants called Gog and Magog who guarded the entrance to a prominent building in the City of London. 'They say that when they go to war, the war ends,' said John, who at over six feet tall and seventeen stone was something of a giant himself. At his suggestion, I called my tank Magog and he called his Gog.

I was looking forward to going into service with it when, out of the blue, I received a summons to report personally to Brigadier Schreiber – 'Immediately!' At first my heart sank but then I thought to myself, 'Well, you haven't done anything wrong, Tom, so I can't think what this is about. And what can he do to you anyway – you're only a second lieutenant.' I presented myself to the intimidating South African who informed me that the unit urgently needed dispatch riders to pass messages to and from the front lines. 'I am appointing you Brigade Motorcycle Trainer, as of NOW!' he said, adding that I could find myself a 'batman' or personal assistant-cum-driver and that I had the use of one of the brand-new American Willys Jeeps we'd been given. 'Go to the Arsenal, get whatever you want and order whatever you need.' What more could a man wish for than that? The brigadier was what I called 'a passer', who passed on jobs to people to get something done. The message was always: 'You do it. That's your job now. And do it well.'

Having lost command of my tank before I'd taken one step inside it, I was officially designated an Extra Regimental Employment (ERE) reporting directly to Schreiber. Disappointed as I was not to be commanding 'Magog', from that day on I was untouchable. Nobody dared say a word because I was working for the brigadier. What would Lieutenant Savile have thought?

I appointed a good, solid trooper called Leslie Parsons to be my driver/batman who would be wholly responsible for my Jeep, take me where I needed to go, be in charge of moving all my gear, and would even fetch me a cup of *chaa* if I wanted one. Once I had him by my side, I chose my 'company car' and set to work. I have to say that I fell in love with the Willys Jeep from the first day, and it even replaced motorbikes in my affections for a while. It was lightweight, four-wheel drive and as manoeuvrable as a motorbike. Not only could it go anywhere but it had the advantage that it could also transport three passengers and a gun. I'd still have one to this day, given the choice. Les was a good driver, older than me and very personable; a good Sheffield lad and – best of all – we spoke the same language. He chatted to me about his hometown, his wife and his daughter all the time and I enjoyed his company.

Although I undoubtedly had a good job and I was pleased to be working with bikes again, I also worried that it was rather a poisoned chalice. If it all went well, then OK, but if it didn't I'd be dead in the water. Plus, this new position might be detrimental to my career path because I wasn't being absorbed into the regiment. Everyone equivalent to my rank had been given his own troop of tanks to command but I'd just lost mine, which would make me a spare part and – in many ways – an odd bod. My commanding officers had clearly identified me as a good all-rounder, knowledgeable about different practical things including mechanics, map reading and navigation. Also, not much fazed me. But would those skills get me to Captain?

Having been informed that twelve DRs (dispatch riders) were needed in all, I set about providing them. I ordered twelve bikes and took delivery of brand-new 500cc BSA M20 side valves, not dissimilar to the one I had at home, which is just as well because they were the only option apart from the tatty motorbikes the locals used. As with the Valentines, they weren't fit for purpose because they were designed as touring road bikes and not for cross-country. They were slow and heavy when what we really needed were competition bikes like a Velocette K series with studded trials tyres, lower gear ratio, higher ground clearance, and a different gearbox. Frankly, even though I wasn't much of a fan, a horse would have been better at the job, but at least the BSAs were reliable and relatively easy to maintain, so they'd have to do.

I went to the Arsenal in Kirkee as instructed, holding my rare and valuable order giving me carte blanche for anything I wanted, only to be bitterly disappointed. The stores were largely equipped for an expected campaign on the North-West Frontier so, if I'd been in charge of a mule train, I'd have had all that I needed – including the mules. As it was, I left empty-handed. From Supplies I ordered the necessary fuel, oil and lubricants, equipment and goggles – vital for the ubiquitous dust in the dry season. There was no chance of getting helmets and, besides, they'd have been too hot to wear. I had a list of what was needed as each rider had to become familiar with the bike and all its replaceable parts including belt, tube, valves, repair kit, spark plugs, magneto, piston rings, nuts and washers. Uncle Billy would have been in his element.

With the brigadier giving the orders, the motorbikes were delivered in days, so I set to training up British soldiers straight away. Most of them learned fairly quickly but I had to be selective as some were far better than others and several were downright useless. Then there were those who simply didn't want to do it, so they were directed towards something they were better suited for. It was also my role to find locations for initial training and more challenging routes for practice and testing. Just as we'd learned with weapons training, the men had to understand how a motorbike worked and what riding one on the sub-continent might involve. Regular inspection parades checked fuel and oil levels, lights and tyres. Once they'd grasped the basics it was straight out into the bush for starting and stopping, manoeuvring and rough terrain riding.

That aspect took me straight back to the Yorkshire Dales and the bikes trials I had so enjoyed in my youth. As in England, motorbikes take a real hammering out in the wild – especially in the hands of novices – so fault-finding and checking was essential and any major problems had to be reported to the RASC Mechanical Engineers' tent for repair. Once I'd got my trainees through that, they had to learn about dress, equipment, weapons, ammunition, radio (if available), tactics, reconnaissance and message delivery for the success of the mission. There would be a final passing-out test before I had to arrange the changeover of students for the next course.

Dispatch riders were the unsung heroes of the First and Second World War, receiving little recognition, although they played a vital role in maintaining secure communications between headquarters and the troops, often in extreme danger. In places like India and Burma there were few, if any, over-ground telephone lines and even if there were these were frequently cut or damaged by conflict. Wireless sets offered radio operators only a limited range and their messages could be easily intercepted, so the humble dispatch rider was often the only way to get top-secret orders and other messages through – always with the instruction to go via the most direct route and in the shortest possible time. The maps they were issued with were often unreliable and virtually useless once the monsoons washed away primitive tracks or turned passable roads into uncrossable bogs. Each rider therefore had to learn the skills to navigate solo, using their own wits and sense of direction, whilst riding 'off road' as much as on, often under enemy fire.

Because Japanese foot soldiers travelled rapidly and often at night while the Allies preferred to move and fight in the day, riders had to deliver messages between units in all hours, regardless of weather conditions or terrain. Despite their importance, they were never provided with armed escorts and had no other protection than the standard-issue Smith & Wesson .38 revolver, which would have been all but useless against a division of the Imperial Army. Speed and agility was a dispatch rider's best defence, and a breakdown could be fatal, so they carried a few basic tools and had to have enough knowledge to fix a minor problem. Being a rider often suited loners like me who were attracted by the autonomy and sense of freedom, even though the risks were enormous. If the enemy spotted you then they'd do their best to intercept, read or destroy the messages, which usually resulted in the death of the poor devil carrying them.

The men I trained wouldn't automatically become dispatch riders – and many of them would have done so only reluctantly – but, once trained, they could quickly step into the role if any of the DRs were killed or injured – which was something of an occupational hazard. I enjoyed the work and was surprised at how easily teaching came to me. A life in the Army had never been something I'd considered before, but I realized that this was something I was suited to and could potentially stick at even after the war was over. Although that all seemed a long way off.

I should say that there was one great advantage to being the Brigade Motorcycle Trainer for an opportunist like me, and that was that at the end of each course the trainees had to complete a passing-out test before being sent back to their battalions. This involved a long road trip across country, so I devised the brilliant idea of taking them the 120 miles to Bombay and back, driving there in the daylight, staying overnight and returning with me the following day. If they made it there and back they passed. What they did overnight in Bombay was their business, and what I did was mine.

Our road trip to and from the city was always something to look forward to because it was a beautiful ride across plains and valleys, along a main tarmacadam road (not as we would have it, but good enough) with very little traffic and most of it only the old and highly decorated lorries. Once fully fuelled with four gallons of diesel each in our tanks, we'd set off and probably only encounter the odd bullock cart and ubiquitous cow. Aside from that there was nothing to slow us down as we rode in convoy through towns and villages, with me either up front leading or dropping back to monitor their progress and versatility.

I must confess to having an ulterior motive for my repeated trips to Bombay, however. Her name was Sylvia. She was half Indian, half French and the pretty younger sister of the girlfriend of a pal of mine called Russell Curl, a butcher from Cumbria whom I'd first met in battalion training and who was now a cashier for the Army in Bombay. After I met Sylvia there with him I knew I had to get back to her arms as often as I could. She was delightful, in fact, so lovely that I started rushing the men through their training just so I could get to her every weekend. Sylvia and I would go to a bar for a drink and then out for a meal before returning to the house where she lived. Brigadier Schreiber had been pressing me to speed things up, so I was pushing the men partly for him, and partly for Sylvia.

I'd always been a fast learner and I knew that if you put your mind to something in the Army then you could get away with murder. All you had to do was think hard about it and figure out how to work the system to your advantage. Lots of people walked around with clipboards and some blank paper, having discovered that nobody ever asked them what they were doing. I had a clipboard too, but it had a purpose and I worked my own way through the Army to the benefit of us both. I was a bit too efficient for my own good, however, because by hurrying the men through the course I quickly ran out of British soldiers.

Brigadier Schreiber then ordered me to start training up the Indian Army, part of the largest volunteer force the world had ever known. From every caste, race and religion, many of these slender, slightly built men had volunteered to fight for the Empire even though they knew nothing of military life. The majority came from remote rural areas and, although eager to learn and often a good deal more attentive than their

ABOVE: Grandfather John, far left, outside his barber's shop and general store.

Granny Fanny, my guardian angel.

My mother as a young woman.

I loved shopping trips with Mother and Freda to Keighley market.

Low Street, Keighley, shortly before I was born (the corner shop on the right is where Mother ambushed Father to win him back).

Club Nook, the house built by my grandfather that we moved into after his death.

The unveiling of the Keighley war memorial, built by my grandfather, attracted the biggest crowd in the town's history.

ABOVE: Uncle Billy leads the way through the mud in a local trials.

ABOVE: Freda and I befriend a goat in the Dales, with Dad's prized new Rover in the background.

ABOVE: Picking primroses with Mother and Freda after school in 1929.

LEFT: Standing on a wall to get a better view of motorbike trials.

LEFT: The Tower Circus in Blackpool featured Doodles the clown, my father's favourite performer.

BELOW. The Keighley Gala was one of the highlights of the year.

BOTTOM: I was thrilled to go on a pleasure flight from the beach during a family holiday in Southport.

LEFT: Adorned with swastikas as war was looming, the ill-fated German airship *Hindenburg* visited Yorkshire in 1936.

BELOW: I visited the Isle of Man at the age of fifteen to watch my hero Stanley Woods win the annual TT race.

Stanley Woods at Governors Bridge. Senior T.T. 1935.

RIGHT: Mother, Arthur, Freda and Father on the step at Club Nook.

FAR RIGHT: Uncle Billy in his MG with Elsie, shortly before his untimely death.

Mother in her wartime WVS uniform.

Second Lieutenant Moore.

Freda in the ATS.

ABOVE: My favourite Bradford department store, Lingard's, was bombed early in the war.

ABOVE: HMS *Repulse*, later sunk by the Japanese, escorted our convoy to Capetown.

LEFT: SS *Duchess of York*.

ABOVE: Picture of innocence.

LEFT: With my sister Freda on my twenty-first birthday.

RIGHT: Second Lieutenant Moore in Ranchi.

LEFT: The Dukes. The crest of the Duke of Wellington's West Riding Regiment.

ABOVE: Me with my troop in Poona.

ABOVE: Here I am sitting between Philip Thornton and Captain da Costa, third row from front and 3rd left from Major Spong and 'Pig'.

British counterparts, they had never fired a weapon or used modern machinery. As such, there was no mechanical awareness or knowledge, and few could read or write.

None of this bothered me (or mithered, as we'd say in Yorkshire), as all my life I'd enjoyed the company of the illiterate labourers that worked in my father and grandfather's business, all of whom were good and diligent workers. I'd been raised to treat everybody the same, unlike many of my comrades who weren't always pleasant to the Indians and took out their frustrations on them. Once I started with these Indians, however, I did feel sorry for them because these eager but ill-prepared regulars were simply not suited to warfare and the fastest most of them had ever been was on a bullock cart. I knew then that the Army must have been desperately short of soldiers. Don't get me wrong, the Indians were lovely to work with and always tried their best. They were also terribly polite and treated me with the kind of reverence drummed into them by the Raj. In fact, it was more than that because they were so relieved and surprised when I was kind to them when so many were not. Endearingly, they'd put their hands together and say, '*Sahib*, you are my mother and my father now. Tell me what to do.'

But attitude alone wasn't enough. It was up to me to get them into shape, but as most were unfamiliar even with a pedal bike, it was going to take some time. Just as when a child first learns to ride a bike, it takes persistence to work out how to balance without tipping over, so they suffered a lot of spills and falls. Each time this happened, they'd immediately jump up, stand to attention, to salute me and clamber back on their bikes, keen to try again. They were a joy to be with and no trouble at all. You really couldn't fault their effort. There was one major disadvantage with them, however. I didn't dare take the responsibility of leaving these rural farmers to their own devices in a city like Bombay because – even if I got them there in one piece – I feared I would never have seen them or their bikes again. Sadly, that put paid to my weekend jaunts and marked the end of a beautiful friendship. I never saw sweet Sylvia again.

9.

'It is better to let a victory, if it comes, speak for itself;
it has a voice that drowns all other sounds.'

Field Marshal William 'Bill' Slim (1891–1970)

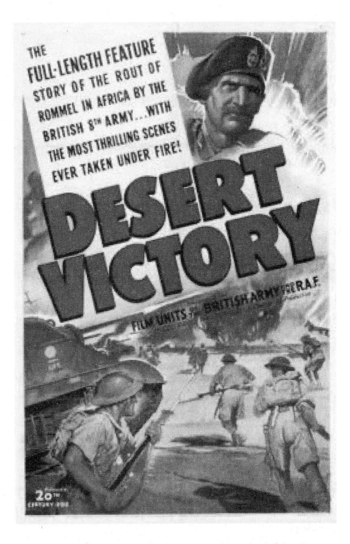

The Allies finally secured victory in North Africa in 1943.

THE MONSOON SEASON WAS a welcome break from the punishing humidity and heat, but our tanks were rendered virtually useless in the wet clay that clogged up the tracks and de-railed some clean off their suspension.

Unable to train with them, we were ordered to break camp and mobilize the whole battalion, including twenty lorries, mortars, an armoured car and 500 men. Our destination was 900 miles further east to an area called Lohardaga and Camp Ratu in Ranchi, East Bengal, where we'd be held as mobile reserve. The tanks were wisely sent forward by train. As I had feared, once we broke camp I was suddenly a spare again, which meant being given whatever job was required, and there were a lot to choose from because the journey to Ranchi was challenging, with exercises en route. Only the British Army could think to relocate an entire armoured regiment with two-wheel drive 15 cwt lorries, petrol trucks, water wagons, troops, cook's wagons and armoured vehicles in the heaviest rains I'd ever seen in my life. I still have photographs I took of vehicle after vehicle bogged down in riverbeds as the roads were virtually washed away and vast areas flooded.

We traversed every kind of landscape from forests and palm trees to wetlands, stopping every 100 minutes for maintenance and rest. When we halted at a place called Mhow the men discovered that some British nurses worked in the hospital there so we had a sudden epidemic of 'tonsillitis', blamed on a change of water, which meant that those afflicted could spend a happy night or two gawping at the girls. Then we resumed our month-long journey travelling through places like Kalpi, Cawnpore, Benares and Hazaribagh. My love for the India of Rudyard Kipling – whose poem 'Gunga Din' about a British Army officer's respect for his Indian soldier I'd only recently read – grew and grew. I couldn't help but marvel at the exotic sights, sounds and smells of the India we passed along the way, not least the ancient Hindu temples and the tenacity of the colourfully dressed people. Benares, now Varanasi, was especially interesting as a site regarded as the spiritual capital of India, drawing thousands of pilgrims who bathed in the River Ganges and performed funeral rites.

By this time I'd been appointed Regimental and Brigade Navigator, largely on the basis that I could read a map. In truth, after my childhood on the moors, being tested by my father during our drives to the coast, and travelling to remote places in my first 'company car' – the waterworks van – I barely needed one. I had long been able to gauge prevailing weather conditions and tell compass points from the stars. India was nothing like the moors, however. The landscape was unfamiliar, key landmarks were often unrecognizable because of the rains, and there were countless unexpected obstacles. We weren't supposed to cross the paddy fields unless we could help it because rice provided a living for the locals, so we had to circumvent them if we could. In some cases this couldn't be avoided and the poor villagers whose crop would be destroyed by all our vehicles and heavy artillery would have to apply for compensation, making us less popular than we already were.

It was easy to get lost in that strange country, although I don't believe I ever did, even if it sometimes felt as if we were going round in circles. One day a major known as 'Cocky' Haslock publicly took me to task during another of our meandering all-day journeys. He halted the convoy, marched up to me in the lead vehicle and, in his clipped accent, said, 'Moore, you haven't the slightest idea where we are, have you?'

I jumped down from the truck and stood briskly to attention. 'Yes, sir, I do.'

'No,' he countered. 'Admit it, Moore. You don't have the foggiest idea.'

Resisting the temptation to look smug, I told him, 'Sir, if you look up that hill you will see a bush, and if you look to the right of the bush you'll see a milestone. That will prove we are on the right course, sir!'

'Rubbish!' he replied but he sent someone to look and of course the milestone was there.

Lieutenant Colonel Woods was with us but said nothing, as he was next to useless with a map or anything mechanical. A charming man – and someone I wouldn't say a word against – he was an excellent hockey player, but map reading or driving wasn't his forte. If ever we were taking part in an all-terrain exercise or due to cross something remotely difficult he'd say, 'Drive me, would you, Moore?' because he knew I could manage his heavy armoured car. He trusted me completely and especially loved it when we'd encounter another unit who were lost and going the wrong way when we were on the right track. He always thought that was a hoot. Thanks to him and my own resourcefulness, I always seemed to find some kind of gainful employment because I was useful, I was willing, and I could do what were basically simple tasks. The Army at my level wasn't intended for brilliant people.

After we arrived at the busy Ratu camp in July 1942 we found ourselves a corner and carried on with our training and exercises. The great advantage of the place was that it had a nearby lake in which we could bathe to get ourselves clean and cool. I took several photos of the men relaxing by it, including one of Lieutenant Colonel Woods in his bathing suit. And I was delighted to reconnect with Lieutenant (Lord) Savile, who'd been transferred there with the 1st Battalion Lincoln Regiment and seemed just as pleased to see me. He always showed a great interest in everyone under his command and was unfailingly gracious and kind.

Over the next few months I continued to be assigned to whatever job was required of me, but one of the things I was fortunately not enlisted for was a night-time tiger hunt encouraged by the local maharajah. His Highness Gaekwar of Baroda, who was known as a bit of a playboy, came so often into our camp that he was eventually given the honorary rank of major. One of our genuine majors, named Bucknall, went on the tiger hunt with him and shots were fired – much to the alarm of Brigade HQ – but all they came back with was a hyena. There was also a jungle shoot with the one-eyed Lieutenant Colonel Woods who was concerned that someone might wound a tiger rather than kill it outright. He needn't have worried because all they bagged was an Indian hare.

As well as the wild animals in India there were a lot of rather skinny stray dogs, some of which attached themselves to the men. They made me homesick for my Billy, being cared for by my parents at Club Nook. I'm pleased to say that I never witnessed any cruelty to the dogs, and in India the animals rarely fought each other or attacked anyone. It was too hot for that. We also saw elephants on the roads and lots of cows, which wandered around as they pleased and couldn't even be moved out of the way because they were sacred. Naturally, the locals were horrified whenever we ate beef. One officer named Arthur Spong adopted a black piglet called 'Pig' as our mascot, which appeared in many a regimental photograph – until it vanished. The rumour was that a rival regiment had stolen it and cooked it for their mess dinner, which seemed shameful but plausible.

Another of my random jobs was to give talks to the regiment about anything that might be relevant to our campaign. One day I was handed a big sheaf of papers about the Japanese, their culture and the geography of their islands, and was told, 'Read this, Moore. You are to give a talk about Japan in the Officers' Mess tomorrow afternoon.' Being the diligent twenty-two-year-old officer that I was, I read everything and duly gave my lecture to the fifty or so men on a very hot afternoon, telling them about Hokkaido island, the Japanese customs of anything from tea drinking to *hari kari*, and their devotion to their emperor. I did my best with the information I was given but the beauty was that, whatever I said, they couldn't correct me because they didn't have the slightest idea – and neither did I.

The funniest thing was that after I'd been talking for some time, I looked up to see that a third of them were asleep, a third were half asleep, and the final third weren't listening at all. I couldn't blame them, because if I'd been forced to sit in a sweaty marquee following a jolly good lunch in order to hear someone droning on about something I wasn't interested in, then I'd have nodded off too.

*

The terrain in Ranchi was similar to what we were expecting to find in Burma – overgrown scrub and heavily wooded with deciduous sal trees, as well as paddy fields and the deep tributaries of rivers that snaked across the land known as *chaungs*. These, we were warned, were used to good effect by the enemy in Burma, who often positioned themselves behind them so that they acted as natural tank traps. We did several exercises to negotiate the wretched things without getting stuck – many of which were unsuccessful. It didn't help that we were often plagued by rain, which made getting around the camp difficult and rendered many of the roads impassable by anything but four-wheel drive vehicles. One night the rains were so bad that all our bedding was drenched and we had to break camp. There were times when we forgot what it felt like to be dry.

As we received so little information about what was happening with the Japanese, we still had no idea what to expect. We just knew that we would be part of the Burma Campaign and that was what we were there for. First, though, we still had to turn ourselves into a proper fighting force, so the training and brigade exercises never stopped and included everything from signals to flanking tactics, camouflage lessons to grenade throwing – often in driving rain. Groups were also set to digging latrines and slit trenches and erecting one-man bivvy tents. There were mine clearing exercises, firing range practice, battlefield first aid, and instructions on how to use the new sun compasses sent to us from the desert campaigns and virtually useless in India. Just to keep us on our toes, we were regularly inspected by various commanders, including Lieutenant Generals Sir Charles Broad and Lieutenant General Noel Irwin, commanders of the Eastern Army, India.

Our new commander-in-chief, the Great War veteran William 'Bill' Slim, acting lieutenant general of the Burma

Corps, was revered by the men, not least because he'd been wounded three times in both wars. Unusually interested in the welfare of his men and determined to reduce the sickness rate from 60 per cent of total strength, he introduced strict anti-malaria practices and had every man inoculated against cholera. I always found this process amusing because we'd stand in line waiting for our injections and it was usually the biggest, toughest soldier who flaked out at the sight of the needle, even before they got to it.

We were also issued with mosquito nets, water-purification tablets that made everything taste foul, mosquito cream and – later – yellow Mepacrine tablets. These latter were to guard against malaria, tapeworm and giardiasis, any one of which we could contract in the tropics. Thousands of British soldiers across the Far East, including several of our own men, had already been hospitalized with malaria, cholera, dysentery, smallpox and other endemic tropical diseases in this, the hottest and most humid part of the world. I had a touch of malaria and lost a bit of weight, but aside from that and the odd rumblings of 'Delhi belly' from the food (that often included local goat meat), I'd managed to stay fit and well despite being pestered by insects.

The Mepacrine tablets were rumoured to make men impotent (which we doubted), but the one thing they did do was turn us all yellow. There weren't any other side effects although I did feel a little unwell at one point so I went to see the Company Medical Officer. He can't have been out there long because he took one look at me and announced, 'You've got jaundice.'

'No, I haven't,' I replied. He insisted I had until I explained that all the men were yellow after taking the anti-malaria medication. He soon changed his tune.

In September 1942 we undertook a major brigade exercise in which we were informed that the 'enemy' had landed an infantry division on the Indian coast at Orissa and the 50th Indian Tank Brigade was ordered to destroy them. This proved to be a success and the invading force was crushed. We were getting the sense that things might be happening for us and this only grew when a few senior officers were sent on a recce of the Calcutta area 350 miles east to see if it was suitable for tanks.

In November I was appointed Intelligence Officer (IO) of our unit, another nice little job. The joke amongst regular soldiers was that there's never been an intelligent officer in the Army, and they may have been right. All that it involved – as far as I could see – was communicating with the other regiments and gathering the little information that was coming and going between exercises. I must have done something right because just before the year's end I was made up to Lieutenant, having completed eighteen months of commissioned service. A few days later, I was also appointed Unit Photography Officer (UPO), probably because I always had my camera with me. This was an additional job to the others I was collecting like scout badges along the way. My brief was to take and develop photographs of the men, the unit and everything from the weather conditions to the exercises, which I did quite happily. My evenings at the Keighley Photographic Club with my father hadn't been wasted.

After so many months of training, we were itching to see some action and on 24 January 1943 a handful of our number, including my friend Philip Thornton, were finally given their chance. Assigned to a tank in a troop of 'A' Squadron, which was added to 'C' Squadron to increase its strength, they were moved out as a combined force, destination unknown.

This naturally caused a bit of a stir as it was the first unit of our brigade to go into action and we wished we were going too. Good for Philip, I thought, as I shook his hand with a brisk, 'Good luck!' He and I had been together since Winchcombe so I was sorry to see him go, along with several others I'd been shoulder to shoulder with for the previous nineteen months, some of them, like Sergeant Dennis and Troopers Bird and Lister, ever since Otley. I couldn't help but think that if I hadn't inadvertently become a spare, I might well have accompanied them with my very own tank troop.

We had no idea where they were being sent or what had happened, and nothing more was heard for three weeks. Then at 12:00 hours on 13 February, Brigadier Schreiber, as Brigade Commander, summoned all ranks to a talk, which was unusual. With a grave expression, he told us that on 1 February, our small troop from 'C' Squadron had been sent into action against the Japanese and there had been some casualties, although he couldn't at first tell us how many. The CO added gravely that the action 'had not been a great success', but insisted that valuable information had been obtained. He said the Valentines had stood up 'quite well' against the fire of captured British two-pounder guns that had been used against them by Japanese at ranges as low as ten yards. There was no news of my friend.

The following day, Major Moody from the 50th Indian Tank Brigade gave a more detailed talk on the action to the officers and NCOs. Three of eight tanks, including one commanded by Philip, had been ordered to take part in a combined attack on an FDL or Forward Defence Line at Donbaik on the 90-mile long Mayu Peninsula of the Arakan, a jungle-covered region on the Burmese coast. Donbaik was an enemy stronghold on the lip of the Bay of Bengal and dominated by a notorious bunker called 'Sugar 5' that the British had already failed to take twice, both times with considerable loss of life. As the Army had already discovered to their cost, the razor-edged ridges, treacherous tidal streams and thick mud were such that it was rarely possible to deploy more than a few tanks at a time into any one field of combat. The feeling was that, if they were well enough supported by infantry, they might be more successful as the Japanese weren't equipped with effective anti-tank guns. Thanks to one of those short-sighted decisions that sometimes happen in warfare – and against the advice of Lieutenant General Slim – this group was sent into a heavily defended area without enough of that support and it quickly became a massacre.

On 15 February the casualties were published in Daily Orders:

Killed in action, 1 Feb 1943, Trooper R. Bird. Reported missing since the action on 1 Feb 1943, Lieut. P.H.T. Thornton, Sergeant Dennis, Corporal Willie, Troopers Carpenter, Bedford, Lister, Heywood, Inman, Nicholson.

Ten in all – missing, dead or taken prisoner. Three tanks went in, with three men per tank, plus a trooper who'd been shot. None came back. It was the most dreadful shock to our unit and had a severe effect on morale. The grim news hit me hard and I couldn't help thinking about Philip's parents back home and wondering if they had yet received a telegram.

I didn't find out what really happened at Donbaik until much later when I heard details from some of those who were there. Philip and his fellow soldiers had been in training for a different assault on Akyab Island, a few miles south of Donbaik, when they suddenly received orders to assist 55th Indian Brigade on the orders of Lieutenant General Irwin, who'd been put in charge of this part of the Arakan offensive. The intelligence received had been deeply misleading as the men were told not to anticipate much resistance. The tanks were to be supported by a unit of the Dogra Regiment of the Indian Army, as well as artillery and Bren Gun Carriers with additional fire support. But instead of only a small contingent of Japanese, the cunningly constructed hilltop bunkers at Donbaik were crammed full of men from one of the most feared divisions of the Imperial Army. They were well armed with machine guns and they'd also captured the British anti-tank gun which they used to good effect.

When Philip and the other tank commanders went in, they not only faced a huge number of embedded enemy soldiers but found the going beneath them appalling. Almost as soon as they entered the field of battle, they realized their mistake, but it was too late. One by one, the ground fell away beneath the first three tanks and they nose-dived into a heavily camouflaged *chaung* adapted as an anti-tank ditch. Despite their desperate efforts to reverse out, as we had been trained to do in exercises, there was no grip and they were unable to extricate themselves.

The rest of the squadron was then hampered by poor visibility caused by smoke, failed radio communications and weapons that jammed because of the humidity. They said later that from the noise of firing, the men in the three tanks must have put up a very gallant fight before being overrun. In the chaos that followed Captain da Costa, the officer in charge, tried three times to turn his troop around to help the others but without success, because he could no longer reach his men by radio and when he raised the 'rally' flag no one could see it for smoke. When they came under even more sustained mortar fire, one of the tanks was disabled and Captain da Costa towed it to safety before they were forced to withdraw. A rescue attempt was made within the hour but the Japanese resisted so fiercely that it too had to be abandoned.

Of the five tanks that managed to escape, three suffered serious damage, Lieutenant Carey was badly wounded in the leg and his gunner killed. The men stood by for some days hoping to attempt another rescue but were eventually ordered back. Before he left, Captain da Costa climbed to a hill over-looking the site and, through binoculars, saw that the tanks and the men inside them were – as he reported simply later – 'unrecoverable'.

What happened at Donbaik was rarely talked about amongst us, and the details of the tactical errors made were kept quiet at the time so as not to further lower morale. Slim was incensed that his advice had been ignored and Irwin – who blamed the equipment, training and motivation instead of admitting any personal responsibility – was relieved of his command and returned to Britain, where he was given a much reduced role in Scotland until the end of the war.

Lieutenant Colonel Woods was devastated by the loss and went on immediate leave. I was sent on an instruction course to Barrackpore, north of Calcutta, which included training in Map Reference Points Codes. From there I wrote to Philip's parents to express my condolences, beginning a correspond-ence that lasted for several years. I didn't know them and I never went to see them, but I like to think they took some comfort from the fact that one of his friends vouched for his courage, good humour and his popularity among the men.

On my way home from the course at Barrackpore, I found

myself on my own in a hotel in Calcutta, seriously unwell. I can't even remember how I got there, but I know I spent several days in bed with a horrid fever, a nasty headache and nobody to tend to me. Aching all over and unable to eat, I was too ill even to take myself to a doctor, but eventually the fever broke and I was able to make my way back to my unit. I'd always been thin but I lost so much weight that Lieutenant Colonel Woods, who found himself walking behind me, said: 'Moore, you haven't got a bottom. You've only got tops of legs.'

Almost as soon as I returned I was ordered to give a lecture on what I'd learned about map reference codes. It was the unit doctor that informed me that I'd had dengue fever, a viral infection spread by mosquitoes and rife on the Indian sub-continent. He said I was lucky that it hadn't become life-threatening, but I told him that having grown up in a family where you either got better or you didn't, there was no choice to be a softie about it – or anything else.

10.

'The only thing we have to fear is fear itself.'

Franklin D. Roosevelt (1882–1945)

6 June 1944. D-Day marked the beginning
of the end of the war in Europe.

FOLLOWING THE FAILURE OF DONBAIK, there seemed to be little chance of going into Burma again because the Valentines were simply not suitable and their weaponry woefully insufficient. As one senior officer put it, 'Burma is untankable.'

It was perhaps telling that the Japanese, who were far more accustomed to jungle warfare, only used a few tanks in that region – mostly light Type 95 *Ha-Gos* and usually in small groups. Then in March 1943 we heard that the remainder of 'C' Squadron, including Lieutenant Carey who had recovered from his injury, was successfully involved in the action on the Mayu Peninsula with a battalion of the Black Watch. This, at least, was something. When they returned to Ranchi the brigadier invited them to tea at Brigade HQ. Bravely, I thought, Lieutenant Carey also gave us a talk on the lessons learned from the deaths at Donbaik.

The months rolled on with continual exercises and training as well as ever more rain to contend with. Then in May 1943 we were finally sent back to Poona – this time by train – where we would sit out the monsoon and remain for nine long months. The tide of war in the rest of the world had turned dramatically at this point. North Africa had been wrenched back from the Germans, the Russians were reclaiming their besieged cities, and the Italians had surrendered to the Allies. I kept up with British developments via the newsreels and had occasional missives from home when my parents' letters made it through. One came via China and contained a delightful surprise: a photograph they'd had taken of Mother, Father, Freda and Uncle Arthur in the front parlour at Club Nook with a framed photograph of me on the mantelpiece. My beloved dog Billy, looking greyer in the muzzle than I remembered and with the telltale glint of cataracts in both eyes, sat on the couch between the two women. I read the accompanying letter and learned that Mary, the Princess Royal, had visited Keighley as part of 'Wings for Victory Week', and that even more evacuees had arrived from London to be cared for in the community. The Yorkshire Dales and my beloved moors seemed a million miles away from Kirkee and, although I was still only twenty-three, I felt ten years older. I wondered what age I'd be when I returned to them all.

In November 1943, after a series of catastrophes for the British in the Far East with various missions hampered by the harsh conditions, there was fresh military impetus with the formation of the South East Asia Command (SEAC) under Admiral Lord Louis Mountbatten, a close friend of the royal family. Expecting a full-scale British invasion of Burma, the Japanese Army was first plotting an advance on India's North-East Frontier. Things were hotting up. That Christmas was marked in the barracks with the usual festive food and celebrations, but soon after came news that we might be required for action after all, which sparked some frenzied speculation.

We were drafted to Alipore Transit Camp in Calcutta, a journey of 300 miles or so, where it looked to be all systems go for a foray into the region where Philip Thornton and the others had lost their lives. But, in an attempt to cut off supply lines, the Japanese Air Force had carried out air raids on Calcutta's Kidderpore Dock, killing hundreds and causing massive destruction to ships and warehouses. Our mission was then switched further east to help defend the port of Chittagong in what is now Bangladesh, a critical naval, air and military base for British and American forces during the Burma Campaign. This we did, just as the Japanese 15th Army began their advance with an attack on the British supply bases in India, on the Imphal Plain and Kohima in northeastern Nagaland.

Somewhere in the middle of all this confusion, and with our orders changing frequently, I found myself in a tented camp with forty or so men deep in the jungle about three miles from Chittagong. It was a spartan place with very few creature comforts but, for a while, it was home. One sticky afternoon, a charming young Englishwoman appeared in our midst out of nowhere, like some sort of vision. All smiles, she pushed her way through the bush on foot, and was quite a sight to see. Everyone snapped to attention immediately and hurried over to say hello to the first British woman we'd seen in months. We also wanted to find out what on earth she was doing there. We quickly learned that she was part of the Entertainments National Service Association (ENSA) whose job it was to raise the spirits of service personnel. Their random concerts and camp sing-alongs were something we were growing accustomed to, and we'd already been visited in previous camps by the comedic singer Stainless Stephen from Sheffield (wearing a waistcoat made of Sheffield steel), as well as the British satirical comedy duo and BBC radio stars Elsie and Doris Waters, who played the comic characters Gert and Daisy.

But the appearance of this young lady who was about the same age as me was very different – not least because Lord Louis Mountbatten was accompanying her. Their arrival attracted a great deal of attention, but several of us still didn't have a clue who she was. 'It's Vera Lynn!' someone said. 'You know, the one who sings "We'll Meet Again"'. Although I was familiar with the tune, which came out soon after war was declared, I'd never registered the singer's name before or knew that the *Daily Express* had dubbed her the 'Forces Sweetheart'.

Not that it mattered. We were all just happy to see her, whoever she was. Miss Lynn chatted sweetly to the men and offered to sign anything from shirts to hats. She then sang us a little song or two, completely unaccompanied, including 'We'll Meet Again', which resounded magically through that sorry little excuse for a camp and raised our spirits enormously. This blonde-haired, blue-eyed angel from back home helped us feel that we weren't so far from those we loved. I will never forget what she did or the fact that she wasn't at all precious about being there. I had to admire her for that. Mountbatten was pleasant enough and I noted that there were a few other top brass accompanying Miss Lynn – lucky devils. I can remember thinking to myself, 'You see, Tom – only the top people get the top jobs.'

Her visit was something to remember and a welcome distraction, because soon after she left us, and at short notice, I was placed under the command of the Indian XV Corps and Lieutenant General Philip Christison, part of the British 14th Army, and ordered into Burma and the Arakan, where battles were raging almost continually. I would be going in with a squadron and a small 'HQ' with reconnaissance vehicles as well as the Valentines. We were told that we'd also be working alongside American Lee and Grant tanks as well as a few 75-mm Shermans left over from Africa. The Sherman especially was an iconic American tank that came to represent victory in WWII for many, and all of them were bigger and more sophisticated than ours, with crews of between four and six, which meant they had room for a wireless operator. From a mechanical perspective, the Lees were something of a concern as they were fitted with air-cooled radial aircraft engines that needed aviation fuel and if not started carefully in such a warm climate, tended to burst into flames. Someone had to be standing at the ready with a fire extinguisher in case it happened (which it often did), so everything hung on not flooding the engine.

Despite these minor risks, everyone was excited to be going into action, but in the end the squadron was held back, while only a small contingent of us were sent ahead with the rest. This time I was driving my own Jeep, as there was no need for a batman in combat. Shortly before we set off for battle, we heard the distressing news that the Japanese had overrun a British main dressing station (or medical tent) in the region we were heading to. They'd killed not only the handful of West Yorkshires guarding it but bayoneted the doctors, orderlies and patients in a senseless act of barbarity. Thirty-five people lost their lives. The reaction within the 14th Army was one of rage and a renewed determination to crush the enemy. Perhaps in light of what had happened, we were each given a tablet of cyanide to take with us, a lethal dose to take if we were captured. Death by poisoning must have been considered a preferable option to what the Japanese might do to us. I don't recall keeping the tablet long, as I didn't even like to carry it on my person. We were also given a map and a little hacksaw to slide into the sole of our boots, presumably to saw through a prison bar. None of this was worth dwelling too deeply on.

My two campaigns in Burma seventy-six years ago are a long time since and, as a relatively junior officer with no access to the strategies of the generals, I rarely had a clue where I was from one day to the next. We were constantly on the move through jungle and across open country towards destinations I'd never heard of and likely couldn't have pronounced if I had. Our skirmishes were many and varied in all sorts of conditions, from open scrubland and paddy fields to bamboo forests and dense jungle. I do know that on my first campaign I was involved in the Battle of the Admin Box in February 1944, which proved to be one of the decisive moments of the Campaign.

This battle happened because the Japanese, who were about to launch their assault on Assam, tried to distract Allied forces by attacking the Indian Army's 7th Division on the Mayu Peninsula, a hundred or so miles north of where Philip and his comrades had been killed. Their offensive was codenamed Operation *Ha-Go* after their tanks. The Indian Army had managed to capture the port of Maungdaw but the Japanese launched a surprise counter-offensive and over-ran the 7th Division headquarters, forcing its commander and staff to flee to a clearing that became known as the Admin Box when they hastily re-established it as an administration area.

It was there that they were surrounded and trapped.

Our orders were to go into the region in support of several other tank and infantry brigades and help them. As they held the line against overwhelming enemy forces, time was of the essence, but our progress was not easy.

Moving from one map reference point to another, our

biggest problem was the many weak or sabotaged bridges that created flashpoints and stalled our advance. Such were the hazards of live warfare. Every time we had to stop, the resourceful sappers of the Royal Engineers would arrive with all kinds of kit and hastily erect a temporary interlocking pontoon bridge sturdy enough to carry us across. Dugouts similar to the trenches of the Great War were created for us while we waited, and although we were relatively safe inside them, the biggest risk was that if the enemy were watching we'd be easy to pick off as we emerged. There was always an underlying tension in the air as we stayed alert to the possibility of attack, but luckily for us, the Japanese seemed to have other targets. For now.

On we went across a lot of open country that was a mix of bush and paddy fields, constantly keeping an eye out for small pockets of nimble, unpredictable enemy that seemed to be more interested in hindering and tracking our column's progress than in risking the launch of a a full-scale attack against a numerically superior force. The commander of our group was Lieutenant Colonel Richard Agnew, a Northamptonshire cavalryman from the 15th/19th King's Royal Hussars. I don't think he ever forgave the Army for putting him in charge of an armoured corps battalion full of Yorkshiremen, because he barely understood what any of us were saying. One day, he summoned me and a couple of captains to inform us that the Japanese had reportedly severed the road behind us, as was their way. Agnew ordered us to go back and find out where and how badly we'd been cut off. I remember his words as clearly as if he said them yesterday because, before sending us on what seemed like a suicide mission, he added casually, 'And I say, you chaps, if you get yourselves killed, I shall be very displeased with you.'

As the three of us climbed into my Jeep and headed back along the road with a pistol each between us, I have to admit there was a certain amount of trepidation about what we might encounter. Would the Japanese be lying in wait? Might we be injured, or killed? What if we were taken prisoner? I'm sure the minds of my companions were racing as fast as mine, because we were all in the same boat. The longer I spent at war, however, the quicker I learned that the anticipation of something bad happening can often be a lot worse than what actually happens, so I tried to focus on the job in hand. Fortunately, it paid off this time because before we'd made it very far a vehicle raced up behind us with the message that another unit had radioed in to say that they had already cleared and secured the road.

As we progressed deeper into Burma we found ourselves in rugged, near impenetrable jungle in extremely hot and humid conditions, which only made the journey more arduous. We were headed for our first major objective, which was to help clear what became known as 'Tunnels Road', a series of long tunnels through the Mayu Ridge which peaked at 2,000 feet atop the long mountain range that cut through the peninsula. This road provided the only route between Maungdaw and a village called Buthidaung, both of which had strategic importance, and was heavily defended by troops of the Japanese 55th Division. Our orders were to push them back and clear the way for an Allied advance. Once we arrived, we found ourselves in a dangerous bottleneck with many other vehicles and men, all stuck in a ravine under enemy bombardment, waiting to get through the first tunnel. The reason for the hold-up was that the tunnel was heavily defended by the enemy, with men and arms positioned all around and a 105 mm cannon positioned menacingly at the far end of it.

The approach to the tunnel mouth was a winding hill track that eventually veered off into the entrance at something of an angle, which meant that tanks couldn't easily be positioned to fire down it and disable the cannon. But unless we could, anybody who entered it would likely be blasted. In addition, there were well-defended Japanese positions on the hillsides all around us, delivering a constant barrage of fire throughout. The crack and splinter of the enemy rounds as they echoed around the valley certainly brought an element of discomfort and you had to be sure to keep your head down, but I wasn't too afraid because we had British and Indian infantry in full support. I think you're more excited than frightened when you're that young.

Being the best equipped, the trusty Shermans were drawn up to the tunnel as best they could with the help of sappers who cleared enough space and, turning their searchlights on, they fired into what they could see of it at point-blank range to flush out the enemy. The powerful thump of their 75 mm main guns punctuated the sounds of gunfire. At the same time, infantry went over the top to drop smoke bombs and disable the hillside bunkers, which often involved close-quarter combat with small-arms fire and bayonets. Meanwhile, the guns of our Valentines, Lees and Grants joined the cacophony as they fired repeatedly over and into the hill to bomb the Japanese holding the other side, and sometimes we fired clean through the narrower stone ridges and out the other side, creating mini landslides. And all the while Hurricane fighter-bombers harried the Japanese still further and fired directly on those they could see.

Nothing prepares you for the sights, sounds and smells of live action. The noise is incredible and almost continuous as one weapon after the other unleashes its fury on to an intransigent enemy. The smell of smoke mixed with cordite fills the air and all around you there is a teeming ants' nest of activity as sunburnt, unwashed men soaked through with sweat push aside their discomfort and fear to get on with the job in hand. There can be no conversation unless shouted into an ear (something I was a dab hand at), and at all times you are aware that a shell might land on your position or a Japanese sniper could have you in his sights. This was what we'd trained for. This was the British and Indian Army at its best.

By continually firing down the tunnel as well as bombarding enemy positions from the ground and air, our infantry were eventually able to knock them out and disable the mighty cannon. The Shermans withdrew and the traffic began to shunt forward bit by bit as men and machines passed without incident through a fiercely defended thoroughfare long denied them. I saw some footage on the Pathé News about this later in which someone with a sense of humour had erected a wooden sign on the road that read: '*About Turn! Only Those Killing the King's Enemies & Supporting their Troops Allowed Beyond This Post.*'

Having attained our objective, it was important that the tunnels were kept open so we were ordered to dig in and hold our positions, something that we did in extremely hot and sticky conditions for several weeks. As we were in very enclosed country with no access to supplies, sortie after sortie of twin-engined Dakota transport planes flew overhead, dropping thousands of tons of vital rations and ammunition to consolidate our positions and those of our many comrades further forward on foot. Spitfires piloted by brave young men also wheeled around the skies protecting the Dakotas from the Japanese Zero fighter aircraft and thwarting any enemy attempts to drop similar supplies to their men. The sight of them further stiffened the resolve of the troops on the ground. There was no wind, not even a breeze, so it was impossible to keep cool, even at night. A sound sleep, a clean body and any form of comfort were all distant memories. Once daylight began to fade you couldn't sleep for the noise of the insects, but there was one consolation about the dark that we didn't mind at all. In fact, we welcomed it, because thousands of fireflies took to the air all around us, lighting up the jungle with their illuminated ballet like in some magical fairy kingdom. And, best of all, they didn't bite.

It took a while but eventually our tactics of holding fast with airdrops prevailed and ultimately helped win this important fight. Out of ammunition and food, the enemy had no choice but to retreat. But it had been hard won and bloody, characterized by vicious hand-to-hand fighting that saw one soldier awarded the VC, and another fight off an attack from an opponent wielding a samurai sword. The Battle of Admin Box had claimed the lives of 6,600 Allied and Japanese soldiers, with more than 2,000 injured, but it was an important and decisive action. It not only turned the enemy's tactics against them for the first time but was also a massive boost to our morale, because it proved that we were finally gaining the upper hand. I am proud to have played my small part in this crucial action that turned the tide of the war in Burma.

Returning to Poona for the monsoon season, having seen real action at last, was a very good feeling. None of our chaps had been lost and I must have done something right because in July 1944 I was promoted to Captain. My salary – on what was called 'the Imperial pay rate' that I was eligible for in India – was £12 a week. Some of the men I'd signed up with never made it to Captain, so I have to say I was chuffed.

Having done my bit in the Arakan I was owed some leave, so I decided to take a 2,000-mile train and road trip to Kashmir in northern India, a place I'd heard was very beautiful. I travelled alone as most of my colleagues who had leave headed instead to Ootacamund, better known as 'Ooty', a hill station in Tamil Nadu that is said to have a permanent spring climate. Happy in my own company, I journeyed through the interesting landscapes around the cities of Ahmedabad, Udaipur and Amritsar, and finally arrived in Srinagar. I wanted to see Shalimar for myself, a seventeenth-century Mughal garden on the shores of Lake Dal and a place I'd only ever heard about in a popular Deanna Durbin number of the time called 'Kashmiri Song' with the lyrics, *'Pale hands I loved beside the Shalimar.'* It didn't disappoint. Then I travelled by car to the hill station of Gulmarg at 8,690 feet above sea level, a Garden of Eden that brought back powerful and fond memories of my happy trip to Switzerland with Uncle Arthur.

Once there, I checked into a colonial bungalow that had been converted into a small hotel with lovely gardens and was treated extremely well by staff long familiar with the British. Best of all, they served English food and a half-decent South African brandy. 'Gulmarg' means meadow of flowers and it certainly lived up to its name. The area had long been used by the Raj to escape the summers of the North Indian Plains. Far to the southeast I could see the snow-capped Himalayas and, in my mind at least, the summit of Mount Everest on a good day. That was something I'd always wanted to see so I had to be satisfied with that distant glimpse of the range.

Gulmarg proved to be highly enjoyable for another reason because on my first night, sitting in the bar of my hotel, I met up with a very pretty Anglo-Indian woman who reminded me of the lovely Sylvia. Her husband, she told me, was a Japanese prisoner of war and she'd gone to Kashmir to wait for news of him. We started chatting and became friendly and I enjoyed my time with her very much. I hadn't expected to find romance in the mountains, but there it was, and I wasn't one to argue. She was an unexpected delight.

There was only one tricky moment when one morning she said, 'Why don't we go for a ride today?' and I realized that she didn't mean motorcycles but horses. Thinking back to the day John Driver had tricked me on to a steeplechaser and almost broken my neck, I had serious reservations but knew that if I refused that could have been the end of us. So I got on the horse as if I'd been doing it all my life and, after years of practice on a motorbike, managed to hang on once more without incident. Mercifully, I lived to spend another day in paradise with my delightful companion before returning to Poona.

Kirkee felt like home these days, so during the rainy months we got back into our routines of exercises, debriefings and drills, waiting for our next chance. There were infantry battle schools, experiments in river crossings, marksmanship lessons and exercises in which the RAF also took part. As I had already learned, life in the Army veered between long periods of boredom and short bursts of excitement. The inactive periods were often the hardest for the men to bear and that was when they missed home the most and wished the war would soon be over. Britain felt so very far away and the news we had of war in Europe with D-Day and the Normandy landings in June 1944 only made people more homesick. A lot of the men read and many of them caught up with their sleep, while others played sports or games to while away the long, wet days. I filled any spare time I had by tinkering with tanks, bikes, Jeeps and anything else mechanical that I could find. I have found that if you have a love of something, you will never be bored.

After victory in the Battle of Admin Box the Allied tactics changed and the generals stopped repeating mistakes from the past. Bill Slim recognized that at Admin Box and elsewhere, some of our greatest successes against the Japanese had been won because, instead of trying to advance or retreat once surrounded, we held our ground and used defensive and guerrilla tactics whilst being constantly supplied by air. When, in March 1944, the Japanese went ahead with their assault on Assam in their quest for a supplies and air base from which to attack India, this proved vital. Although the Japanese did well to begin with and quickly surrounded the strategic British positions of Imphal and Kohima with a total strength of 85,000 men, it proved to be a disaster because they underestimated our new defensive skills. During some of the fiercest fighting of the campaign, and in simultaneous battles fought over five months in some of the worst monsoon conditions, the Japanese suffered heavy losses from starvation, disease and exhaustion while the British were kept well supplied with airdrops.

Our side managed to hold firm and the enemy was finally driven back into Burma. It was the worst defeat the Japanese Army had ever suffered with 53,000 dead and missing, compared to our 4,000. The 14th Army's stunning success at Imphal and Kohima was the turning point of the whole Campaign in Burma. From here, working in tandem with American troops, the plan then was to advance south from the plains of northern Burma, which – they hoped – would ultimately lead to Rangoon and, in Bill Slim's words, turn defeat into victory.

II.

'We may allow ourselves a brief period of rejoicing;
but let us not forget for a moment the toil and efforts that lie ahead.
Japan, with all her treachery and greed, remains unsubdued.'

Winston Churchill (1874–1965)

War leaders Churchill, Roosevelt and Stalin meet
at the Yalta Conference in February 1944.

In NOVEMBER 1944, it was back to Burma where after a long struggle following defeat after defeat in South East Asia we were finally winning under Bill Slim. My latest job description was Technical Officer and with a very different role. But first we had to get there, travelling by train and river steamer to Chittagong and then via the Naaf estuary, landing on the west bank at Kayagyaung to set up camp at a place called Waybin.

We spent Christmas at Waybin, building defences, doing reconnaissance and creating bamboo shelters for the tanks that proved to be insubstantial. There was the odd skirmish with an enemy that seemed committed to sabotaging our defences and nipping at our heels, but we soon saw them off. In January 1945 Lieutenant Carey and two other officers travelled to Donbaik to see what more might be learned from the deaths of Philip Thornton and his troop. It had been two years since that fatal battle, but the area was so strongly defended that this was the first time the British had been able to access the site. They found the tanks stripped bare and the bleached bones of five of the nine crew laid out in the dirt nearby. Their remains were eventually removed and laid to rest, first in a cemetery at the natural fortress of Razabil, and later in the Commonwealth War Graves Cemetery at

Taukkyan in Burma, a site that holds the remains of 5,580 Allied and Commonwealth servicemen, and a place I would love to visit one day.

Before too long Major Bucknall's squadron was sent to take part in a successful amphibious assault on Ramree Island with the 71st Indian Infantry Brigade, as part of Operation Matador. We were under orders to remain where we were and many of us thought that we might not be deployed again. This proved to be unfounded because a few days after 'B' Squadron had departed we were sent with 'A' and 'C' Squadron on a reconnaissance mission to the vicinity of Cox's Bazaar, named after an eighteenth-century captain of the British East India Company.

Much of this region consisted of tidal creeks and mangrove swamps, but we landed on a wide sloping beach. It was warm weather, quite pleasant, and I was still a spare, so not with the tanks but part of infantry support. As we advanced, there was little opposition and no hand-to-hand fighting. We did receive some overhead fire deeper in but it was minimal, so we just put our heads down and kept going. I suppose there was some element of danger at that point, but it didn't feel as desperate as things had been on my previous visit and we were the lucky ones, spared much of what the infantry were facing up ahead.

Our orders were to move across country through thick forest towards the Japanese front lines. As we had learned to our cost, tanks weren't ideal for the terrain and it wasn't easy to advance with so many trees in the way and the soft mud in the valley bottoms. Plus, we were always on the lookout for landmines, which the Japanese were in the habit of laying. We eventually made it, using the lead tank as a battering ram, but only after a struggle, by which time the tanks needed to refuel. Hunkering down for the night, we took whatever cover we could from the natural hollows. The war in the Far East for tank crews involved a lot of sitting around and was often a rather static affair between battles because we were mostly in a holding operation in support of the infantry.

We rested for that first night and the infantry sent out patrols, as vigilance was constantly necessary. By this time we were well aware of the fact that the Japanese liked to sneak around behind us at night to lay roadblocks or cut off routes, so we needed to keep track of what they were up to. Masters of psychological warfare, they would sometimes cry out in English as if they were wounded, or make strange noises to disconcert the guards. A few of the men were involved in skirmishes with those enemy soldiers who were continually badgering them on the periphery. Some were injured but I don't believe anyone died, and I think one chap later won a medal for gallantry.

Realizing that the Japanese tactics hadn't changed and that they would continue with their attempts to surround us and pick people off one by one, it was decided that a line of communication needed to be set up between fronts. That's where I came in, or should I say that's where my motorcycle and I came back into the picture.

I often wonder what would have happened if I hadn't turned up at Weston Park on my BSA, because my connection with machines went on to define much of my war, leading to me being drafted to the Royal Armoured Corps, training men first in tanks, then as dispatch riders and now this. Back in Burma in 1945, I was not only still the spare but everyone knew I could ride a bike pretty well, so they added the title of Infantry Liaison Officer to my list and made it my job to warn the regiment if the enemy had doubled back, blocked our path or were lying in wait. During the night, I was to remain at the forefront with the Indian Army but early in the mornings, when I prayed that the Japanese had all gone, I was the one who had to go back and check.

There were no roads as such – just winding tracks through a bamboo forest, and the belief was that if I successfully made it through several miles of bamboo and scrubland from one command post to the next then each unit would know the path was clear. The only way to cross that kind of terrain was on a motorbike so I was, in effect, to become a dispatch rider without carrying a physical dispatch. In fact, I was the dispatch. This was about to be the most dangerous period of my war and some might say I was a sitting duck, as I could very easily have been intercepted, killed or captured.

Eager to do what I knew was important work and with lives at stake, I prepared myself as best I could before I set off each time by checking the latest intelligence reports on enemy movements. Even though I remembered from my time as an Intelligence Officer that these were often far from reliable. Every journey took just under an hour and I'd be lying if I said I wasn't frightened. I knew from training the DRs that speed and agility was my best defence so I leaned forward, gassed the engine and roared off through the jungle as fast as I could, trying not to think too much about the noise my machine was making in the quiet of the forest or how close the enemy might be – in most cases, a stone's throw away.

In all the many time trials I had witnessed in Yorkshire as a lad, I had watched time and again how Uncle Billy and the other riders kept low to their machines to negotiate bumpy ground or unusual cambers. I'd seen how they used their own body weight to keep the bike from toppling on trickier sections. In this, perhaps the most dangerous time trial of all, I deployed all those tactics and used my own instincts to get through. I don't recall ever being shot at or chased, but I was well aware that the enemy was always just out of sight through the trees, so I didn't hang around anywhere long enough to find out.

All I had on me was my loaded Smith & Wesson revolver and a heavy radio strapped to the back of the bike with which to wireless if the road was clear – or not. There were a few times when I made it through and attempted to contact the other command post but couldn't get any reply. I often wondered if the radio operators were asleep, in which case I'd risked my life for nowt.

The biggest risk was often not so much when I was out on my own dashing through the scrub but once I reached my destination. That was the real danger point because I never knew what I was going to find, and the Japanese might easily have overrun the camp I was heading for. The Indians were fearless and admired, but they had limited experience and weren't especially well equipped to deal with the enemy. I could have been shot by friendly fire just for riding into their camp. Fortunately, they didn't and were very pleased to see me, because I'd always looked after them.

Incredibly, in all of my missions back and forth, I managed to stay clear of the Japanese and only ever heard the odd gunshot or the sound of men and machines through the trees. Granny Fanny must have been watching over me still. Thanks to luck – or to her – I never came face to face with an enemy soldier, which is just as well because it would have been a bit like me in the LDV armed with an ancient rifle and ammo I wasn't supposed to use.

Little Tommy Moore, aged just twenty-four, would have been a goner.

Having survived all that, and spent a largely uneventful final few weeks in Burma, my time there drew to an end in the waning days of February 1945 when the brigade received orders to move to Madras, which meant a sea voyage of several days over 1,100 nautical miles. My hope and expectation was that, after regrouping in Kirkee, I'd one day return with my unit to help finish off our ferocious and determined enemy. That is what we all wanted and we believed that we had earned the right to see it through. And on a personal note, I also hoped to one day fight under the command of my new hero, General Slim.

In what seemed like a world away, the war was almost over in Europe and the Middle East, with the liberation of Belgium, Greece and much of Italy, and the conclusion of the North African campaign. Even the Home Guard had been stood down in Britain, so the fearless patrolmen of Riddlesden would have handed back their rifles and taken off their armbands for good. In Japan, however, the fighting was far from over and it felt clear to those of us who had encountered the enemy that the Japs would fight to the last man.

On the slow voyage back to Madras along the east coast of India, I became unwell and developed a sore throat. It wasn't too bad and I put it down to the dust. I didn't intend to do much about it at first, but my brother comrades and the Medical Officer seemed strangely excited by this development and decided that I had tonsillitis – not for my benefit but for theirs. They did this for exactly the same reasons that the throat infection had been used to great effect before – they'd booked me into Madras Hospital when we landed, one of the few in India where the nurses were British. I was to be offered up as the human sacrifice.

They were as disappointed as I was when the minute we disembarked I was summoned to headquarters in Madras for new orders. I was to be sent straight back to England on temporary duty for four months' training as 'a matter of great urgency' and there would be no time to say goodbye to my comrades. My destination was the Royal Armoured Corps AFV School at Bovington Camp in Dorset, fifty miles southeast of Southampton.

A rather uninspiring colonel stuck in a hot office told me, 'You are to train for the role of Technical Adjutant at Southern Command, Captain Moore. Once qualified, you are to report straight back to Kirkee and train up your men with the new Churchill tanks.' Whoever issued the orders must have been told that we were getting these new tanks and wanted the men to be fully prepared by someone who knew what he was talking about. Who else to send but Captain Moore? It was made perfectly clear to me that my size 11 feet were not to touch the ground.

Instead of being tended by a pretty British nurse in a starched white uniform and cap, I had to forget about my sore throat and my friends, get back into khaki, grab my kit – including my greatcoat and cold weather clothing – and make my way to the railway station to catch a train to Bombay. From there it would be on to Calcutta from where I'd be 'emplaned' and flown back to Britain. Although I liked the idea of quickly learning about these new tanks and then bringing this important information back to the Far East with me, I knew that I was embarking on a long and lonely journey.

Most importantly, I was leaving behind the men I'd served alongside for the previous three years; men who I knew might well be sent back into combat in my absence. Philip was gone but several others had taken his place in my coterie of close comrades I'd have invited to tea, so it was with little pleasure that I took my place in the back of a staff car and headed for the station.

It was March 1945 and I would be returning to a country that had survived five years of bombardment and privations. I had no idea then that I would be leaving India for good.

12.

'Discipline strengthens the mind so that it becomes impervious to the corroding influence of fear.'

Field Marshal Montgomery (1887–1976)

VE Day in London, May 1945.

My passage to india had taken me eight weeks but it took just six days to get back. For a twenty-four-year-old who'd long been interested in all things mechanical, the journey home by train and plane enthralled me. The best part was taking my seat in a large RAF flying boat called a Short Sunderland.

Specifically designed by Short Brothers as a long-range reconnaissance aircraft and bristling with bombs, machine-gun turrets, mines and depth charges, the Sunderland had four Bristol Pegasus radial engines and was fitted with radar and other detection equipment. Its chief role in the war had been in finding and destroying U-boats, but it was also used in the evacuation of Crete when more than 16,000 beleaguered Allied troops had to be rescued from the Germans in 1941. A purely functional aircraft, the Sunderland was never built for comfort, so I sat on a fold-down seat next to a few crates of cargo having my bones jolted around for hour after hour. With typical British Army bureaucracy, and even though my appointment was supposed to be 'a matter of urgency', my journey home was a tortuous and convoluted affair. From Calcutta I was sent to Karachi, then flown from Karachi to an RAF base in the deserts of Bahrain, then to Alexandria in Egypt, before flying on to Sicily and finally to England.

Cruising at 5,000 feet, our low altitude allowed me to peer out of the window to see people and livestock, camels, buildings and deserts below. We travelled in the daytime, stopping overnight three times and staying in some extremely comfortable requisitioned hotels, for which there was never a bill. The war wasn't yet over in Europe as the Germans fought to defend what territory they had left, and our pilot had to remain vigilant for enemy aircraft and attacks from below. I was the only male passenger but there were also two ladies – the British comedian Joyce Grenfell and her pianist Viola. They'd been in India and Burma as part of the same ENSA initiative that had flown Vera Lynn out to entertain us earlier in the year. I didn't recognize Ms Grenfell at first but once we were introduced I remembered hearing her on the wireless. She was later famous for doing a funny monologue as a harassed nursery school teacher forever ticking off a boy called George, and became a perfect comic sidekick to actors like Alistair Sims. She was definitely a lady with a pedigree and I was told that her husband was a lieutenant colonel in the King's Royal Rifle Corps. I am pleased to report that she didn't have any airs and graces, however, and was delightful company throughout the long journey home.

We eventually landed in Poole Harbour on 16 March 1945, where I was collected at the quayside by a corporal and driven the twenty or so miles to Bovington Camp. The weather was bitterly cold and windy, with a feeling of impending snow. Even though I'd swapped my lightweight tropical shirt and shorts for full khaki battledress and a greatcoat, I shivered at the change. Britain was familiar yet strange; quite drab and monotone compared to the vibrancy of India. All I could see out of the car window as we drove through Poole was sandbags, barbed wire and civilians in hats scurrying to and fro, heads down. There was a general sense of gloom. Spring 1945 was still a difficult time for the home front, with the last of the V2 rockets raining down on London and random German air raids on selected cities, including Hull. In retaliation, Berlin was heavily bombed and the historic city of Dresden firebombed with the loss of tens of thousands of civilians. Prime Minister Winston Churchill attended the Yalta Conference in the Crimea where the leaders of Russia, the US and Britain came together to discuss the end of the war and its aftermath.

The sprawling military encampment of Bovington, known affectionately as 'Tin Town' for its many tin-roofed barracks – some from the previous war – was the unofficial home of the Royal Armoured Corps and the biggest military camp I had ever been in. It had sections as far away as Bournemouth in Hampshire and Catterick in Yorkshire. A teeming hive of activity, it was crammed with servicemen and women, and every kind of Armoured Fighting Vehicle. There were also marching columns of new recruits going through basic training before starting on their technical training. Seeing those green young men eager for war took me straight back to Weston Park four years earlier. Back then I'd been a naive lad in a flat cap who leaned his motorbike up against a wall and walked towards a war without a clue what being a soldier in the British Army would entail.

I was shown to the officers' quarters in the Allenby Barracks, which were practically the first proper buildings I'd lived in for years. An orderly provided me with everything I needed and offered me a hot meal in the Mess before pointing out the air raid shelters and informing me of the bombing drills. I wasn't surprised to learn that the camp had been attacked many times. At night I could see the searchlights from nearby Warmwell Airfield, a huge base near Dorchester for many valiant British Spitfires and Hurricanes and for the American Lockheed Lightning fighter aircraft – known by the Germans as *der Gabelschwanz-Teufel* or fork-tailed devils. As I unpacked my belongings I discovered that I still carried my Smith & Wesson revolver in the pocket of my greatcoat. Holding the cold weight of it in my hands, I thought back to the days when I'd sped through the Burmese bush on my motorbike wondering if I might have to use it one day to save my life. Then I packed it, and the memory, away.

The following morning I put in a telephone call to my parents to let them know I was safe and in the country. Mother was so pleased to hear from me at last and made me promise to visit them as soon as I was given some leave. Without further ado and with no time to lose, I was put straight to work because my Technical Adjutants' course – under the auspices of the Driving and Maintenance (D&M) Wing – was to start imminently. I quickly discovered that although the camp had hundreds of tanks it only had one Churchill, a beast of a machine named after the Prime Minister and known for its heavy armour, large chassis, better manoeuvrability and ability to traverse slopes. Rushed into production in 1941, the version I'd be training with was the Mark VII, equipped with armour plating far thicker than anything I'd worked with before, and carrying an Ordnance QF 75 mm gun. It also had far better tracking for getting it out of a tight spot. As I walked around this machine that was twice the size of a Valentine with tracks double the width, I couldn't help but think that if it had been available at Donbaik then ten men might not have been lost.

*

After a few days' familiarization with the camp I was given a thirty-six hours' pass, so I bought a train ticket and travelled home to see my parents for the first time in four years, sending them the details of my train.

I was looking forward to being reunited with them all, although I can't now recall if I already knew that Granny Fanny had died in March 1941, not long after I went away, but I think I must have. Maybe my parents had written or perhaps Mother told me on the telephone. I was sad, of course, but my kind, sweet grandmother seemed to me then to be a very old lady at eighty-two, and had seemed ready to go.

I will never forget her parting words – 'It's not goodbye, our Tom . . . it's goodnight.' – and was deeply touched to hear of her dying promise to look after me from Heaven. As I told my mother, it seemed to have worked.

Aside from seeing everyone back home, I was especially eager to see my dog Billy who would have been eleven by then and must have missed me as much as I missed him. In the photograph I'd been sent I'd been surprised by how old he looked, and I hoped he would still be capable of a long walk with me across the moors.

I arrived at Keighley Station as scheduled and found Father waiting to meet me. He'd always been a quiet sort of man but I could tell from the joy in his eyes that he was very pleased to have his only son home, and in one piece. It was good to see him again too and he looked well, although perhaps a bit more hunched over than I remembered, his spine curved by the arthritis that is a Moore family trait. We warmly shook hands and I pressed my mouth to his ear and told him, 'It's good to be home, Father,' as his eyes glistened. Then he walked me to his car and drove me home. The first thing I noticed was that he'd hoisted a Union Jack on to the flagpole at Club Nook to mark my return. I'd never seen a flag up there in my life so that really touched me because he was telling Riddlesden: 'Our Tom's home!' Mother also looked well, possibly a little thinner than before, but she was beaming with happiness as she held me tight and kissed me on both cheeks. To my delight, Uncle Arthur was at the house too, so everything felt much the same, apart from Freda who was still with the ATS. Well, almost.

'Where's my Billy?' I asked, soon after I'd greeted everyone.

'He died,' Father replied quite bluntly, as I took a step back.

'He went blind, Tom,' Mother added, more gently. 'We had to put him down.'

I was a grown man now and we were not a soft family, but that did upset me terribly. No tears allowed, however. I knew the drill. Then my father informed me that he'd also sold my BSA motorbike, as it was just sitting around 'gathering dust'. I couldn't blame him but I was sorry not to have any transport of my own.

I spent a day and a night in Club Nook and heard all about Freda working as an RAF plotter with her friend Daisy, and about Mother's work with the Women's Voluntary Service, along with all the Keighley gossip. The mayor's nephew had been killed in a plane crash in France, people were donating furniture and household goods to people bombed out of their homes, there was a measles epidemic locally, and an egg collection for patients in Keighley and Victoria District Hospital, with the slogan, 'One egg is not too small a gift'.

Rationing hardly seemed to have affected my parents at all but then it was different in the country. Farms surrounded us, and the black market was thriving there as much as in the city. My father still had his orchard so we had plenty of fresh fruit and we knew people with pigs and chickens, plus there were always friends with whom you could barter. It was a case of wheels within wheels. Mother seemed to have everything, including fresh eggs, and she made me my favourite roast beef with Yorkshire pudding for the Sunday roast – or perhaps that was all just for my benefit. It was good to be home but it felt a little strange, too, and I was eager to get back to the routines and familiarity of the Army. Leaving early the following morning, I caught the first of a series of trains all the way back to Devon, keen to return before the blackout.

My first task at the Armoured Fighting Vehicles School was to spend a few days fully familiarizing myself with the Churchill tank and its guns. Sitting inside one never failed to impress me because, for all a tank's faults – the claustrophobic interior, vibration, noise, lack of visibility and general stuffiness – it was a machine with enormous power and weight, its massive steel tracks rotating to roll it forward, and its armour almost invincible as it lurched towards the enemy.

The mechanics alone were impressive, with a huge 21-litre, 350-horsepower Bedford truck engine that was effectively two engines operating on a common crankshaft. I also found the Churchill's steering a great improvement and liked that it could turn 360 degrees within its own length. There were a few elements similar to the Sherman but they were really chalk and cheese. The Sherman was faster but it was the sheer weight of armour that limited the Churchill to a top speed of 15 mph.

Once I felt fully acquainted with the tank I set about investigating the M24 Chaffee, a little American tank made by Cadillac and equipped with a 75 mm gun. These were to be used as subsidiary vehicles to the Churchills and had been given to us from the United States under a wartime Lend-Lease scheme. It was the first tank that had an automatic gearbox and, although lightly armoured, it proved popular. I was also given a quick tour of the latest 'B' vehicles that we might come into contact with, such as the soft-skinned support vehicles like the 15 cwt trucks, Jeeps and other wheeled vehicles, some of which could also be armoured. And, of course, I took a special interest in the motorbikes and sidecars. Then I explored the various courses and ranges that Bovington had, over some 1,500 acres of coast, including the Bindon Range at Lulworth, the only fully equipped AFV range in the UK. There were also the workshops to investigate, along with the Wireless and Trials wing, before I was set to work on my four-month course on 22 March.

The instruction at Bovington was excellent but I can't say that I found it as challenging as it might have been for those who didn't know their way around a tank. My experience in India with Valentines, Stuarts, Lees, Grants and Shermans had served me well so there was nothing that really surprised me. It might sound a bit big-headed, but I came out nearly top on every section of the course, earning the comment '*Very Good*' in almost all categories. I suppose I was still trying to be the best I could be, or at least as good as anyone else.

My time in the camp improved enormously when I met a delightful Scottish nurse by the name of Jean Robertson from Dundee. She and I became good friends and enjoyed each other's company in whatever spare time we had. Unfortunately, quite soon after we met she was transferred to a new hospital at Fleet in Hampshire, which was a long way from

Bovington. As I didn't have a car or a motorbike and the bus and train services were limited, it looked as if our friendship was over, but Granny Fanny must have been smiling on me again, because my course included three weeks learning about AFV design at the British Tank Research Centre at RAF Chobham in Surrey, fourteen miles southwest of Fleet. I'd also be given weekends off, and so would Jean.

When I arrived in Surrey I was pleased to find that my billet was a lovely room in the grand white-stucco neoclassical mansion of Chobham Place, which had been requisitioned by the War Office. This was far more luxurious than any barracks. Determined to see Jean and not to be beaten by the distance, I borrowed an old bicycle without lights or gears and cycled to Fleet and back along unmarked roads each weekend. It was worth the effort and my time with Jean was a joy. It was only when I returned to Bovington after my course that our friendship fizzled out, although we stayed in touch for many years.

In my spare time in Dorset I set about finding myself a means of transport in order to drive around the coast and, on my next weekend off, return to Yorkshire to visit my parents. My military pay had accumulated over the years with little or nothing to spend it on, so I was wealthier than I'd ever been. I heard through the grapevine that someone in the camp was selling a two-seater 1936 Morgan Model F four-cylinder three-wheeler, which was bright red. Its registration was FGC 787, and its style reminded me a little of Uncle Billy's heavenly blue Bugatti. I bought it for £169 but my next problem was finding enough petrol to get it as far as Keighley and back, as Britain was still under strict rationing rules. A three-wheeler's tank didn't use much, but if I went north that would mean driving on winding country roads with few petrol stations as the A1 was an ordinary two-lane road and motorways didn't exist yet. As a member of the armed forces who had everything provided for me, I didn't even possess a rationing book or petrol coupons with which to purchase fuel, which meant I had to source whatever I could in the camp. My years in the Army hadn't been wasted, however, and I knew that with a bit of cash and a friendly contact in POL (Petrol, Oil and Lubricants) at the Stores anything could be bought.

Driving around the countryside in that little red sports car was great fun and quite different from any I'd done before. Because of rationing and air raids, there were hardly any cars on the roads, so the rolling hills of Dorset became my own personal speedway track. Even though it was nine years old I could get the Morgan up to 70 mph, although bits kept dropping off it – but that may have been more to do with my driving. As a precaution, I ended up carrying a ball of wire and some tools to strap things down. The car had no heater or radio, but for winter there was a hood and some side screens. I loved that Morgan and it certainly turned a few heads, especially when I went home to Keighley. My father was probably a bit impressed too but he wasn't the sort of person to say so. Then it was straight back to Dorset to continue my course, with the goal of returning to my unit as soon as I could.

The longer I stayed in Bovington, however, the more I began to wonder if I would ever rejoin my men in India. The war in Europe seemed closer to finishing than ever with Germany on the brink of collapse. And there were other, darker considerations too. Following the liberation of Auschwitz in January 1945, news was gradually beginning to emerge about Nazi atrocities against the Jews. This had been well hidden during the war and we knew nothing about it until we saw the shocking newsreels. I was utterly appalled and couldn't understand the reasoning behind it or how one human being could inflict so much suffering on another.

There had been several German Jews in Keighley who'd set up business in the textile trade shortly before the war, all of them hard-working refugees from fascism who'd started from nothing. They all seemed to have the surname Black, which wasn't their real name but it was the one they'd chosen when they fled. Interestingly, the one man who didn't change his name and whose family had lived in Keighley for two generations was called Mr Hoffman and it was his shop window that was broken during the war by those in the town with anti-German feelings. Before I'd left, I'd been aware of some anti-Semitism, but it wasn't something that I really knew about or understood, so to see the camps was beyond comprehension. We were – as yet – ignorant of the Holocaust's vast scale, or that Japanese camps were treating British POWs just as appallingly in the occupied Far East.

The good news was that Japan was now under enormous pressure not only from the Brits but also from the Americans who were pouring thousands of men and arms into the region. The sheer might of the US Army was always going to win in terms of firepower, but Japanese loyalty to their emperor meant that not only the soldiers, but the entire civilian population, might well be prepared to die rather than surrender, which could only lead to a prolonged and bloody campaign.

Although it might now seem strange, I very much wanted to be part of whatever happened out there next, or at least felt I should be. To have been brought back so unexpectedly had been a shock and felt like unfinished business. With my thoughts never far from my comrades, when Winston Churchill declared that war in Europe was officially over on 8 May 1945, sparking the national celebration that became known as VE Day, I didn't feel able to participate. I watched on the newsreels as London and elsewhere were packed with people dancing about, all absolutely thrilled that we'd got through the war in Europe at last. It was, indeed, a great victory, and we did well to win against the might of the Germans thanks to the enormous effort of many different countries working together, but it still felt like a bit of an anti-climax to me. I was unhappy about those I'd left behind who were still getting a pounding in the Burmese jungle. None of them were getting the day off. Perhaps because of this, I have few memories of VE Day. There was a bar in the camp and plenty of ATS girls and officers under training, so I'm sure they had a pleasant day, but I didn't take part. I was still Burma-orientated, so for me it was business as usual and I was eager to push on.

And push on I did, even though all around me men and women were being demobbed, most of them more than happy to relinquish their uniforms and return to loved ones. Getting so many people home from every corner of the Earth was a massive task that took a great deal of organization and would likely take years. As everything around me was wound down to peacetime levels, I focused on my studies, kept my head down and carried on through what felt like another kind of Phoney War. At the end of my course in early July 1945 I earned myself a good final report with an official stamp confirming that I was now a Technical Adjutant. I still have a flimsy carbon copy of it, an abbreviated version of which says:

This officer has worked very hard and has a good knowledge of the limitations, use, care and maintenance of hand tools and of general principles. He is familiar with the constructional features of common power plants and of transmissions, and is capable of the diagnosis and repair of faults . . . He has gained a very good theoretical knowledge of the Churchill and has shown considerable ability in his own use of tools in practical work on the tank . . . This officer has a very good grasp of the AFVs and is quite outstanding for his theoretical and practical knowledge. He should prove to be a very satisfactory Technical Adjutant.

I couldn't help but think that Uncle Billy would have been happy with that.

I was now ready, willing and able to get straight back to India and the continuing battle against the Japanese, but it wasn't to be. And, in the end, I discovered that I only had myself to blame. I seemed to have caught the eye of the senior officers in charge of Bovington. 'You'll not be going back, Captain Moore,' I was informed brusquely. 'We're claiming you for ourselves. You are an exceptional Technical Adjutant and we need you to stay on here as a Captain Instructor at the Specialist Training Section.'

The news was disappointing, if flattering, and I knew that there was no point arguing. If there was one thing I'd learned since Weston Park it was that from the moment I put on my uniform, my life was in the hands of others and that was that. My orders were to be obeyed. On the plus side, I knew that being a Captain Instructor was an important and necessary role, especially for those still fighting the war thousands of miles away. It was vital that the men sent out there knew how to operate the tanks and AFVs with which they'd be facing the Japanese. I'd seen that for myself. I also reminded myself

that I should be grateful for my reprieve from further conflict, as staying on in Dorset would offer greater comfort and
a far better chance of survival. Quietly, I thanked Granny
Fanny for saving me once again from what could potentially
have been the end of me in Burma.

13.

*'A hero is someone who steps up
when everyone else backs down.'*

Anonymous

Nagasaki, 9 August 1945.
Japan surrendered six days later.

In bovington i was assigned my first trainees, a group of about a dozen men that I was expected to train up in three weeks. The clock was still ticking and I set to work. Just as I had been taught, these young men needed to understand all the characteristics of Churchill tanks, including its armour, engine and similarities to the Sherman. They were also taught gunnery, driving methods, and how to operate its many controls and its gun sight.

They needed to be well versed in signals including Morse code, wireless procedure and maintenance, and train as tank commanders before driving the Churchill up and down the muddy hills, obstacles and false canyons of the camp's tank testing ground on the surrounding heathland. This area, incidentally, was where they also trained dispatch riders so I watched with great interest as instructors scrambled across the bumpy landscape on Matchless, Norton and Royal Enfield 'Flying Flea' bikes. Uncle Billy would have loved every minute.

By this time the recruits knew that if they saw any action it would likely be in the Far East, so they not only had to be familiar with how the tanks worked, but with how to fix them in such a hostile climate. I, of all people, knew how abused vehicles were out there so I drummed into them the sort of problems they might face and how the heat and humidity could affect all of their machinery. Because of my experience, I suppose I was perfectly placed to teach them, which meant that I became invaluable to Bovington and remained in a senior training role there for almost a full year. I enjoyed the work but it became repetitive and boring after a while, going over the same syllabus again and again.

The greatest irony was that in the end only one Churchill tank was ever sent to India and it had hardly covered itself in glory. On the first occasion it was called into battle its ammo hadn't yet arrived from the UK, then its carburettor failed and there were other technical problems, so it never saw action there at all. The same could not be said of the rest of the 14th Army. I continued to keep a watchful eye on the news from Burma and was happy to follow the reports of Field Marshal Slim's marvellous success in crossing the Irrawaddy River, but there was never any information about my unit.

By this time I had another good reason to stay on in Dorset because I was dating a member of the women's ATS, a lady called Ellen May Page from Bedfordshire, who regularly came to my office to deliver messages and cheered me up no end. With Britain at peace and weekends off, I took her out in my Morgan three-wheeler, driving through pretty villages as we explored the beautiful Purbeck hills. Dorset is a truly delightful county. A favourite destination of ours was Weymouth where we could gorge ourselves on fresh lobster and crab or have tea and a bun at the Salvation Army canteen near the station. I also returned home whenever I could to see my parents, although I never took Ellen with me. Our relationship was just a bit of fun and introducing her to my parents might have suggested otherwise.

Mother and Father were keen to know when I might be

demobbed and it quickly became clear to me that – after the death of Uncle Billy and then the war – I was no longer expected to finish my training as a civil engineer. Besides, those kinds of things had virtually come to an end since the war. Instead, it had been decided that I was to join the family building firm, even though I'd never expected or wanted to. In fact, after five years in the Army I'd got quite settled to it and could easily have stayed. I think I would have done all right if I had and had an entirely different life. I might even have made it to Major, my new goal. This was no longer an option for me, though, as my sixty-year-old father was completely alone – and deaf – running a floundering company that he'd inherited unwillingly.

But first the war had to end.

Rangoon had been captured at last. I had been sorry not to have gone back to fight alongside my comrades at the battles of Imphal and Kohima where they achieved such a decisive victory – even if no one in Britain knew much about it. And when Burma was saved I finally felt as if Philip and his men hadn't died in vain. Still the Japanese refused to surrender, however, so in the summer of 1945 the Allies launched a campaign of sustained bombing raids on scores of its cities in an attempt to force the government's hand. When even this didn't work, they demanded the country's unconditional surrender or warned of 'prompt and utter destruction'. Japan, seemingly believing herself invincible, ignored this ultimatum too. With Britain's consent, the United States surprised the world by detonating two atom bombs over the Japanese cities of Hiroshima and Nagasaki on 6 and 9 August. This was modern warfare and something that had never happened before. Emperor Hirohito described the bombs as a 'new and most cruel' weapon.

To begin with, I think we all thought that the attacks were a necessary evil because it proved to the Japanese that the American military was a far superior force. They surrendered on 15 August. It was felt that their intransigence had left the Allies with no other course of action than something so severe that they'd finally realize they couldn't possibly win. Then, when news started to filter through from Hiroshima and Nagasaki that an estimated 200,000 civilians had died in such an unpleasant way, there was a great deal of hand-wringing about how terrible and immoral it was. I understood that and I wish it had never been necessary. I have no desire to ever visit the sites of the bombs, because I know that it would be too painful to see. Having faced that generation of Japanese soldiers in battle, however, I am also of the belief that if the war hadn't ended then there would have been even greater numbers killed. It was a question of trying to balance one horror against the other. This is impossible to do.

Victory in Japan (VJ) Day was marked over two days of national holiday on 15 and 16 August, but not – I felt – celebrated as wildly as VE Day had been. People were pleased that the war there was finally over, but so many more had fought in Europe and the Mediterranean that it had felt much closer to home. Those who'd been in the Far East justifiably felt rather forgotten then, especially when more than 9,000 British, Indian and Commonwealth soldiers had been killed or wounded and 130,000 captured, including 2,269 dead in Burma alone. When Field-Marshal (later Viscount) Slim heard one of his men complain, 'People call us "The Forgotten Army",' he replied, 'Forget that! Nobody has even heard of you.' His message was get on with it and stop complaining.

To mark the Battle of Kohima where more than 4,000 men lost their lives, a war memorial was later erected and inscribed with the poignant wording: '*When you go home, tell them of us and say, For your tomorrow, we gave our today.*' The Burma Campaign, fought in a country far, far away when so much of the focus was on Europe and Africa, never got the same attention or sympathy. Because of this it will forever be known as the 'Forgotten War'.

But not by me. Not ever.

On VJ Day my orders changed and I was assigned for a time to the Royal Armoured Corps depot at Catterick Barracks in Yorkshire under the 61st Training Regiment, where I carried out much the same duties as I had in Dorset, only closer to home. I didn't stay long, though, and went back to the AFV School to await my discharge from the Army.

Demobilization was still taking time, as the dismantling of the military had to be completed in stages. We all took the *Daily Express* because it was given the news first and listed those groups of people who were being demobbed next, depending on age and length of service. As I waited and the months rolled by, I remained in Bovington instructing those who'd decided to remain in the Army. The routines of camp life with its meals and lessons, exercises and lectures changed with the arrival of the wives and families of the officers based there. The whole atmosphere of the camp had altered and then my girlfriend Ellen was demobbed and went home to Bedfordshire, which made my remaining time there rather dull.

My name finally appeared on the list in June 1946 and, with leave taken into account, I was officially demobbed in October. Like everybody else, I was sent to a demobilization depot to be issued with a complete set of civilian clothing. This was given to every member of the armed forces who might no longer have suitable clothes after years at war. The demob outfit comprised a rather grim brown two-piece suit made of coarse woollen material, which was nevertheless hard-wearing. Many people discarded it in a snobbish way because they considered it to be too common, but I wore mine every day and wore it out. I was given the option of a felt hat or a flat cap (I chose the cap), a pair of shoes, a raincoat, two shirts, a tie and some undergarments. The majority of these demob clothes were made on commission by Burton the outfitters, known as 'the fifty-shilling tailors' and owned by a man called Montague 'Monty' Burton. It was this that led to the expression 'getting the full Monty'. I was allowed to keep my uniform and took it home as a memento. I still have it in the wardrobe and did try it on recently but it was a little tight.

Having served in the Far East I received notification that I was entitled to four medals – the 1939–45 Star, the Burma Star, the Defence Medal and the War Medal. These were to be sent in the mail and not presented to me in any formal way, as there were too many to issue. Most people received a medal of some sort, including Freda for her work with the ATS. Getting them through the post was a strange end to my war, but I knew I was fortunate to have come through unharmed. Many thousands, including friends and comrades, had not been so lucky.

At the age of twenty and a son of the fading British Empire, I had given five years of my life and been prepared to lay it down because I believed in our cause to fight a greater evil. I am sorry that the reputation of the British in India has been tarnished by the mistakes of colonialism. Although the Raj have much to answer for, they also did a great deal for India with the building of vital infrastructure, the establishment of education and law, and the construction of many fine buildings that still exist to this day. In the words of Mark Antony in Shakespeare's *Julius Caesar*, '*The evil that men do lives after them; the good they do is oft interred with their bones.*'

Once I was back in Keighley the name of the family building company was altered to W. Moore & Son (Builders) Ltd, and at the age of twenty-five I officially became the 'Son' in the title, much to Father's delight. Putting my hand to as much as I could, I started off by driving the lorries and organizing the materials. I wasn't a bricklayer or a stonemason and had no building experience, but I was a practical young man and was determined to work hard.

My first wage at the company was £7 a week, which was far less than my Army pay. I found it ironic that my mother, who was in charge of the wages, had always told me never to accept a job less than £10 a week. There were fringe benefits because I was living at home rent-free and – having sold my Morgan – I had the use of my first ever company car since the Jeep, a Wolseley 12. Having a car at my disposal was to become an important indicator of my status and of my own self-esteem in the coming years.

Being back in Club Nook with Freda and my parents and sleeping in my old room was certainly an adjustment and very different from my time in the forces, so it all felt rather surreal, as if nothing much had changed. And yet I'd been through a lot and there was a great deal that I missed about Army life, but there didn't seem to be any other options open to me. I knew what was expected and I was a dutiful son, so I did the best I could. I also had to adjust to other aspects of civilian life. As I was out of the services and no longer provided with all my needs, I was issued with ration books for clothing, food and petrol and found that I couldn't even buy a pair of shoes unless I had the relevant coupons.

The building company was much reduced from my grand-father's day. Wartime restrictions had effectively shut down all building work unless to fix bomb damage, so there wasn't much money, and without the driving force of Billy, my father only took on little local jobs, mainly repairs and extensions. Rationing didn't help. If you wanted timber, cement or any other building materials you had to formally apply for it to the authorities, state what you needed it for and wait for a certificate to be issued that allowed you to purchase it – a process that could take weeks. The black market was as healthy as ever, but for a big building project paying its prices was unaffordable. We just had to do what we could with whatever we were allowed.

Just as I had done in the Army by starting at the bottom and climbing through the ranks, so I wanted to build the company back up to what it had been. With hindsight, this was probably too ambitious for the times. Historically the company had built homes, so I managed to secure a contract for us to build a few houses on a council estate and, happily, Father went along with whatever I was suggesting. He was so relieved and grateful that I'd come back to help him that I suspect he indulged me, but then we'd always got on very well. We were father and son but we'd always been friends, too, after years of going to the field trials and the speedway together, watching silent movies at the Cosy Corner, or me bidding for his building machinery as a boy. We both knew that there would have been no one else for him to call on to remove my late Uncle Billy from his car, and not another soul in the world that he'd have raised the Union Jack for on my return from war. What we had was special.

One thing that was a bit odd when I think about it now is that my parents never once asked me about the war, and I didn't volunteer much information either. We simply never talked about it. When Freda came home from her RAF base it was the same. We never discussed the war, not even between us. That was in the past. Like me, she settled back into Club Nook and took up sewing from home because her apprenticeship with the Wright sisters was over. It had always been her intention to become a seamstress and – with war forgotten – she also did what was expected. My father was delighted because he'd always wanted his only daughter to stay home so that he could look after her in a rather old-fashioned Victorian way. This arrangement seemed to suit Freda, too, who was a homebody, and the only time she went out was to visit her wartime friend Daisy who'd moved back to Bradford. Other than that, she lived quite peacefully at home helping Mother around the house and pleasing Father by keeping away from boyfriends. And that is where she remained for most of her days, which is a shame because she could have been married to some nice, kind man and had children, and I would have had nieces and nephews to spoil.

When work was over each day Father and I came straight home. We never went to the pub and just slotted back into being the happy little family unit we'd been before the war. There was no more rug making but we still sat around the wireless together as my father read his *Yorkshire Dalesman* magazine, Freda and Mother sewed, knitted or read, and I caught up with the news. I bought myself a Pentax single-lens reflex camera that was ahead of its time and carried on taking photos whenever I could, but there wasn't much to take pictures of apart from construction sites and the company works. On the few occasions I went out of a night, Father would often wait up for me, even though I was a grown man. One night when I came home around 1 a.m., I found him standing at the top of the stairs. 'Thomas,' he said (so I knew I was in trouble), 'you are getting in very late. If you're not careful, you'll be called a "Stop Out".'

There were times when I sorely missed the camaraderie of the Officers' Mess and the cocktails we'd enjoyed together at sundown. As everyone had returned to their respective homes and lives after the war and because I wasn't a great letter writer, I'd had very little contact with my Army comrades from India and Burma. The region was very much on my mind in 1947 because the government divided British India into two dominion states – India and Pakistan – with the most terrible consequences. To me, it looked like it was going to be a disaster from the outset and I was right. When we heard it was going to be partitioned, we all said, 'Surely the British Army will stay?' The feeling was that if they didn't there would be a civil war. The Army didn't stay, so millions who'd been abandoned were displaced and hundreds of thousands killed. It never should have happened – not the way it did. For many of us who knew and loved India that was unforgivable.

Happily, I would soon have an opportunity to discuss it with some of my former comrades-in-arms because that same year I was delighted to receive an invitation to a reunion of ex-officers from the Duke of Wellington's Regiment in London. The person who organized it was a lovely chap I'd known called Lieutenant Jim Stockley, whose father was the head of Fyffes Bananas. Eight of us gathered at the Olde

Cheshire Cheese pub in Fleet Street, where we had a jolly good lunch and a catch-up. Even the grim news from India couldn't dampen our spirits and it was so good to see everyone. Someone suggested that we should organize not just a reunion of officers, but an all-round regimental one. Because nearly everyone invited would be from Yorkshire and I was the only Yorkshire officer present – and still living there – I was nominated to organize it for later that year, a task I took on with relish. Before I went home by train to York that day I took a wander through the still devastated City of London to see if I could find the statues of the pagan giants Gog and Magog described to me by my friend John Billham before we named our tanks. To my disappointment, I couldn't, because the originals were destroyed by fire in the London Blitz.

The first full regimental reunion of the 9th Battalion, the Duke of Wellington's Regiment (West Riding) took place on a very foggy night six months later in November 1947 at the Guildford Hotel in Leeds. The evening that began with a toast to: 'The King!' was reported in the regimental magazine *The Iron Duke*. There were 120 men of all ranks, including Lieutenant Colonel Agnew and Major Bucknall. Captain John 'Gog' Billham made it as far as Manchester but had to give up due to the fog. Russell Curl, who introduced me to the lovely Sylvia, sadly couldn't make it either. The colonel of the regiment General Christison – under whom I had served in Burma and who'd been the British officer to whom the Japanese surrendered in Singapore – was tied up elsewhere, but we had plenty of others to catch up with. Dressed very tidily in our blazers and ties with berets, badges and shiny new medals, we enjoyed dinner with a pay bar and the evening was a huge success. Wives weren't invited, which may have been a mistake because it became rather raucous towards the end. I remember that as people were leaving, a little the worse for wear, a few of us had to check their pockets for cutlery – anything that could be lifted was taken.

A few months after that I received an unexpected letter in the post from Lord Savile, who'd heard about the reunion and was interested to know how the regiment was. I was surprised to hear from him and even more taken aback when he invited me to his gentleman's club in London for lunch. I put on a suit and my maroon and grey-striped regimental tie and we had a very pleasant meeting during which I told him how everybody was. I also invited him to the next reunion, which we'd decided to try to hold on the first Tuesday in November every year (little did I know that I'd be responsible for hosting the reunions for the next sixty-five years). Lord Savile – who always said, 'Please call me George,' thanked me but politely declined. Just as had happened with our first encounter at Weston Park, I didn't appreciate the protocol. He'd not only left the 'Dukes' but had gone back to being a lord looking after his estates, so it wasn't appropriate. He never held my ignorance against me, though, and we agreed to write to each other and meet occasionally for lunch, which we did for several years.

A devout Christian and a local magistrate, Lord Savile had been forced by his mother to sell his family seat before the war, although he kept hold of the land, and had never married. In later life he returned to Burma and tried to get to Donbaik to pay his respects to those who were killed, but the authorities wouldn't permit it. Over time, we lost contact and I was sorry to read in 2013 that he died, childless, at his sixteenth-century home, Gryce Hall near Huddersfield, at the age of eighty-nine. The *Yorkshire Post*'s obituary described him as in some respects 'one of the last of the P.G. Wodehouse landed gentry to inhabit the twenty-first century . . . charmingly eccentric and every inch a gentleman.'

They had him spot on.

14.

'The medical arts of science and healing should be made available to people when they need them.'

Aneurin Bevan (1897–1960)

Minister of Health, Nye Bevan, visits a Manchester
hospital on 5 July 1948, the day the NHS was founded.

AT THE AGE OF TWENTY-EIGHT I, too, was unmarried and childless but I was so focused on doing my best for Father and the company that there was no time even for a girlfriend. Not long after I returned I did bump into pretty Ethel Whitaker in town, pushing a pram. She was married and when she showed me her baby, she said somewhat wistfully, 'It's your fault, Tom Moore, that he isn't yours.'

I also had something else to think about by then as I had decided to save my wages and buy myself a vehicle to satisfy my love of speed. Although it didn't come in red, the car I desperately wanted was a Jowett Javelin made in Bradford, way ahead of its time in streamlining. I also liked the look of the Chrysler Airflow and the Singer Airstream, which had a unique waterfall bonnet and the slogan – 'The car of tomorrow – today'. In the end my budget only ran to the purchase of a motorbike, hopefully good enough to one day ride in the TT on the Isle of Man, a childhood dream since seeing Stanley Woods race his Norton in 1935. Somebody I knew sold me a 250cc Excelsior Manxman that I absolutely loved and managed to get up to 90 mph on one of the top roads above the moors, pushing it to the limit. I didn't wear a helmet, just my tweed cap pulled firmly down over my ears so that it didn't fly off.

The next person I bumped into in Keighley was my old school friend Charlie Dinsdale, who'd had an interesting war. Within a few months of the outbreak he'd been sent to France, only to be trapped at Dunkirk. The boat he was rescued on was sunk but he survived and got out on one of the last vessels to leave St Malo. From 1942 he was with the 1st Battalion in North Africa and fought his way through Italy, Palestine, Syria and Egypt until, having made it to Regimental Quartermaster Sergeant, he was demobbed around the same time as me. Soon after he came home, he married a lovely girl called Hilda Watson from Silsden whose father was a member of the Temperance Society, so only tea was served at their wedding. Charlie described this as 'an absolute hoot', but I knew that it would have been torture for a genial fellow like him.

I also reconnected very happily with my friend Brian Booth from Bradford Technical College, who'd been a prisoner of war in Germany. His father Leonard still owned the limestone quarry near Skipton and – like me – he went home to work in the family firm. Brian had a very nice girlfriend called Pat and one night when I was over at his house she arrived with an attractive young lady called 'Billie'. That wasn't the name she was christened but her father had always wanted a boy so that's what he called her. As the Billys in my life had all been special to me, I took this as a good omen. Either way, I was immediately taken with this delightful young lady and began courting her. She had a little local job when we first met but soon packed it in, as 'ladies don't work in my family'. Her father was high up in the wool trade and her mother came from a wealthy background.

Once we started to get serious, I was invited to meet Billie's grandfather who was a prominent freemason. I was appalled to discover that he had a black manservant who lived in a shabby outhouse. I never saw this chap in person but the mere thought that I was under the roof of someone who was continuing the ethos of the old slave trade which had been abolished over a hundred years earlier bothered me enormously. I never went again. The old man was rather Victorian in other ways, too, because halfway through my visit he took me to one side and whispered, 'Come with me, please.' I followed him upstairs where he quietly showed me the lavatory in case I needed to use it. His attitude was that normal bodily functions were something secret and disgusting, never to be discussed in company. I remember being very taken aback by that and thinking, 'Hang on a minute. I've been in the Army and seen everything, especially the latrines!'

Billie, Brian, Pat and I went everywhere together and made a nice little foursome. Then one day I took her home to meet my parents. Father could see straight away that I was smitten with this beautiful girl and I could tell that he was disappointed. He wasn't a controlling man but what he wanted more than anything was for our family to remain together, and never break up. He certainly didn't want me to get married, even though I was almost thirty, but it was too late. After Brian and Pat were wed, I proposed to Billie despite hardly knowing her at all. When she said yes, I was delighted. We were married not long after in a church in Esholt, near Guiseley, which is where her people came from. Brian was my best man and Pat our bridesmaid, but we didn't have a big do because there was still rationing, so it was family only. The year was 1949 and my father wept. It didn't augur well.

Our honeymoon was spent at the Grand Hotel in Scarborough on top of the headland, and then we moved into the top-floor flat of a house called North Villas in Skipton Road, Keighley. The landlady was prim and proper, a well-to-do lady, who rented us a bedroom, living room, little kitchen and an attic. It was all I could afford, as we didn't have much money. It would have helped enormously if Billie had worked too, but she'd made it clear from the outset that she never would. As soon as I married, I sold my Manxman and gave up all thoughts of ever riding in the TT. The harsh reality was that, as a newlywed working all hours, I'd never have the time to practise every day and was unlikely to find the kind of sponsorship I'd need to compete. It was the end of that dream but – I hoped – the beginning of a new one with Billy. So, instead, I bought myself a 125cc Royal Enfield from Pride & Clarke in Stockwell, London, which they were selling cheap for £25. To begin with I kept it at the back of the house, but the landlady didn't approve of that so, when she wasn't looking, I carried it all the way up to the attic.

Billie and I were happy enough to begin with but, looking back, I realize that the first few months of our marriage were the happiest we ever had. To my disappointment, things weren't quite right between us from the start. She was very shy and restrained and I assumed that she'd relax in time, but sadly she never did. When I tried to talk to her I discovered that sex wasn't something her family ever discussed and, having had that odd experience with her grandfather, I could well believe it. I don't think Billie even knew what intimacy was and I soon came to realize that all she wanted was to be married, stay home and keep house. Because I thought so much of her, I tried to be patient, but as time went on I became increasingly unhappy and frustrated. I must accept some responsibility, however, because I couldn't believe that anyone could be the way she was, which was so far removed from how I felt. And the longer it went on the more I thought she was being difficult, and not just about the physical side of our relationship. Even so, I continued to believe that – with time and patience – things would improve. Whenever I went to bed with unhappy thoughts, I reminded myself that the next day I'd wake feeling brighter in the knowledge that it was a new day.

My mother must have sensed that things weren't quite normal between us because in 1950 she gifted me a family property she'd inherited in Granby Drive, Riddlesden. I think she thought that in a three-bedroom house with a garden, we might think about starting a family like our friends Brian and Pat, who had asked me to be godfather to their baby girl. Billie and I moved into our nice new semi-detached home and lived together pleasantly enough, in our own way. She was affectionate to me – well, as much as she could be – and as long as I didn't discuss the elephant in the room we never had any trouble. But things hadn't changed and it was clear to me that Billie had no intention of doing anything about it. I didn't feel that I could talk to anyone else about the problem either, as that would have been disloyal. Nor could I suggest that she speak to her mother or Pat because it was a subject that she refused to discuss with anyone. So we muddled along and I threw myself into trying to build up the company, which meant I didn't have too much time to think about what I was missing.

My marriage to Billie represents the darkest period of my life and I think now that it was my fault. I was too impulsive and should have got to know her better. I shouldn't have married the girl, but I really did care for her to begin with. As the years passed, I felt as if I had sunk into a deep hole and couldn't get out. We had little or nothing in common, and because her family would never have accepted us separating or divorcing we were stuck with each other. I could have been unfaithful but I didn't believe in that. I had signed a contract, I had a wife and that's just how it was. There was no one I could turn to because this wasn't a conversation that could be had by shouting into my father's ear and, although I'd always felt able to talk to Mother, I had no idea how to broach this. I could never discuss sex with Freda who, I imagined, was a virgin, and I didn't think Uncle Arthur would understand. I was on my own, in every sense of the word.

Looking back, I realize Billie had mental health problems that only became worse in the absence of professional help. Maybe I should have spoken to my GP about it, but nobody did that in the 1950s. The free-to-all National Health Service was a brand-new concept, established in 1948 by Labour's Health Minister Aneurin Bevan with the aim of preventing and curing disease. The emphasis was on the physical, not the psychological, and there was still a great deal of fear, stigma and prejudice around problems of the mind. The threat of being 'sent to Menston' was as real as ever. It was still operating and anyone suffering from mental health issues was still considered defective or a 'lunatic' to be locked away in places where there was little incentive to treat them because they were believed to be incurable. It wasn't for another decade that psychiatry started to gain ground as a science, and even then mental health remained taboo, and not to be aired publicly. Besides, I kept reasoning, Billie just needed more time and I needed to be more patient with her. Things would turn out all right in the end, I told myself, only half believing it.

Keeping myself busy, I divided my time between work and home and was still organizing the regimental reunions, which took a lot of time and effort, although it was always a joy to see everyone each year, including Major Spong (without his pig), and 'Cocky' Haslock who, I think, had accepted by then that I was a man unlikely ever to get lost.

I was never much of a gardener but at weekends I'd mow the lawn and then relax by watching the kinds of cowboy films I used to enjoy with my father, the ones where the good people always win. Or I'd play my favourite country music records by artists such as Patsy Cline, Jim Reeves and Glenn Campbell. I also loved the songs of Dean Martin and Frank Sinatra. Closer to home, I liked Anne Shelton and, of course, the ever lovely Vera Lynn, especially her song 'Look for the Silver Lining', with the lyric, *'Whenever a cloud appears in the blue, remember somewhere the sun is shining.'* That's very true. A bit of optimism goes a long way in this life.

And I loved to watch all the Formula 1 races on TV, especially if they featured my hero Stirling Moss, who I'd seen race on a solitary trip to the brand-new racing circuit at Silverstone in Northamptonshire. Nine years younger than me, Stirling was truly the gentleman of the race track and I was so impressed by the fact that, although he drove dozens of different marques, he preferred to race British cars like Coopers and Vanwalls, Jaguars and Aston Martins, saying, 'Better to lose honourably in a British car than win in a foreign one.' In one year alone he competed in sixty-two races and although, famously, he never won the title, he became the English driver with the most F1 victories. He was a champion to me.

Every now and again Billie and I would meet up with Brian and Pat at one of the village pubs near Otley. Brian was still working at his father's quarry and never one to turn down a pint, while Pat and Billie would sip their popular 'Gin and Its' (gin with Italian vermouth). I'd nurse my half-pint of Timmy Taylor's and we'd have a pleasant enough evening together, before Billie and I returned home to our loveless bed. This became the pattern of our lives.

Needing something just for me, I decided to take up the motorcycle time trials that were still popular amongst the owners of pre-1915 machines. Most of them were run by vintage bike clubs and sponsored by local newspapers. I couldn't afford a vintage bike of my own but I'd remained friends with Oliver Langton, the Leeds builders' merchant who'd raced for the famous Belle Vue Aces Father and I used to go and watch. Oliver owned several old bikes and a few vintage cars, and he couldn't possibly ride or drive them all, so he lent me a 1912 Scott Flying Squirrel, registration DN 3612, made in Saltaire, Shipley – just like the ones Uncle Billy used to race. It was a great bike and did me proud by winning me all sorts of cups and trophies, so when I recently discovered that it is still in existence and held in the collection at Bradford Industrial Museum I was delighted. It would be grand to be reunited with it one day.

Just as when I was a lad, the trials took place all over Yorkshire and in Lancashire for up to a hundred riders, smogs permitting, that is. Those deadly clouds of fog and pollution in the 1950s were just like the winter fogs of my youth and were triggered by the burning of coal in factories and homes, which often created virtual blackouts. Driving or riding was impossible, and when you blew your nose it turned your handkerchief black. That was a filthy time and the smog seeped into houses so that you sometimes couldn't see across a room. It caused all sorts of problems for those with chest conditions and killed people in their thousands.

Thankfully there were enough clear periods and bright days for the trials to go ahead and I travelled all over for them. There was one at Bridlington that covered the West Riding, and another in Morecambe. Although great fun, they were nothing like as exciting as the trials my Uncle Billy had ridden in because they were all on main roads and timed from A to B. The biggest and best was the forty-five-mile London to Brighton 'Pioneer Run for Ancient Motorcycles' that I completed on several occasions. Started in 1930 by the Sunbeam Motorcycle Club for pre-war bikes, trikes or combinations, the Pioneer Run traditionally set off from Tattenham Corner railway station on the Epsom Downs racecourse, taking riders through Surrey and Sussex, past the village of Pease Pottage and on to finish on the seafront at Madeira Drive, Brighton. The 250 or so restored motorbikes taking part had names few will know now, like Alldays & Onions, Kerry, Ariel, Rudge, Arno and Minerva, which attracted admirers from far and wide. There were even a few 'fore-cars' (now obsolete) that carried the passenger in front of the motorcycle like a reverse rickshaw. None of the bikes had clutches, so to get started the rider needed to push it and run alongside before jumping on, making it largely a young man's sport. Sidecars were made of everything from baskets to leather and often came with racks for luggage or even champagne.

The Pioneer wasn't really a race – you simply had to get from one point to the next within a period of about four hours, regardless of the weather or conditions, and there were secret checks along the way to make sure nobody cheated by arriving early to wait on the outskirts. It was run on main roads with other vehicles and traffic to contend with, and if you were early or late because of a delay or breakdown you were given a penalty. Each driver was responsible for running and maintaining their own bike, with no support vehicles allowed. At the end of the trial your timekeeping was added up and the rider with the least penalties won either a medal or one of the larger First-Class trophies. I won several of each; many of the ones I was allowed to keep are still on my shelf. Oliver Langton was so pleased with my performance, which of course also reflected well on him and his collection, that he also lent me another great bike – a 1912 BSA that I also enjoyed putting through its paces. I attached a wicker sidecar to that one just for fun and because I was interested to see how it handled. The experiment *was* interesting, but I really needed a passenger for it to work properly. Sadly, Billie wouldn't go near it so I dismantled the sidecar and returned the bike to how it was.

Riding vintage bikes in trials was an enjoyable all-weather endurance sport but only really for diehard enthusiasts like me. It wasn't the kind of sport you could easily watch as a spectator – unless you were standing at the start or the finish – so I don't recall anyone ever coming to support me, not Billie or my parents, who were both in their seventies by then. And nobody apart from Oliver Langton helped me, either. I rode for me and me alone and in fond and grateful memory of dear Uncle Billy.

15.

'*If you don't believe in God, all you have to believe in is decency.
Decency is very good.*'

Harold Macmillan (1894–1986)

Britain's first motorway, the M1, was opened in 1959.

IN 1955, AT THE AGE of thirty-five, I decided that I wanted to do more for my community so I joined the Keighley Round Table, where several people I'd known all my life were making a valuable contribution to the community. After showing my eagerness to get involved, I was quickly elected chairman – a position I held for a number of years. My intention right from the start was to introduce as many events and interests as I could to attract new members, and encourage the towns-people to take collective responsibility and care for its less fortunate inhabitants.

Not long after I joined there was a dreadful event in Keigh-ley that impacted on the whole community. In a three-storey worsted-spinning mill called Eastwood Mills, a fire broke out when workmen were installing some pipes and then spread so rapidly in the noisy mill that there was no time to raise the alarm. Eight people died, including a sixteen-year-old girl, and when the fire brigade were finally able to get near they found most of them trapped behind a locked door. A later inquest discovered that fire precautions were almost non-existent in the mill and several of the fire escape doors were locked and barred.

The Keighley mill fire was one of four that occurred within a month in the Yorkshire woollen mills and made national headlines. Questions were asked about it in the House of Commons and that led to important changes in the law. More than 40,000 factories nationwide were checked for fire safety and thereafter fire alarms and regular inspections made compulsory. This was a matter of considerable interest to everyone in Keighley and we at the Round Table donated money to the Mayor's Fund to help the families of the victims, and did all we could to help the authorities and ensure that nothing like it ever happened again.

Separately, I also instigated the setting up of the Keighley Disabled Club whose mission was to: '*Provide a much-needed meeting place for people who are lonely, confined to their homes or live alone.*' Having grown up with a father who was deaf and Aunt Elsie who was crippled, I knew what it was like to feel isolated from the rest of the community. With Round Tablers providing free transport to the club at Keighley's Westgate Clinic, our first meeting had over seventy-five new members, some of whom had to be carried in bodily. The disabled of the town had been variously affected by polio, injured by war, in industrial accidents or had disabilities from birth. Some were even younger than me, including one girl with Parkinson's who I remember bursting into tears she was so happy and grateful to have been invited to such an inclusive and social venture. Older members were gnarled with arthritis or had other long-term health problems that confined them to their homes. Few of them had means so we set up an appeal for funds and raised other monies from subscriptions, bring-and-buy sales, teas and the sale of used stamps. Refreshments were provided as well as entertainments with concert parties and lectures. We also paid for a specially fitted holiday home in East Anglia that people could visit with a carer, created and planted them a little garden, and took them for afternoon tea in the grounds of Harlow Grange residential home in Harrogate in a convoy of more than twenty volunteers' cars.

The man who helped me greatly with the project was Alderman John Taylor, heir to the local Timothy Taylor brewery. While my meagre consumption of their product can't have done much to recommend me to them, I'd known the family all my life and they were charming and generous people. I am proud to say that the club is still going strong more than sixty years later.

With my help, the Round Table and the Lions Club also joined forces to organize a charitable treasure hunt in aid of the disabled club and other local organizations. This took more than fifty competitors on a forty-mile route from Riddlesden to Ilkley via the Dales to find fresh eggs that had been hidden in strategic places. The evening concluded with a buffet supper, dance and charity auction and was a great success.

I was already a member of the Keighley Young Conservatives, which I'd joined before I married, as this was very much a social club for like-minded friends to meet once a month and organize larger events. While my parents had always been Tories, I joined because the Party felt to me like a rising force, especially with John Taylor as our local MP under the leadership of Winston Churchill. As Churchill was the leader that helped us win the war, I was proud to be on his team.

Like many, I was shocked and amazed when he'd been ousted the first time and lost the 1945 election to Clement Attlee, which must have felt like such a betrayal after all he'd got us through. I suppose people were ready for a change and tired of the war, of rationing, and of broken promises. They'd also had enough of being told what to do. And then when Churchill returned to Downing Street in 1951 at the age of seventy-seven, he was so tired and unwell that he eventually had to resign. He handed the baton on to Anthony Eden, who got kicked out because of the Suez Crisis, when he foolishly launched an invasion of Egypt in order to regain control of the Suez Canal after it had been nationalized by the Egyptians. Eden didn't realize that people had lived through enough conflict and weren't prepared to put up with Suez-related petrol rationing on top of the food and other rationing that was still firmly in place. In a little over a week Britain was forced to withdraw, humiliated, before Eden resigned. It was undoubtedly an embarrassment, but it did nothing to dim my deep patriotism to my country or my loyalty to the Conservatives. I just wished Eden hadn't let the side down.

Billie wasn't interested in politics and I think she only ever came to one party gathering and never again. Similarly with the regimental reunions I was still organizing every year and to which wives were eventually invited. She wasn't comfortable and the idea of an evening of small talk with strangers was terrifying to her. Thus, as with almost all my committees and clubs, I made excuses for her and went alone. She always said that my friends weren't 'her thing', but then I never really knew what 'her thing' was.

This was the mid-1950s when Frank Sinatra, Vera Lynn, Bill Haley and the Comets, Elvis Presley and Cliff Richard all had No. 1 singles and chimpanzees started pouring PG Tips tea in adverts on the telly. The last Avro Lancaster bomber, that magnificent workhorse of the European theatre of war, had recently been retired by the RAF and the 'Queen of Crime' Agatha Christie brought out a new novel every year. Mike Hawthorne became the first British racing driver to win Formula 1, and Donald Campbell pushed the world water speed record up and up towards an astonishing 260 mph and beyond with his beautiful *Bluebird*. And in 1957 the USSR launched Sputnik into space. The world was changing fast. All of this interested me and more, but not our Billie. She wasn't even interested in talking about any of these momentous events.

Closer to home, I was kept busy. As chairman of the Young Conservatives, I was involved in everything from supporting our local MP at the hustings to helping the town commemorate the death of George VI in 1952 and then the Queen's Coronation the following year. For the latter the town was strewn with red, white and blue bunting and the war memorial my grandfather built was gaily decorated with flowers. Despite the unseasonable June weather, beacons were lit at Keighley and Bingley as well as bonfires that were visible for miles, although the fireworks display had to be cancelled because of the rain. There was a joyous week of street parties, afternoon teas, concerts and fancy dress competitions as well as various pageants, tableaux and sporting events in honour of our lovely new Queen.

All the town's schoolchildren received a silver spoon and a souvenir mug as the church bells chimed. A fleet of pleasure boats took to the Leeds and Liverpool Canal at Silsden followed by a regatta. A Coronation Ball featuring a ten-foot crown made by local art students of crêpe paper was lit with coloured bulbs and suspended from the ceiling of the Municipal Hall, where a television was installed so people could watch the ceremony live from Westminster Abbey. We watched it at home in the parlour on a black-and-white television Father bought specially for the occasion. That was certainly was a day to remember. After the austerity of the war years and with the end of rationing on the horizon, the country's future felt bright.

After a few years in the family firm I was feeling more settled. We were building houses again and I felt I had found my niche. Communication with my father was as difficult as ever, though, with every conversation still yelled into his ear. It seemed to me that he'd become even deafer over the years. He'd tried a rudimentary hearing device for a while, with headphones and an amplifier that he wore around his neck, but it never really worked and he didn't believe anything else could help. I wasn't so sure. I hoped that recent technological advances might make a difference, so I booked him an appointment with a specialist and took him there myself. The expert conducted all sorts of tests and asked Father to listen to various beeps and sounds but, after half an hour or so, he looked up at me over my father's shoulder and simply shook his head. There was nothing that could be done.

Resigning myself to having to shout at Father for the rest of his days, I continued to work very hard at trying to grow the business and gradually felt better able to contribute more to the practical side of things. I wouldn't say I was a leader, but I'd trained and led men in the Army and been brought up to take responsibility, so I hired a few labourers, including the former lance corporal who'd taught me how to use a Bren gun at Weston Park and came looking for a job. I also liked helping out in the joiner's shop and working with the circular saw whenever we were busy.

One day I was doing just that, cutting a small piece of wood into a pattern and rushing a job that was running late, when I momentarily let my attention slip. The next thing I knew, the blade had sliced off the top of my left index finger. Strangely, it didn't bleed at first even though half an inch was missing, complete with fingernail. I must have called out because some of the workmen came running, but I don't remember anyone making a huge fuss. I got in the car and drove myself to hospital – it never occurred to me that I shouldn't – and it was only when the nurse unwrapped the cloth around my finger that it started spurting blood all over the place and they made me lie down on a stretcher.

'Where's the tip?' a doctor asked when he came to examine me.

I looked up at him blankly. 'I've no idea.' I hadn't thought to bring it with me. Later enquiries revealed that the men had scooped it up with the sawdust and thrown it on to the fire. The medical staff did a great job, folding over the remaining skin and stitching it up, sending me back to work with nothing but a small bandage wrapped around the stump. Best of all, thanks to the marvellous NHS, I didn't have to pay a penny. I can't remember who suggested that I make a claim on the industrial insurance but I went ahead and received £164, which seemed like a lot of money in the days when I was earning around £12 a week.

In the summer of 1956 our family suffered a sad loss with the death of Uncle Arthur from cancer, aged sixty-six. He had a long and painful decline and moved into Club Nook towards the end so that Mother could care for him until he had to go into the local St John's Hospital that had originally been the infirmary for the workhouse. He was buried with his lovely mother, my Granny Fanny, in Keighley cemetery. Arthur's death filled several local obituary columns and the one in the *Keighley News* praised him for his long links with local amateur dramatics dating back to 1910 when he starred in a production called *The Princess of Kensington* at the Keighley Hippodrome. It added, 'At heart he was a "Savoyard",' (a devotee of Gilbert and Sullivan) and said he'd spent a great deal of time encouraging the arts in churches, chapels and neighbouring villages.

I remember him with such fondness as the kindly uncle who took me to London for the first time, escorted me on my first ever foreign holiday, was waiting to meet me on my return from the war, and always provided food, laughter and song at our family gatherings. He would be sadly missed by us all.

Around this time, W. Moore & Son, which had long since moved from its original Alice Street premises, where Prince and Duke once had stables, to a yard in Lime Kiln's Yard, Riddlesden, moved again, to a site in Fleece Street. We were still building houses and the best of them were a row of five stone-built bungalows on a sloping site in Carr Lane, Riddlesden.

These were quite modern for their day with hidden wall heating, open-plan staircases and garages at the front of the house that framed the substantial front gardens. We were keeping our heads above water with all this but still not developing quite as quickly as I would have liked, due to a lack of working capital. My hope was that our properties would be well enough received to lead to further contracts. I had no reason to think otherwise or suspect that there was anything seriously wrong.

Then, not long after Arthur died, my father surprised me by announcing that he was selling Club Nook and the family was moving into one of our new bungalows in Carr Lane. He was seventy-one that year and Mother was seventy. His reasoning was that they weren't getting any younger and that it made sense to live somewhere more manageable with Freda, who was soon to be forty. The garden was big enough to grow his dahlias, he said (as he had long since sold his orchard plot), and living somewhere more modern would, as he put it, 'make a nice change'.

I had lived in Club Nook since I was eleven years old after we moved there from Cark Road. It was only seven years previously that I'd left, so it still felt like home to me. Taking one last walk around our airy four-bedroomed house with its oak-panelled hall, inglenook fireplace, large garden and separate garage – the one with stained-glass windows that had once housed Grandfather Thomas's beloved French automobile – my head was full of memories, all of them happy ones.

The house went on the market with local agents Dacre, Son & Hartley, and was described as,

A superior residence in first-class structural and decorative condition situate [sic] in attractive position . . . pleasant garden with heated greenhouse, garage and central heating chamber. The property has been well maintained and would be ready for occupation without further expense.

The records don't state how much it sold for, but it was put on the market in the July and by January 1957 my parents and Freda were living at 52 Carr Lane.

Two years later, in February 1959, my life took another unexpected turn. The firm's accountant summoned my parents and me to a meeting and told us that we would have to put the company into liquidation with immediate effect. We were almost broke, he announced, and unless we wound up the company voluntarily we wouldn't be able to pay off our creditors, which was not an option for a reputable local firm.

This news came as a terrible blow. I knew we'd stretched ourselves and that we'd had a lot more local competition in recent years from rivals prepared to do the same jobs for less, but I'd always believed that our name and reputation would see us through. I never suspected that we were on the brink of collapse.

My parents didn't seem at all surprised, which made me realize that they'd been expecting this for some time – possibly even as far back as the death of Uncle Billy. I now understood that a lack of funds was almost certainly the reason Father had sold Club Nook. Had he been trying to save the firm with his own money so as not to disappoint me? My head was in a spin as I wondered how this could have happened and what I was going to do. As with my situation at home, I worried how much I was responsible for and blamed myself. Had I been too ambitious in taking on bigger jobs, or did I not cost them properly? In the Army I'd not been content to be Private Moore and was determined to be an officer, so maybe I'd pushed too hard while not watching the money. My father was the official head of the company but he was old and stone deaf, so I'd been the *de facto* person in charge, but I'd been too busy running around trying to drum up more work to pay attention.

There was nothing I could do about the closure and there was no further discussion. The decision had been made. Over the next few months a liquidator by the name of Geoffrey Kitchen was appointed and he made a formal announcement about our closure in the *Keighley News* and held a public meeting at the town's Temperance Hall so that our creditors could present us with their bills. I was kept on for a while to sell off the assets, pay off our debts and help close the company that had been started by an illiterate farmer's boy after whom I'd been named, and which had come to what felt like a shameful end on my watch.

I'm sure my mother shed tears over the loss but I'm certain my father was somewhat relieved, as he'd been shouldering too much responsibility for far too long. He retired to enjoy his photography and gardening, and never spoke of the losses that must have touched him deeply. There was no money left over for me either and with very little in the bank I had nothing to fall back on. One day I was working hard to build us a future and the next day there was nothing.

I am not a man for regrets and I still don't have any, but there were times then when I couldn't help but think that if I'd remained in the Army things might have been different. Instead of being unemployed, I could have become a senior officer on a regular salary, expanding my horizons at home or abroad. I'd have liked to make it to Major, as I think that would have suited me in terms of command. If I'd been in such a position, I may even have been able to save Club Nook, and fulfilled my ambition to see Mount Everest closer than a dot on the far horizon. Instead I was forty years old, out of work and still living in my hometown, not far from my parents. I didn't imagine anybody local would be interested in employing me after I'd let the company slide, and I didn't have any qualifications that anyone particularly wanted. I'd just have to find something else to do – whatever job was going. I needed to be away from the house, working and earning. I was prepared to do anything and never had time for anyone who said that manual labour was beneath them.

One of the first things I did was sell my Royal Enfield motorbike as I couldn't afford it any more. Billie had never liked me riding it anyway and used to say motorcycles were dangerous, but I always told her, 'Rubbish. They're inanimate objects. It's the riders that are the problem.' I never possessed a bike again, and all thoughts of time trials and racing were abandoned for good. That decision probably saved my life because although I was a good rider, the average speed of machines had risen massively from my day and the more powerful they got, the more dangerous they became. One little mistake at 130 mph and you're dead, which was the reason why more and more people were dying in the TT races I still followed. I reasoned that if ever I'd tried to compete there I'd have probably killed myself. After all, there was only so much Granny Fanny could do to keep me safe.

The days immediately after the company folded were dark ones for me, but I had a good friend in Brian Booth who stepped up and offered me a job at his father's quarry, ten miles out of Skipton. He apologized that he didn't have anything better but said there was an opportunity to be a labourer there if I wanted it. I agreed immediately and with gratitude and, from that day on, things turned out differently for me.

As Duke Ellington once said, 'Grey skies are just clouds passing over.' I have always believed that after every storm, the sun shines brightly. I think you have to go through a bad period to appreciate the good and, although that period wasn't a happy one, I never gave up hope. Never.

Just as I had set out to be the best soldier I could be and then the best builder, so I decided I would try to become the best labourer. It might seem boastful, but I can honestly say that I achieved this at the quarry and I learned so much along the way. I wanted to try everything so I started working with the crushers, which suited me fine because they involved using heavy machinery. Huge lumps of stone blasted from a forty-yard-high wall of limestone would be loaded on to a conveyor belt and dropped into a machine that pulverized them into smaller ones – anything from three-inch pieces to gravel, all to be used in construction, road building and concreting. It was unbelievably noisy and none of us wore ear defenders. I'm not sure they'd even been invented. My ears still ringing, I moved on to working with explosives to blow up the rock face, which was even more exciting. The quarry's limestone wall had natural cracks in it so I learned to look for those and then place the explosives at the bottom to take advantage of any weakness. I especially loved lighting the fuse or plunging the handle on the detonator and then making a run for it as the noise of the explosion echoed around the rocks and the smell of cordite filled the air. Once the smoke and dust cleared it was always gratifying to see the results.

I'm sure Billie disapproved of being married to a manual labourer, especially one who was paid £10 a week, which was considerably less than I'd been earning at the family firm towards the end. She never said anything, of course, remaining – as ever – entirely neutral. Unexpectedly, I really enjoyed the quarry work and I liked working with the quarry manager, a cousin of Brian's, as well as the twenty or so other labourers, many of whom were older than me. I think I could have stayed there forever if I hadn't any ambition, but I had no intention of remaining a labourer on £10 a week. Brian and his father Leonard had been kind to give me a job but they worked together in the main office over Ilkley way and I knew there was no room for me, so after six months I left when I heard about a promising job opportunity.

On the face of it, this looked like an unlikely change of direction. But everything happens for a reason and my decision to become a door-to-door salesman for *Woman's Own* magazine ended up changing my life. To begin with it was all just part of my plan to move higher and higher up the ladder until I could find myself a management job. No one in my family was ever work-shy. The advertisement in the newspaper seemed to offer the world, with all sorts of chances to earn bonuses on top of commission, and I thought it would be a step up. Women's magazines were incredibly popular in the decades after the war with 12 million copies a week sold. Competition was intense between rivals so sales tactics became more aggressive. I had no idea really what my job would involve but my hope was that if I did well enough as a salesman they'd promote me quickly and invite me into the office.

I don't know what I expected, but I didn't think the work would be so soul-destroying – knocking on people's doors and trying to con housewives into buying something they couldn't afford. I was cold-calling and selling subscriptions, for which I was paid commission, but once a customer signed up to the magazine they were stuck with it long-term and I hated that. It went against all my principles. To begin with, though, I had to stick with it as I had nothing else. I started knocking on doors further away from home, as I didn't want anyone I knew shutting the door in my face. In the end no one did and everyone was extremely trusting and polite, which only made me feel worse. I only sold one or two subscriptions in about three months because I couldn't bear tricking people. I was constantly on the lookout for another job, but before I found anything the sun shone on me at last because I called on one woman when the man of the house happened to be home. As I chatted to his wife, he listened to my sales pitch and seemed impressed.

'I'm a salesman too,' he told me. 'And my company is looking for people just like you. Why don't you apply? I could put in a good word for you.' This was music to my ears and I will always be grateful to that man, Ken Rosier. He gave me the name and number of a company called Nuralite in Gravesend, Kent, and I called and was invited there for an interview whereupon they offered me the job of travelling salesman straight away. The office manager was a pretty young lady by the name of Pamela Paull, who was terribly nice to me. I was very attracted to her and felt we made an instant connection, but I knew that I couldn't do anything about that because I was married. I wasn't prepared to break my marriage vows, even if I didn't really have a proper marriage to break.

My new title was Nuralite Representative for Cheshire and Manchester, working side by side with Ken, who covered Yorkshire. Nuralite was a roofing material that came in great sheets and rolls. Made from a mixture of asbestos fibre and asphalt (in the days before anyone realized asbestos was deadly), it was half the price of the traditional lead although it had to be heated to become pliable. As a former builder I found myself perfectly placed to seek out builders' merchants and persuade my fellow tradesmen to become stockists of this new product. I was good at my job because I genuinely believed in the product and, with plain Yorkshire speaking, told them how good it was. The job increased my pay to £15 a week and I was given my second ever company car, an Austin 7, which cheered me up no end, even though I had to buy my own petrol. Overnight, I had a regular income and a means of transport all in one giant leap.

To celebrate I took Billie on a special journey in the new Austin. It was early 1960 and the first stretch of the M1 motorway had recently been opened between Watford and Rugby as part of the planned London–Yorkshire motorway. I wanted to see what it would feel like to drive down a public road as fast as I could go without any speed restrictions (these weren't introduced until 1967). Motorways were the future for the British economy and would make a huge difference, especially to salesmen like me, but unfortunately British cars like the brand-new Ford Anglia or the Singer Gazelle just weren't up to it yet. The manufacturers had never anticipated that their vehicles would be expected to go full speed, hour after hour, and that's when the problems like overheating and excessive oil pressure started.

I'm not sure Billie was as impressed as I was with our outing as she just kept twiddling the dial on the radio to find some music she liked. It was the era of the Everly Brothers who were number one with 'Cathy's Clown', beating the likes of Anthony Newley, Adam Faith, Roy Orbison and The Shadows. It wasn't music that I was especially fond of, but I was always impressed when someone made it to the top of the charts and idly wondered what that must feel like. My focus was strictly on the road and the car and the experience, however, and I was surprised by how few drivers had come to test it out. Even with clear lanes, my big drawback was that the Austin's top speed was only 65 mph, so I didn't exactly break any records. As I pulled off on to the slip road at Rugby, pleased that I'd tested the new surface to my satisfaction, I had no idea just how often I'd be driving up and down it in the coming years.

16.

'It is so important to keep going,
keep smiling, and keep hoping.'

Dame Vera Lynn (1917–2020)

US President John F. Kennedy addresses the
crowds in West Berlin in June 1963.

MY WIFE'S MENTAL HEALTH dipped further when we moved house. Needing to live more centrally for my job, I decided to sell the Riddlesden property Mother had given me and move to Manchester. I looked carefully and found us a nice detached house, with a coveted carport, in the suburb of Northenden which I bought outright with no mortgage. We were fortunate to be in a position to do so, but our move up the housing ladder was not easy to enjoy thanks to Billie's anxiety.

I thought she would be pleased and hoped she'd like making a new home for us there, but sadly the sixty-mile move away from her family and all she'd known seemed to trigger more psychological problems. That's when she developed what would now be called obsessive-compulsive tendencies. This had already manifested itself in different ways to do with cleanliness and other things, but in Northenden it became a fear of fire. We had to go around the whole house together every night checking that every electric switch was off before she'd consider going to bed.

We hadn't been in the new house very long before I changed jobs again, first to work with a company based in Hemel Hempstead that sold water pumps, then for a firm that sold industrial conveyor belts, and then for a dewatering company in Bishop's Stortford. Each switch meant a promotion, with more money and a better company car. Whilst I enjoyed the work, being in one sales job after another wasn't, it has to be said, as stimulating as I'd have liked and so for me it became all about the cars. If I'd had the choice they would all have been in red like my Morgan, but companies gave me whatever they could get for the best price so they came in every hue. And all took me away from home.

Whatever the vehicle, I was travelling as much as 45,000 miles a year, using my now well-honed navigational skills more often than maps to find my way around Britain, and stopping at transport cafés for a quick, cheap meal before trying to get home if I could. Every company I ever worked for was impressed by how well I looked after my vehicles – keeping an eye on tyre pressures, oil and water gauges – and delivering them for servicing at exactly the right mileage. Uncle Billy and the Army had taught me well. The Hillman Minx was pretty reliable, and the Triumph Herald even better, but sadly the Austin often overheated despite my best efforts. All these were displaced in my affections by the Ford Cortinas I had after that – good solid workhorses. They had to be. I virtually drove them into the ground.

I stayed away overnight as little as possible because of Billie, but if I really was too far from home or had to be back in the same area the following day, I'd find a B&B or a pub for the night. My first foreign sales trip was to Barcelona for the dewatering company, where I advised those building the new airport which pieces of our equipment would be best deployed to drain the land. Interestingly, I flew to Spain in a de Havilland Comet, the world's first commercial jet liner which was launched in 1952. Within the first two years, three of them crashed and they eventually discovered why – stress and metal fatigue caused in part by the large square windows. These were redesigned and relaunched with oval windows and I was relieved that the one I flew in was one of the later versions that continued to fly without incident until the 1980s. They were beautiful machines. Having arrived in Barcelona in one piece, I was put up in a nice hotel and so enjoyed what I saw of the place that I thought I might take Billie there one day.

With my work back in the UK taking me further east than Manchester, I decided to sell the Northenden house and buy a two-bedroom flat with a balcony an hour away on the out-skirts of Leeds. This was more convenient for work and also netted me a small profit. I hoped that a little less time on the road would help, but again the move only made things worse for Billie. It was my fault, I'm sure. I should have realized that all the moving about and the uncertainty of my work would tip her over the edge. Plus she was home alone all day while I was working hard to keep us afloat. And in what little spare time I had I was still organizing the regimental reunions, which called upon my limited secretarial skills in confirming addresses, booking hotels, sending out invitations and man-aging the finances.

I was too busy to register the impact of my absence on Billie, and I'd somehow become too preoccupied with things to pay much attention to world events such as the Cold War or the erection of the Berlin Wall. I remember Churchill gravely saying: 'An iron curtain has descended across the Continent.' But it took something like the assassination of President Kennedy in 1963 or the death of Churchill and the sight of his coffin being loaded with great solemnity on to a barge on the River Thames to really cut through. We'd moved into the era of the Beatles, the Rolling Stones and rock and roll, but I was never much of a fan – although I thoroughly approved of the mini-skirts that went with the era and Billie was still a very beautiful woman who looked terrific in hers. My nod to the swinging sixties was to wear suits with wider lapels and the occasional floral tie, but I drew the line at flared trousers.

One day in October 1964 I returned home from a long day on the road to hear Billie tell me that my sister Freda had called. This was unusual so I put down my case and reached immediately for the phone. 'Mother died,' Freda told me, her voice flat. I heard her words and had to sit down. At the age of seventy-seven, the huge heart of the four-feet ten-inch tall Isabella Hird had simply faded away and she passed away peacefully at home, with Father and my sister by her side. She didn't suffer and, like Granny Fanny, she died in her own bed. It was a huge loss to us all, as she was a warm, life-enhancing woman who had looked after us all so beautifully. My mind conjured up images of her picking daffodils in the Dales, kneading bread in the kitchen at Club Nook or selecting butter at the market. I saw her smiling face through the glass of the Morton Banks Fever Hospital when I was a nipper, and her pinched expression when I went off to war. Father especially felt the loss, as she'd been his ears and his right hand for forty-nine years and had given him the happy family life that he might never otherwise have had. Once again, though, none of us wore black armbands or keened in public. We Moores dealt with our grief quietly and privately and remembered her each in our own special way.

Our dear little mother was buried at Morton cemetery in the Moore family plot that Grandfather had erected – a four-faced mottled grey marble memorial beneath an obelisk. Father's name would be added to it one day and I expect he thought Freda and I would join them, too, thus reuniting the

ABOVE: Vera Lynn entertains the troops in Burma.

RIGHT: Riding a Valentine tank to work in Burma.

BELOW: A pair of Valentine tanks crossing a river. My friend John Billham and I called ours Gog and Magog, after two mythical giants.

ABOVE: A Lee tank travelling along the Ngakyedauk Pass to engage Japanese positions in an operation I took part in.

RIGHT: My photo of our Shermans in action in Burma.

BELOW: Entrance to one of the heavily defended tunnels on the Maungdaw–Buthidaung road that we captured from the Japanese 55th Division.

ABOVE: A Sunderland flying boat like the one that flew me home from Burma in the company of Joyce Grenfell.

ABOVE: Tank tracks. The mighty Churchill on which I trained as an instructor at Bovington camp in Dorset in 1945.

RIGHT: Two wheels. With my beloved 1912 Scott Flying Squirrel, clutching some of the trophies I won in trials.

BELOW: Three wheels. Back in the UK I bought a Morgan F3 three-wheeler like this one.

LEFT: In business back in the day with quite the 'tache.

BELOW: Wedding day in Kent, with Pamela's mother and my father.

LEFT: Pamela. The office manager who stole my heart.

BELOW: An advertisement for the Nuralite Company where I worked on two separate occasions. And where I met the love of my life.

Nuralite gives you a 1st class return

Photograph by kind permission of BRITISH RAILWAYS

British Railways' Bexhill Station is roofed with Nuralite; one of several places where British Railways use Nuralite for roofing and therefore keep their roofing costs down.

Nuralite the new thermo-plastic roofing material supersedes roofing metals at a fraction of their cost. It is ideal for guttering, ridging, flashing, flat roofs, etc. It is permanently weatherproof and a craftsman's material to work. Its fire resistant qualities satisfy the requirements of Model Bye Law 49.

WILL WEATHERALL

Nuralite **SUPERSEDES ROOFING METALS**

THE NURALITE COMPANY LIMITED
WHITEHALL PLACE • GRAVESEND • KENT

Telephone: Gravesend 6176 (3 lines)   Telegrams: Nuralite, Gravesend

TOP RIGHT: My father gets to meet Lucy, his first grandchild.

BELOW: Dressed to kill with Pamela.

BELOW: My sister Freda with little Hannah on holiday in the '70s.

BELOW: Our trusty Austin Maxi took us all the way to Italy for a wonderful camping holiday.

BELOW: On the *Blankety Blank* Christmas special with Terry Wogan in 1983.

Burma star medal.

Receiving my regimental statue from General Sir Evelyn Webb-Carter, the last Colonel of the Dukes, on the sixtieth anniversary of the 9th Battalion Burma reunions that I started in 1947 and ran for sixty-five years.

Proud father. With my two lovely girls at Hannah's wedding.

Visiting an old friend at Bovington Tank Museum.

ABOVE: A return to India, after Pamela's death in 2006.

LEFT: With Lucy and Hannah, in India, in 2012.

BOTTOM LEFT: In Nepal, anticipating a flight over Everest, in 2010.

BELOW: With my four wonderful grandchildren: Thomas, Max, Georgia and Benjie.

On my 100th birthday,
with a card from Her Majesty the Queen.

LEFT: I'd only been planning to walk a hundred laps and raise £1000!
TOP RIGHT: The RAF flew over on my birthday, eighty years after I saw my first Hurricane.
BOTTOM RIGHT: Back with the Dukes. Celebrating my 100th birthday with my old regiment.

family that meant the world to him. The grave stands just a few yards away from the German POW's memorial that the *Hindenburg*'s flying priest had wanted to commemorate. We had a quiet family funeral for Mother and then we went home. The passing of the daughter of the town's once popular barber, stationer and hairdresser wasn't deemed worthy of a mention in the *Keighley News*. A far cry from the coverage of my grandfather's death or that of Uncle Arthur.

Mother always said that Father had to die at least one day before her, 'For, without me, he'll starve.' And yet she did go before him, but probably only because she knew he'd be in safe hands. At the age of forty-seven, my sister Freda was still living in the Carr Lane bungalow and it was quietly accepted that she'd never marry and would take care of Father for the rest of his life, just as he'd always wanted.

As if Mother's death hadn't shaken me enough, there was more heartache around the corner. When Billie announced that she'd found herself a job I was so taken aback that I could hardly respond at first. She'd never worked for the whole of our fifteen-year marriage, not even when the company was shut down and she knew how worried I'd been about money. When she told me what the job was I was flabbergasted – she'd accepted work as an assistant to a doctor in Leeds who treated patients with sexual disorders. I couldn't believe it and protested, 'But, Billie, love, you are completely the wrong person for that.' She was determined to do it, however, and I was so busy working and driving all over the country that I didn't have the time, or the energy, to argue.

Increasingly worried for her mental health, I made sure to get back to Billie when I could because, left to her own devices, I could only imagine the obsessive rituals she would put herself through. One day I returned to Leeds unexpectedly early to discover a strange man in our flat. This was unusual in itself but even more so when he appeared suddenly as I walked in and then wouldn't talk to me. When I asked Billie who he was she said he was her psychiatrist and that he was helping her with her problems. Confused and puzzled, I nevertheless managed to convince myself that this could only be a positive development, so I didn't ask too many questions.

From then on, she started to see him regularly and always at the flat when I was away, which I thought odd as he surely had an office she could visit. And I wondered who was paying for her treatment because I couldn't afford to. As time went on, I began to suspect that Billie had developed a crush on this chap because she never stopped talking about him. Matters finally came to a head when I arrived home one February to hear her declare, 'I'm moving in with my psychiatrist, Tom. I want to have sex with him. He says that this is what I need to do.'

I was shattered by the shock and audacity of it. I had been such a loyal husband and so very patient and it felt like the worst kind of betrayal. I decided there and then that enough was enough. It was dreadfully sad, but our so-called marriage was over. I packed a suitcase with a few belongings and walked out, leaving her and everything behind me.

Too upset to tell anyone at first, I went back to my room in the pub at Bishop's Stortford and sat alone, my mind churning over what had happened. I felt wretched.

Within days of me leaving, Billie realized her mistake and, desperate, she wrote and left messages and finally came looking for me in Hertfordshire. Fortunately I was at a sales meeting when she turned up at the pub in tears and she missed me, but it wouldn't have made any difference. My mind was made up. I never saw or heard from Billie again, except through our lawyers. If she hadn't done what she did I would probably have stayed with her forever because loyalty and fidelity is important to me, but she gave me a way out of a union that had made us both unhappy and I took it. Although I wasn't to blame for what happened, I felt as if I had failed, and for a time I was as sad as I had ever been in my life.

Once I felt able, I drove to my father's bungalow in Carr Lane, where I intended to live for a while. Turning up unannounced on the doorstep with a suitcase and telling Father and Freda that I'd walked out of my marriage was one of the hardest things I'd ever had to do. No one had ever divorced in our family, but once I told them the sorry truth of my relationship with Billy they were both appalled on my behalf and extremely sympathetic. Thereafter I stayed with them at weekends and whenever I was in the area. I instructed a solicitor to start divorce proceedings and when I told him everything that had happened between us he informed me that I could seek an annulment on the grounds that Billie and I had never consummated our marriage. This seemed like the simplest and fastest option, so I agreed.

It was 1967, I was approaching fifty, and I had stuck it out with Billie for eighteen of what should have been the best years of my life. Now I had to look to the future.

While my hand had been forced I have always found that the turning tide brings in something better and it did for me then, with an advert I spotted in the trade papers. Nuralite needed a new regional manager so I applied and was welcomed back as the north of England and Northern Ireland manager with a good salary and – to my delight – a wedge-shaped, aerodynamic Austin Princess. Now, that was a company car to be proud of – or so I thought.

My new role involved frequent meetings at the company's head office in Gravesend, Kent, and it was there that I reconnected with the pretty office manager, Pamela Paull. Fifteen years younger than me and in her early thirties she looked terrific, like a model, and – to my surprise – she was still single. From then on, I looked forward to my trips to Kent more than perhaps I should have and over the following year gradually forged a lovely friendship with Pamela, taking her out for a coffee, meals, a drink and a chat. It felt good to have someone to talk to.

Pamela was completely different to Billie – a capable working woman and an excellent office manager who was so highly regarded at the company that she'd been promoted to that position at the age of twenty-four. Slim, blonde and stylishly dressed, she appeared to have nothing like the hang-ups of Billie and I was smitten. It didn't seem odd to me that at thirty-two years old, she'd never married or had children and still lived with her parents in Gravesend. I myself hadn't left home until I was almost thirty, after all. When I discovered that she'd never been abroad either, I took her on her first ever foreign holiday. We drove all the way to the south of France in the Austin Princess (which only just made it) and she loved every minute, commenting on all the Frenchmen making eyes at her. We had a wonderful time in a hotel by the Mediterranean and I was happier than I'd been in years.

I suppose I impressed Pamela in my own way, too, because I was not only someone who'd fought in the war that had defined her childhood but was a senior manager at the company where she worked. Her future probably looked a bit more secure with someone like me, but it didn't start out that way, as I had little or no money and nowhere to live, making me effectively homeless. To be closer to Pamela while I waited for my divorce to come through, I decided to change jobs again. I was happy at Nuralite but I didn't think it was appropriate to date somebody at work and would have hated her to become the subject of office gossip.

In what proved to be my best career move, I became sales manager at a branch of the large Yorkshire company Cawood, Wharton & Co., builders' merchants and concrete manufacturers in Blackwall Lane, Greenwich, east London. Happy for the change, I left the north of England behind me for good. This was another promotion but quite a tough job to begin with. The works made and sold concrete pipes and blocks and special concrete facings for buildings, so I found myself dealing with planners and architects working on projects at least two years ahead of time. This was further complicated by the fact that the building regulations were constantly changing with increasingly high standards to be met. I was able to keep up well enough to soon be promoted to technical manager. My training as a civil engineer had served me well.

Pamela and I were already falling for each other and I decided that there was no time to waste. The time had come to be with someone who could make me happy, so I asked her to be my wife. My plan was to marry her as soon as my divorce came through and then find somewhere for us to live. It was her suggestion that I move in with her and her family rather than pay out needlessly for rooms. This seemed like a good idea, especially as I was still driving all over the country and not often home, but I hadn't bargained for the reaction of her relatives. They were set against me from the start and considered me wholly unsuitable – too old, with a failed marriage behind me, an intruder, and from Yorkshire to boot. In their opinion it couldn't get much worse.

Undaunted, I moved into Pamela's bedroom at the family home, 14 Northridge Road, Gravesend. It wasn't far from the River Thames and within earshot of its passing ships. A three-bedroom house in a row of stone-built properties, it had a living room, kitchen, back room, outside loo and small verandah. Pamela's father Reginald Paull, who'd been a foreman at a paper manufacturers in Gravesend, had early-onset dementia and wasn't really aware of me or anything much. A poor old soul, he'd go out and get lost and couldn't remember where he lived. He eventually had to go into a mental hospital in Dartford for the final few years of his life and that's where he died, in his sixties.

Pamela's mother Kate was a controlling woman, and sometimes – it seemed to me – nutty as a fruitcake. I think I was the first person who ever stood up to her. I did eventually win her round, chiefly I think because I was assisting with the household bills. Pamela's sister Cath, who was fifteen years older, married and lived in Epsom, was a bit of a bossy-boots who also seemed to take every opportunity to put me down, which – of course – failed as I was immune to her and wasn't playing her game.

Not long after I'd been promoted, the managing director of my works had a heart attack and was forced to retire on health grounds. The only person with enough knowledge of the company to take his place was yours truly. Overnight, I became the works manager in charge of thirty staff and with a bit more money in my weekly pay packet. It was then that I began to realize that the company wasn't doing as well as I'd thought and needed a shake-up. I only hoped I was up to the job. And I now had good reason to as, around the same time, the sun shone for me once more when Pamela fell pregnant. This was not by design as we hadn't even discussed children yet, but I was thrilled by the news. I had long ago reconciled myself to the thought that I would never have children, which clearly wasn't an option with Billie (and that definitely worked out for the best, because she'd have been a terrible mother). So, the idea of becoming a father at my age was an unexpected surprise but one that I relished.

One thing I was adamant about was that Pamela and I should be married before the baby arrived so, with the annulment of my marriage taking far longer than I'd hoped because of Billie's resistance, I agreed to admit adultery and be the guilty party in the eyes of the law. My lawyer told me that this would be achieved by the tried and tested practice of us spending the night together in a hotel, so that our names on the register would confirm our night of mortal sin to her lawyers. I thought we'd find a suitable and not too expensive hotel near to Gravesend, but Pamela had other ideas. 'Let's go into London and make a night of it,' she said, excitedly, and I hadn't the heart to refuse. As she always loved to shop, she chose a hotel in Oxford Street so that we could go to all the department stores afterwards. Having made the most of our costly adulterous liaison, that is exactly what we did, laughing all day at the silliness of it.

Billie would have welcomed my gesture, I'm sure, because to her parents and others, she would then be assumed to be the innocent party and her reputation saved. When it came to the division of our assets, I didn't ask for a thing. There was a mortgage on our flat in Leeds but quite a lot of equity, too, which was all that I possessed in the world. I left the lot to Billie and walked away for good.

17.

'*I was taught that everything is attainable if you are prepared to give up, to sacrifice, to get it. Whatever you want to do, you can do it if you want it badly enough.*'

Stirling Moss (1929–2020)

In 1969 Neil Armstrong and Buzz Aldrin
became the first people to walk on the moon.

THE IDEA OF SPENDING the rest of my days with Pamela and having children with her was so far removed from how my life had been that I was filled with gratitude and love. She was a delightful woman and I was very happy with her, although I was aware from the outset that she was far more vulnerable emotionally than the capable office manager she'd first appeared to be. It was her mother Kate I largely blamed for that – a woman who didn't even know she was pregnant until she gave birth to Pamela in 1935.

The family had remained in Gravesend throughout the war and Kate refused to have her children evacuated. Night after night swarms of German planes flew in to bomb London and the nearby docks, while mother and daughters hid under the kitchen table listening to the bombs falling as the flashes of explosions lit up the room. All around their neighbourhood incendiary bombs set whole districts alight, destroying homes, shops, ships and businesses, and they were plagued by the terrifying V1 'doodlebug' bombs that screamed in at height before cutting out and plummeting silently to earth. On a single summer night in 1941 more than a hundred bombs fell on nearby Northfleet, killing twenty-nine people and injuring many.

Pamela survived all this and more, and – just as when I was in the LDV 200 miles north – it would have been drummed into her that German spies, posing as ordinary people, were infiltrating British society. When she reached school age and was no doubt very impressionable, her mother warned her, 'You'd better behave yourself, my girl, because I've hired a man to follow you. He'll be watching everything you do.' At a tender age and in such a fearful time, this seemed to imprint deeply on Pamela's mind and remain embedded there for the rest of her life. It didn't help that her mother used to mollycoddle her to the point of embarrassment, making her wear two school uniforms every day – the summer one on top of the winter one and vice versa – for fear 'she might catch a cold'. She also insisted that Pamela's free school milk was heated – in case of bacteria. If that isn't mental cruelty then I don't know what is. For the rest of her life the smell of warm milk made her feel physically unwell.

Looking back now, I have to admit that on my later dates with Pamela I'd begun to realize that something wasn't quite right. She would behave perfectly normally in the café or pub I'd taken her to but then something would shift. She'd suddenly stop talking and become agitated for no apparent reason. Then, jumping up, she'd announce, 'We have to go. That man over there is watching me over his newspaper.' Before I knew it she'd have abandoned her drink, sandwich or whatever it was that we were about to enjoy, and fled. Glancing quickly around the room I could never see anyone acting suspiciously or taking more than a passing interest in her. Blinded by love, to begin with, I thought it was a rather endearing trait and that she was just nervous of men ogling her good looks, but when it happened several times more I realized that this was something more sinister.

Once we started to live together, I noticed ever more episodes. She'd leave the house on a shopping trip but return a few minutes later to breathlessly declare that someone was following her and it wasn't safe. I tried to allay her fears each time, but it was clear to me from her mother's complete lack of reaction that this was something that had been going on, unchecked, for years.

By gum, I certainly knew how to pick them . . .

I'm not one for navel-gazing (well, not men's navels anyway), but I suppose if I'd met Pamela before Billie I might have run a mile. After my first marriage, however, anything was preferable and – in every other regard – Pamela was a joy. Better the devil you know, or so the saying goes. And besides, I was in love.

Although I didn't think much of Gravesend compared to the beauty and openness of the Yorkshire Dales, Pamela was unusually attached to it and I realized that it was where she felt the safest. She enjoyed trips away to see Father and Freda, but was always mightily relieved to get back. It wasn't just a haven for her – she loved the easy access into central London and enjoyed living close to the Thames Estuary. Every New Year's Eve, we would open the doors out on to the garden and listen to the vessels moored in the docks sounding their foghorns at midnight like the eerie call of whales. It was doleful and moving as it reverberated through the town. If ever I suggested we might not always live in Kent, she'd look horrified and say, 'But there's no place like Gravesend.' I couldn't disagree with her, but for different reasons.

Although Pamela's mental health concerned me, I never once had second thoughts about making her my wife and hoped that I'd be able to help her feel more secure. Unlike my previous marriage, I walked into this one knowing exactly what I was getting into. Her episodes were quite different to Billie's chronic OCD and only happened sporadically by comparison. Besides, Pamela and I had the kind of loving, intimate relationship that I had sorely missed. I also believed that, once she was a mother with a baby to care for, she'd outgrow the delusions that dated back to her childhood.

Pamela and I were married at Gravesend Registry Office in January 1968. The new 'Mrs Tom Moore' looked gorgeous in a white mini-dress and matching swing coat, little white pillbox hat, white tights and white shoes. Her bouquet was made up of her favourite scented freesias. She'd changed her hair colour from blonde to brunette for the wedding – something she went on to do frequently, which I began to suspect was part of her attempt not to be recognized by her imaginary stalker. She looked adorable that day, and I looked like the cat that had the cream as I gripped her hand tightly, determined never to let her go. Our wedding was a quiet affair attended by my father and Freda, along with a few close members of Pamela's family. Afterwards, twelve of us went to lunch at the Clarendon Hotel on the waterfront at Royal Pier Road, but that and the cost of the divorce cleaned me out so there was no honeymoon.

Our daughter Lucy came along a few months later on 16 August. The original plan was for her to be born at home but it was a very prolonged affair and as Pamela's labour wore on, the midwife was growing anxious – especially as, at thirty-three, Pamela was considered old to be having a first child. Eventually, it was decided that she should have the baby at Gravesend Hospital where the nurses looked after her beautifully. She was there for a long time and I sat with her as she was given gas and air and various drugs that made her woozy. After a while, I realized that I hadn't eaten so the nurses took pity on me and brought me a plate of toast. This was a crime that haunted me because Pamela complained forever afterwards that all I did was 'sit there and eat toast'.

When her contractions got worse and they took her into the labour ward to perform a forceps birth, the staff told me, 'You'd better go home now, and we'll let you know when it's all over.' They made it clear that it 'wouldn't be a place for a man'. I waited and waited but eventually I rang them and they told me, 'You have a beautiful baby daughter, Mr Moore,' so I hurried back, grinning from ear to ear.

I never knew I could love someone as much as I did Lucy. Holding this tiny human being in my hands and knowing she was a part of me was an intense and overwhelming feeling. I couldn't imagine that I would ever experience the same sense of attachment to anyone else.

One of the proudest days of my life was when Father and Freda came to visit and I was able to place my father's first grandchild in his arms. It still makes me emotional to think of how tenderly he held her. I could tell he was deeply moved and I'm sure, like me, he wished Mother were still alive to meet this joyful addition to our little family. Lucy gurgled happily in his arms as 'Granddad Wilfred' cooed and smiled, reminding me what a loving father he had been to me too, and why family had always been so important to him.

Right from the start I was a hands-on dad with Lucy, changing nappies and doing night feeds. This was just as well because, soon after she came home from hospital, Pamela declared, 'I'll take care of her in the daytime, as long as you look after her at night.' She'd always been a sound sleeper and was never a morning person, so I didn't mind at all. As soon as I heard Lucy cry I'd get up and deal with her and, thankfully, she wasn't a difficult baby so I never had too much trouble, it was no hardship. Man had recently landed on the moon so it wasn't too much to ask little 'Tommy' Moore to warm his baby's bottle.

Just like Billie, Pamela had given up her job when we were married and decided never to work again, so the burden of paying the bills was all mine. With Lucy sharing our room and the paraphernalia of childhood filling our house, it all became a bit cramped at Northridge Road so I applied for a mortgage and offered to buy my mother-in-law out. Without complaint, Kate banked my money, moved into a small house locally and remained there for the rest of her days. Ironically, towards the end of her life, it was me she turned to for support and advice, so our peace was finally made.

My job at the Cawood Wharton works was extremely demanding but I loved the responsibility. Half of my staff was West Indian and the other half white, and this struck a happy balance that reminded me of my time in the Army. In India, things worked best when neither Hindu nor Muslim soldiers felt overwhelmed or outnumbered by each other. I tried to make sure that the same was true now. Fortunately, everyone got along well. The challenge didn't lie with the personnel, however.

Once I'd had a chance to fully examine the company books I realized that its products were overpriced. The yard was full of unsold concrete blocks, so I re-costed them and cleared the lot. I increased the shifts from eight hours to twelve and, as demand rose, we went to a twenty-four-hour operation. The men were happy for the extra work and the overtime this brought them. Quite quickly the company went into the black so I was patted on the back and made up to a director.

With the demands of work, Lucy's night feeds and keeping Pamela on an even keel, it was a tricky enough time, but then in May 1970 something happened that reminded me of the fragility of it all when my dear old father took to his bed. My sister telephoned to tell me that at supper the previous night Father told her quite bluntly, 'Freda, this is the last meal I shall have. I shan't have another.' As was his way, there was no weeping or keening about it. At eighty-five years old he was worn out and – just like Mother and Granny Fanny – he knew his time had come. The following day he wouldn't get out of bed, which is when Freda summoned me. By the time I'd dashed to Keighley my father was gone. Freda opened the door and told me, tearily, 'Oh, Tom. You're only *just* too late.' He was interred at Morton cemetery in the same plot as Mother and the two of them were finally reunited after a long and happy life together. In keeping with his wishes, no tears were shed, and Freda and I returned to the bungalow alone.

I loved my father very much and even talking about him now makes me emotional, because I always considered that we were the very best of friends. When I think back to our afternoons in the Cosy Corner picture house watching silent movies together, or the times spent driving to Whitby as I yelled directions, or the sight of him cradling his grand-daughter in his arms, eyes glistening, I am so glad for the many happy years we had together. For a long time after his death I sometimes found myself in the cemetery on my own, just to be near him and Mother. I was so very fond of them both and there have been many times in my life when I have wished I could talk to them again and let them know that 'our Tom' is doing all right.

While the death of my dear mother had not merited a mention, Father's obituary in the *Keighley News* paid quiet tribute to his life in the town as part of an established and respected builders, and spoke of his valuable collections of photographs of old Keighley collected over a lifetime as an amateur photographer. He had always wanted to be a professional photographer and it is with great delight that I have recently been able to send some of his iconic pictures to a Keighley historian for safekeeping. Wilfred Moore, who rose above his disability to marry, have children and provide for his family, will now always be remembered for his prescient images of a time long past. It was the end of an era in so many ways, and especially for Freda and me, although she was to remain alone in my parents' bungalow for another fifteen years.

It is a matter of sadness to me that Father died too soon to meet his second grandchild, Hannah, born in the same year as his death. As with Lucy, she was never intended, she just happened in the loveliest kind of way and Pamela was as delighted as I was. Hannah was born quite easily at home with a midwife and I was there the whole way through. When she finally popped out she was handed to me straight away, so I was the first to hold her and it was me who put her in her cot. I had thought after Lucy that I couldn't love anyone as much again, but I was wrong because Hannah was just as wonderful and surprising to me as Lucy had been.

Pamela was a very good mother and having children was all she could wish for, but her mothering remained somewhat conditional, and only between certain hours, so that's where I came in. Not that I minded at all and I am still grateful for the special times the girls and I had together. Because of my age, there was the odd moment when they were growing up that I realized I was much older than all the other fathers. There were also occasions when I was mistaken for their grandfather, but it never mithered me. I was just so thrilled to have children – at whatever age. I didn't feel old, and although I'd started to lose my hearing in my fifties, I was in excellent health. I'd never smoked, I hardly drank and I'd always been very active. Admittedly I loved fatty bacon and pink beef, full-fat cream and the top of the milk – all the things they now say we shouldn't have, but I never gained weight or developed high cholesterol or diabetes. As long as I stayed fit and well, I hoped to live long enough to see my girls grow up, marry and have children of their own. That would be more than I probably deserved. At the age of fifty, I never expected that I would live another fifty years. Oh, the cheek of it.

As I'd always done the night feeds and dealt with any accidents or nightmares, the girls were accustomed to coming to me with their problems and would call out, 'Daddy' never 'Mummy' in the night. This suited me fine, and led to a very special relationship with them from the start. I'd give them a cuddle or make them some hot milk with a dash of whisky and put them back to bed. It suited Pamela even better because, although she loved them dearly and was a kind and thoughtful mother with sympathy in bucketloads, she preferred to stay in bed in the mornings with the cup of tea I always made for her. The way she looked at it, 8 a.m. just wasn't her time to get up. Once they were of school age, the girls knew the routine and would get themselves washed and dressed then go up and see her so that she could check them over and plait their hair.

When Hannah was born, people used to say to me, 'But didn't you want a boy?' and I used to tell them, 'Whatever for? I wouldn't have it any other way.' I never once felt that I'd missed out. Besides, I treated my girls exactly the same as I would have treated boys and encouraged them from the earliest age to be bold and positive and brave. One of my mottos is, 'Anything is possible.' If they climbed a tree, Pamela would squeal with fear but I'd laugh and ask them, 'How high can you go?' If they were grumpy or irritable I'd make a joke of it and tell them to, 'Come on now, buck up,' or try to encourage them with, 'Best foot forward.'

I taught them how to be practical in most skills from cooking to lighting a fire, tinkering with cars, to general maintenance. They knew how to change spark plugs, clean carburettors and wire plugs. As a nod to the hammer, nails and wood Father gave me as a boy, I bought them screwdrivers, spanners and hammers instead of dolls or teddy bears. I also enlisted them early on to help with the gardening and prepare the Sunday roast. And as they will tell you, packing the car for any of our family camping holidays to Europe had me, clipboard in hand, directing proceedings like a military operation. Oh, and we had the best holidays, one of the most memorable of which was when I packed our tent and luggage on to the roof rack of the Austin Maxi and drove us all to a campsite near Rimini on the east coast of Italy. The weather was glorious and the Adriatic a delight, but the trip was made by a lovely couple in the next tent called Dino and Carla who taught us how to make the most delicious Italian food – things like bruschetta with squeezed tomatoes drizzled with olive oil, pasta with truffle oil and all kinds of treats that really turned our heads and opened our eyes. Delicious.

Just as my father had frowned on ill health or minor injuries, few dramas were allowed with the girls and I encouraged them not to whine. They were pretty good, although Lucy badly smashed her two front teeth during a swimming gala and needed surgery. With hindsight, I probably inherited a lack of sympathy from Father, but at least I didn't make them drink

Fennings Fever Cure. As they grew, there were the usual sibling squabbles and, like most children, Lucy – who'd had us to herself – didn't immediately reconcile herself to having a rival for our affections. They also had entirely different temperaments. Lucy was far more easy-going and could be persuaded to do whatever we wanted but with Hannah – never. We always had to negotiate.

I always knew how to distract them, and one sunny day I suggested, 'Let's go for some ice cream.' They immediately agreed but probably didn't expect me to take them ninety miles to Covent Garden for it, just to calm them down. And if ever we went camping in our folding caravan (which Pamela hated), hitched to the back of my company car, the girls would be instantly happy. Likewise if went to visit Freda in Yorkshire, and I took them over the moors. I would drive as fast as I could on the road that rolled up and down like a roller coaster and they'd squeal with delight while Pamela screamed.

Once they became moody teenagers, though, boy, that was quite something. Adolescence is a very strange place, especially for girls, and one that as a man in his sixties I don't think I ever really understood. I don't think they understood it either, so what I tried to remember was that this was a normal part of growing up as they tested us and pushed their boundaries. I told myself that, like all things, it would pass, and it did.

18.

'*That which you mistake for madness is but an overacuteness of the senses.*'

Edgar Allan Poe (1809–1849)

The Bee Gees released their soundtrack to
the movie *Saturday Night Fever* in 1977.

THE MORE TIME WENT ON, the more I came to realize that I had not two but three girls to look after, as Pamela was much younger than the fifteen-year age gap between us and becoming increasingly dependent on me. Emotionally she was probably twenty-five years my junior and, although she cooked everyday meals for the girls and did a great job raising them when I was at work, she started to do less and less once I came home.

People used to tell me, 'You're doing too much, Tom,' because by then I did most of the cooking and the washing, and would probably be the one who ran the vacuum around the house. None of this fazed me one little bit because all my life I'd been trained to do my share of the chores. And it wasn't that Pamela was lazy but she sometimes found it difficult to be practical and would have trouble with things as simple as counting out coins for the girls' lunch money, or even winding up the Hoover cord. I never begrudged her anything, as we still had a lot of fun and a great deal of laughs.

Given that we spent so much time at home, we were lucky to have had lovely neighbours – Stan, Margaret and their two children. Margaret was English and Stan was a Polish refugee who taught children with special needs. Our two houses were so close that the girls could sometimes see Stan sitting in his bathtub, scrubbing his back and singing Polish songs. I often chatted to him over the garden fence or when we were both washing our cars. He was an excitable sort of fellow who spoke quickly and loudly but then went for days on end without talking to anyone, not even his wife. I knew to leave him be during those quiet episodes and the phase soon passed. 'It takes all sorts,' I thought.

Pamela also had a few close girlfriends whose company she enjoyed – especially Jean Marsden and Jean Simmonds, the 'two Jeans' she'd worked with at Nuralite – but she didn't have any hobbies and had never learned to dance. The truth is that I think she simply preferred home to being surrounded by crowds of strangers. It was she who organized the girls' birthday parties with clowns or some other entertainer, and she loved to throw dinner parties in which she'd take over the kitchen to make the kind of fancy food she wanted, dishes like coq au vin that were far removed from my more solid Yorkshire fare. She'd pile her hair into a beehive, put on a pretty maxi dress, and help me entertain our guests in what were always hilarious evenings, watched in secret by the girls on the stairs. She also liked to play practical jokes on me, unbuttoning my shirt and rebuttoning it incorrectly or tying my shoelaces together if I took a nap. When I woke with a start I'd jump up and fall over, which would set her off laughing, and then – as soon as I'd untied myself – I'd chase her and the girls around the house.

Because she didn't like going out too much, we tended not to go to any concerts or the theatre, but I did take her to a London nightclub to see the Bee Gees once because I knew she liked their music. With songs like 'Tragedy', 'Staying Alive' and 'Night Fever' I've got to admit that the three brothers weren't my cup of tea, but she thought they were great with their tight satin suits, gleaming white teeth and well-coiffeured hair and talked about it for ages afterwards. Give me country or a crooner any time. One great treat in our household was to go on a 'booze cruise' to Calais every other month with the girls to buy duty-free food and wine from the Intermarché supermarket, which was always a fun day out. The girls would get to choose whether we went by ferry or hovercraft and I'd encourage them to only speak French for the entire day. Those were such carefree days.

Pamela was particularly fond of the French days out because she loved shopping. She was as happy as Larry if I offered to take her to Marks & Spencer's, something she considered her 'dream day out'. For a special occasion I'd take her back to Oxford Street in London where we had proved our infidelity. It wasn't that she was a spendthrift; she just loved walking around the shops and looking at things, examining all the new styles, buying things first for the girls before trying things on for herself.

Meanwhile, I was one of those exhausted husbands often seen slumped in an armchair outside a changing room, laden with bags. Not that I minded one bit. After Billie, I knew I was lucky to have a sweet, loving wife and the mother of my two girls. I'd do anything to keep my Pamela happy.

The business was still very successful throughout the 1970s but I'd made a rod for my own back. Because of its twenty-four-hour operation, I worked the concrete plant so hard that I wore it out. New machinery was needed, but this would cost more than the company wanted to spend, so in 1981 they decided to close the factory completely and move production to Cawood Concrete Products works in March,

Cambridgeshire, which was already fitted with the kind of updated machinery required.

As with the Woolwich site, the Cambridgeshire works had been run by an accountant rather than someone with a knowledge of building, and it was making a loss. He had recently retired and my fellow directors told me, 'You've done very well for us, Tom. Now go to March and run the factory there and see if you can make it as much of a success. It's up to you – either make it work or shut it down.'

I couldn't help but have very mixed feelings about it. My Woolwich staff hadn't deserved to lose their jobs, but faced with the prospect of also being made redundant and with a young family to feed, I had no choice but to accept the directors' challenge and relocate. My men were by no means the only ones suffering job losses and hardship. The late 1970s and early '80s weren't easy years for industry, with Britain suffering a widespread economic downturn. There were nationwide marches to protest mass unemployment, British Leyland was in difficulty with strikes at Longbridge, the National Coal Board announced pit closures that led to the bitter miners' strike, and there was even more trouble in Northern Ireland with hunger strikes and IRA bombs. Then 1981 was also the year that Peter Sutcliffe – better known as the Yorkshire Ripper – was apprehended at last, Charles and Diana were married, and Salman Rushdie's controversial *Midnight's Children* was published. Within a year Argentina would invade the Falklands, sparking the Falklands War, and AIDS would be rampaging through the gay community in a pandemic that caused untold misery and widespread panic.

As a family, we'd been very lucky and remained relatively untouched by all these seismic shifts in social and political change. At my age, I was lucky to have a job and to be offered yet another opportunity to prove myself to the company. Given the alternatives, moving from Gravesend was a small price to pay, but it was never something Pamela had contemplated, and she wasn't at all happy. Neither were the girls, who – at the age of eleven and thirteen – were forced to leave their schools, their friends and all that they'd ever known.

'Promise me we'll move straight back when it's over,' Pamela finally begged, and – keen to do anything to make her feel better – I agreed. My sister Freda was also sorry to hear the news. Tired of living alone, she'd been thinking about selling the Riddlesden bungalow and moving closer to us in Kent. She had always been a kind aunt to the girls, coming on holidays with us and spoiling them with pretty handmade dresses and embroidered knick-knacks. She was also always trying to fatten them up, claiming they were too thin for her liking. Much as they loved her baking, Freda wasn't helped in her ambition by her enthusiasm for cooking everything else with lard.

Well aware that all four women in my life hoped we wouldn't be away from Kent for too long, when I sold our home in Gravesend, I found us a nice detached farmhouse in the Fens called Poplar Farm with an acre of land that I thought might make the move a little easier for them while we were away. It was in a hamlet called Tipps End near Welney, not far from the Norfolk border and in the middle of nowhere by comparison to our previous home. I think only Lucy was ever really happy there, as she was an outdoors type and loved the land, helping me plant sweetcorn and raspberries, grow mushrooms in the barn, cut the hedges, pick tomatoes, feed the hens and mow the lawns.

Once we were settled, Freda decided to follow us there and found herself a sweet cottage in March village, where she lived

271

quite happily and became a regular fixture in our lives. It was lovely to have a friendly face so close, as we all missed our friends and neighbours from Gravesend. Or we thought we did. Imagine our shock when we found out that not long after we had moved house, our next-door neighbour Stan had strangled his lovely wife Margaret with a dressing gown cord when he became convinced that she was having an affair. It was a terrible event that those occasional periods of withdrawal barely hinted at. It just didn't chime with the man we thought we knew. Stan went to jail and we never found out what happened to their children, who were older than ours. It seemed to me then that maybe there was a little madness in us all.

Focusing on our new life in Cambridgeshire, we enrolled Lucy and Hannah at St Audrey's Covent School and Wisbech Grammar, neither of which they liked because they felt too parochial after London.

Pamela, meanwhile, was counting the days until we could return to 'civilization'. Away from her childhood home she became ever more fearful and would sometimes tell me with whispered urgency and completely out of the blue, 'There are men in the roof, Tom. They're listening to us!' This was a delusion she was to repeat for many years, and not just to me. She couldn't always hide her anxiety from the children and, as had happened when I'd first dated her and when the girls were smaller, if she was out with them she might suddenly say, 'We're being followed, we've got to go.' Other times, she'd come dashing in and tell me, 'There was a man looking at us in the car park and I think he followed us home.' Fortunately it didn't seem to affect either of our daughters because they'd accepted from an early age that their mother had this unusual trait.

As always, I'd try to reassure Pamela and bring some balance back into her life in order to get through her episodes together. It was just one of those things. I couldn't complain. I'd walked into this marriage with my eyes wide open. Unlike my situation with Billie, I knew Pamela's shortcomings and I loved her anyway.

All I wanted to do was turn the company around as quickly as possible and get her back to Gravesend where I knew she'd be happier. I felt the pressure of that from the start. Unfortunately, she wasn't the only one who was unhappy – my new employees seemed downcast and suspicious of me from the outset. Even though I was from Yorkshire, they thought of me as a 'bloody southern foreigner with a lot of bright ideas' who'd come to shake them up. One thing I noticed was that they tended to keep their heads down and not engage with me in any way whenever I was on the factory floor. That wasn't how I worked at all, so I gathered them together just as I would have with a troop of infantrymen, and decided to have it out with them. 'Whenever I walk around this factory, nobody lifts their head up to say "Good morning" or "Hello",' I said. 'And I'd like to know why not.' There was an awkward silence and then someone piped up, 'We're not supposed to.' By all accounts, my predecessor had a rather high opinion of himself and felt he was above talking to his team, which wouldn't do at all.

'Right,' I told them. 'From now, you'll talk to me. We're working here together and I am one of you.' My strategy worked. They were good country folk and once I realized that they bore me no ill will the job became easier. Within a few weeks, I was able to identify those who were good at their job and those who weren't. Some I had to let go, which I was sorry about as I knew a few were unlikely ever to work again, but I needed a team that pulled together. It was a bit like picking my gunner and a driver for my tank. I needed people I could trust and get along with, so my Army experience once again served me well.

Just as I'd hoped, I was able to turn the company around quite quickly and it was soon making a nice profit, with double time for the men and security of tenure for me. My plan was still to get in and get out, but the irony was that I loved being surrounded by open spaces again and so enjoyed having a bit of land. By this time we'd made a nice little family nest that we'd added to with pet guinea pigs, a rabbit, a black-and-white cat called Whiskey and a black Labrador called Nero, my first dog since my beloved spaniel Billy. I also had a new company car, a 3.5-litre Rover that I liked very much, and then I got the powerful sports version of it. I loved that red Rover. Behind the wheel and as boss of my branch of the company, I really felt as if I had arrived.

Keen to involve myself with the local community, I joined the Rotarians and also organized a mini-marathon of ten miles around the countryside for the employees and their families. I persuaded local industry and small businesses to provide prizes for each category – men, women, boys and girls. It was a great day out. I also entered our company in a national concrete boat competition, for which we worked together to design and make a concrete canoe. Barges made of concrete had been used quite successfully in the Second World War, so it wasn't as daft as it sounded. The one we made looked good, it floated and was, I thought, a top contender, but, sadly, we lost out on a prize.

Aside from that disappointment, the company was doing well and the staff were happy, so the powers-that-be insisted that I remain there. Secretly, I wasn't unhappy about settling into country life in the Fens, but that didn't mean I couldn't still be spontaneous. One of my impulse moments was my 1983 appearance on the TV game show *Blankety Blank*, presented by Terry Wogan. I've always loved game shows and Pamela and I used to watch this every week so, on a whim, I decided to apply. The producers wrote back straight away inviting me on, and Pamela and I were put up overnight in a London hotel but told not to tell a soul about our appearance until the special Christmas edition aired a few months later.

It was the first and last time I applied for anything like that and I had no idea what I was letting myself in for. Filming took two days and was quite a palaver, although certainly interesting. When rehearsals began, I sat in my designated seat on the fake snow set looking tidy in my customary suit and tie, and – to my surprise – a group of scruffy people turned up to sit on the tiered podium opposite. I thought at first that they were staff enlisted as stand-ins, but then I recognized a few faces and realized that they were the celebrity guests – before they went into hair and make-up. There was a lady called Ruth Madoc from a popular TV show called *Hi-de-Hi*, the comedian Freddie Starr, as well as Beryl Reid, the stargazer Patrick Moore, and an actor called Roy Kinnear who'd been in two shows we'd liked called *George and Mildred*, and *Cowboys*, which appealed to me especially as it was a comedy about an inept building company.

The format of *Blankety Blank* was a process of elimination. You answered a question and if you got it right you stayed on, but if not you were knocked out. Terry Wogan was a big star at the time, known for his semi-facetious comments. Dressed in a festive woollen scarf with a silver wand for a microphone, he asked me where I came from and I replied, 'Tipps End,' which raised a big laugh, so I added, 'It's a good place.' He asked if I had any family who I'd rather not be watching 'this rubbish', and I said, 'Yes, two girls, one coming up sixteen and one coming up fourteen. They'll be watching at home.' It was scintillating stuff.

The show went on in much the same vein and was quite a hoot. I was doing well but there was a lady contestant who came on who was brighter than me or anyone else. She also had an extremely revealing dress. When she first appeared on camera sitting behind the podium, her top was so low-cut it looked as if she had nothing on so they had to ask her to put on something else. She came back more suitably attired and knocked me out – but not in a good way. She won the show fair and square although I always thought that Mr Wogan was more taken by her than he was with me. Despite being there for two days, my appearance on the show was only a few minutes long in the final episode, but I enjoyed it nevertheless. I was presented with a consolation prize, the famous (or at least it was then) stainless-steel Blankety Blank chequebook and pen that I still have. And after the programme aired that Christmas a few people even recognized me in the street, which was a novelty in itself but not one I necessarily cared to repeat.

One thing I remember clearly as I waited on set for the endless takes and re-takes were the mechanics of the revolving stage, which I'd assumed would be operated electronically. To my surprise, two stagehands appeared each time and turned a huge crank handle that operated the various cogs and wheels. I was fascinated, not least because it took me straight back to the days of my father's first Leyland tipper truck and the men in caps cranking the handle to wind it up and down. When I told Pamela, she rolled her eyes and laughed, 'Tom

Moore, only you could be more fascinated by the workings than by Terry Wogan!'

The years rolled by and the girls grew up, travelling the twelve miles or so to and from college. If Lucy missed her bus in the mornings, which she often did because she was a sleepyhead like her mother, I'd bundle her in the car and chase after the bus, racing across railway crossings – sometimes whipping beneath the barriers as they began to come down – flashing my headlights until the driver stopped to let her on. She and Hannah were quite used to my driving and never fazed by my antics, or my speed. They knew a thing or two about cars by then after all the motoring museums, car shows and racing stadiums I'd dragged them and Pamela to over the years.

After the girls left school, Hannah went to Cambridge College of Art and Technology to do her A levels and eventually moved into central Cambridge. Lucy went to Peterborough Technical College to get her Chamber of Commerce private secretary's certificate but when she qualified she couldn't decide what to do. In the end she was offered a job as a flight attendant with Gibraltar Airways, known as GB Airways, and moved to Brighton in order to commute to Gatwick. She loved her job and was very good at it, especially in-flight sales, for which she kept winning the top prizes in the airline's competitions. That's my Lucy. I had always joked with the girls that when they met the right chap they should elope because, 'It would save me a fortune.' But it was while she was working for GB Airways that Lucy met Tom, a management consultant whose father was Portuguese and whose mother – coincidentally – lived in Gravesend.

In the end, happily, she chose not to follow my advice to elope and had a lovely wedding in a nice little church on the outskirts of Gravesend. Walking my eldest daughter down the aisle at the age of sixty-eight was, without doubt, one of the proudest days of my life, and one I never believed I would see. A favourite photograph of mine was taken of Pamela and me that day because it reminds me of how happy we all were and how well my darling wife was. It would prove to be a memory to cling to.

19.

'The purpose of life is to live it, to taste experience to the utmost, to reach out eagerly and without fear for newer and richer experience.'

Eleanor Roosevelt (1884–1962)

The Berlin Wall came down in 1989, heralding
the collapse of communism across Europe.

AT FIRST, ALL WAS WELL; in fact, it was pretty good. Life has a habit of surprising you and in 1989 it did just that when, not far off my seventieth year, I found myself retired and living in southern Spain with Pamela and Hannah. This didn't happen overnight, of course, and only came about because of hard work and good luck – plus a little bit of courage on my part, but then I'd long tried to live by the regimental motto: 'Fortune Favours the Brave'.

The company had been trading so successfully that Cawood Wharton was merged with a firm called Redwood, which had a concrete works of their own and wasn't interested in taking on ours. Fearing that this conflict of interests would mean that they'd shut us down, with the loss of my livelihood and sixty jobs, I decided to stick my neck out and organize a management buyout. I approached all the managers, as well as some of our best customers, and our local MP Clement Freud.

'I can keep this company going and I can continue to make it profitable,' I promised them. 'I'll put in £10,000 of my own money, if each of you do the same. This will make you a director and give you a share of the profits.' I'd always been quite a good salesman and it seemed that I hadn't lost the knack, because within weeks I had the funds I needed to not only buy the company out, but also to keep it going with working capital. I had to borrow my share from the bank using our house as collateral, so it was quite a risk but I was convinced it was one worth taking.

We renamed the company and kept it going successfully for another four years. The employees were relieved that they'd held on to their jobs and we all worked together to maintain its success. Then in 1987 ARC bought us out, with the arrangement that I stayed on as managing director for a while. By this time I knew that when my obligations ended it would probably be time for me to take a step back. I left with a nice pension pot and the promise from ARC that it would keep on my staff – which it did until the works was closed altogether five years later. My investors made a healthy profit and I suddenly found myself retired and advised to live abroad, where I planned to buy and sell property.

Pamela and I had been camping in the Costa del Sol in Spain on holiday with Freda and the girls when Hannah was still in nappies, and we'd liked it very much. I'd also enjoyed my time in Barcelona on business. We all loved the sun and the sea, and as Lucy had her new job at GB Airways and would be flying back and forth, Spain seemed ideal. I found a brand-new estate of white Spanish-style houses being built around a communal swimming pool near the Valderrama golf course and bought one for us off plan. I also bought myself a Range Rover, a car I had always hankered after. We sold the house at Tipps End, packed up our belongings, said goodbye to Freda who was content to stay in March and, with the cat and dog in the back of the car, we drove to Spain. Pamela was happy enough with the move to begin with, as long as she was able to hold on to the thought that we would move back to Gravesend eventually. Between us, we decided to treat the next few years as an exciting – but temporary – family adventure.

As our new house wasn't ready yet I rented a flat in Marbella where Hannah attended a sixth-form college. None of us spoke any Spanish but we soon picked it up. When she was seventeen I bought her a Fiat Panda, which gave her the freedom to go out, make friends and forge a new life for herself, something she did with her usual gusto. She loved living there. Before we knew it, she had an English boyfriend and was making money in her spare time selling advertising slots on the Costa del Sol radio station. She then moved into selling mobile phones and, ultimately, luxury yachts. My salesmanship definitely seems to have rubbed off on her.

Pamela and I meanwhile enjoyed the weather and travelling around Spain, including a trip back to Barcelona which had changed beyond all recognition since I'd last been there. Her favourite destination, however, was always Gibraltar because it had English supermarkets and shops, including her favourite Marks & Spencer's. Most of all, she preferred to stay home and not go too far. Twenty years of living with me had undoubtedly boosted her confidence and made her feel more secure, but her home was her castle and she still felt safest there. Plus she knew it wasn't forever. I had promised.

Our time in Spain was a very happy one, especially in the beginning, and it's a period I look back on fondly. But it was while we were out there that something changed with Pamela, and she began to behave strangely again. The girls spotted it first and commented on her behaviour. She became more withdrawn and anxious and went back to thinking that she was being watched and followed. And she'd rarely go out alone. Then I had a silly accident, and that affected us both. I was downstairs in the house on my own, so she must have been out with Hannah somewhere, and – as usual – I was rushing. Forgetting that I'd shut the sliding doors to the garden, I walked straight through a sheet of plate glass. I was lucky that I didn't sever an artery, but I did suffer some deep cuts on my hands and knees. There was blood everywhere and I had to wrap my wounds in towels.

Luckily, I had my phone with me so I called Hannah's boyfriend and asked him to come and take me to hospital, which he did. The doctors stemmed the bleeding, but said they'd have to operate. 'OK,' I said, thinking that all they required was my consent.

'You must pay, Mr Moore,' they said impatiently, and, before I knew it I had to cough up £500 before they'd even book the operating theatre. That was even more shocking to me than the accident and made me realize how lucky we were in Britain to have the NHS. While I was recovering, I started thinking about what would happen if one of us were taken seriously ill in Spain, or if Pamela needed treatment. By this time Lucy had moved to Bristol with Tom, because GB Airways had merged with BA Connect, and Hannah was thinking about going back to London because she missed it so much. So in 1993 I finally fulfilled my promise to Pamela and decided to return to the UK, where I hoped she'd feel more settled. I sold our lovely Spanish villa and bought a semi-detached house in Gravesend with a nice long garden.

The worst part about returning to England was that Whiskey the cat and Nero, our Labrador, had to go into quarantine for six months, which Nero especially hated as much as we did. I went to see him often at his kennels, which were ten miles from Gravesend, but leaving him again was heartbreaking, as he never understood. It was torture for us both. He had been such a loyal and super companion and he lived to about twelve, but his back legs went and we had to put him down in the end. I will never forget carrying the weight of him into the vet's that final day. I wasn't sure I wanted another dog after that, as I was so sad to lose him, but Pamela insisted and we went to a kennels where she chose a white Labrador puppy we called Harry. It was one of the best things we ever did. After Billy in Keighley, Harry was the best dog I ever had and we got on so well that Lucy used to say he and I were 'joined at the hip'. He reminded me so much of dear Billy, which was just as well because I came to rely on him a great deal in the coming years.

Not long after we took him on, I began to get terrible pains in my head and eyes, so I went to see the doctor. They referred me to a senior GP who was even older than me, but who knew a thing or two. He diagnosed temporal cellulitis and said I had to go straight to hospital immediately or else I'd go blind. I was sent to the Joyce Green Hospital in Gravesend, where I remained for two weeks. They put me on a far higher dose of steroids than I should have been on, and for a longer period, but I remember one young doctor saying, 'We shouldn't be giving you such a high a dose, but at your age it doesn't matter.' I was seventy-eight. Lucy came to visit, bringing Pamela and our new grandson Thomas, who was in a pushchair. My first grandchild was a lovely little lad and I was delighted that the name of Grandfather Thomas was being kept alive in our family. The respected Yorkshireman who started a dynasty would have been very proud.

Being back in Gravesend wasn't the quick fix I hoped for with Pamela, and her mental state continued to be a concern. One day I came home to find her talking on the telephone, which wasn't that unusual, but she stayed on for ages and was saying all sorts of strange things. When she'd finished, I asked her who it was. 'A man,' was all she said.

The next time she did it I picked up the extension to listen in but there was nobody there. The severity of her delusion shook me to the core. These imaginary conversations continued for some time, even in front of the girls, as we all began to realize that things were getting worse. That was the beginning of fourteen years of slow descent into dementia. When I think back to how her father was when I first met her, I suspect she had some genetic predisposition to mental decline and had probably suffered from it in some minor way for all the years I'd known her. Her hallucinations became more frequent and she was still imagining that strangers were talking to her. The 'man on the telephone' invited her to his house, she said, and could we go? I had to stay calm and tell her, 'I'd like to speak to him first,' but of course he was never there. One day she announced that she was having an affair with a local man who kept taking her out in his car, when I knew she wasn't and hadn't been anywhere. We'd go shopping together and she'd tell me he was meeting her there.

It got worse and worse, and she became so forgetful around the house that if I had to take Harry for a walk or go to the supermarket, I'd lock the doors and take all the knobs off the cooker in case she turned the gas on and forgot to turn it off. It was extremely distressing and I had many tearful phone calls about her gradual deterioration with the girls, who visited when work and family commitments allowed. Worried and exhausted, I eventually followed their advice and went to my GP for help. He sent a health visitor to come and talk to Pamela to assess how bad her dementia had got and to start monitoring her over time to see if it was getting worse.

Luckily, she wasn't cross or upset about this as I'd feared she might be because she never really understood why the health visitor was there. She thought she'd come to see me.

Living with her like that was extremely isolating and – just as with my first wife – I'd never been very good at opening up to other people about my situation at home. As I saw it, this was my problem and I just had to deal with it. The 'two Jeans' – Pamela's friends from Nuralite – were a godsend and would sit with her if I had to go out, but there was no one else to help on a daily basis. Freda had moved from March to be near us but within a few years she died of a heart attack at the age of eighty, literally dropping down dead in the bathroom of her sheltered flat. I had to go and identify her body and it was strange and painful to see my sister lying in a coffin. We'd had our minor differences as children, but dear Freda was a lovely, kind-natured person and she had grown fond of her little brother, as I had of her. She'd had quite a lonely life, I think, and one that could have been filled with the love of someone and maybe even her own children if only she'd defied Father and gone her own way. And yet she'd loved Hannah and Lucy and so enjoyed being a big part of their lives – and mine – for which I know she was grateful. With her death, I had lost the last link with my past in Keighley and to the rest of my family. No one else would remember my parents, Uncle Billy, or Uncle Arthur. The memories of our happy family holidays in Whitby, the drives to the moors, or the spectacular Keighley galas were mine alone now.

My girls were as busy as ever with their own lives and visited whenever they could, but I didn't want to trouble them too much. Lucy was still working for the airlines and, in between always looking extremely tidy in her uniform, selling duty-free like hot cakes and flying all over the world. She had another son, Max, born in 2000, so she had her hands full. Hannah was living away and working first for Laura Ashley, then for a series of companies and ultimately the Swatch Group, where she became responsible for sales, distribution and marketing in the US, Europe and the Far East, making a far speedier rise to management than I ever did. Neither acorn fell far from this tree. She had a Lhasa Apso called Betsy that she loved, but when she moved house she couldn't take her, so I took her in. She was a nice little dog – if a bit yappy – but one day she snapped at Pamela, which was strange because she was as sweet as they come and had never snapped at anyone else. It made me worry that something must have happened with Pamela that she either hadn't told me about or had forgotten, so I kept an eye on them both.

As the twentieth century drew to a close, I heard some very sad news about my old friend Brian Booth, who was still married to his wife Pat and living in Yorkshire, where he had become managing director of his father's quarry until retirement. We had stayed in touch via Christmas cards but hadn't seen each other in years. Then I heard that, at the age of seventy-eight, after suffering from depression for a number of years, he had leapt to his death from the 1,300-foot Cow and Calf rocks near Ilkley that I had free-climbed as a lad. At an inquest into his death, it was said that he had written 'an extremely loving' note to Pat before he jumped. I remember him as a great man, a loyal husband and a good friend to me, who helped me in my hour of need. I often wondered if his years as a prisoner of war in Germany might have contributed to his sad end.

When the new millennium arrived and another century began, I was fast approaching eighty and Pamela was sixty-five. Because of how she was, this milestone wasn't something we marked in any special way. Instead, after Pamela had gone to bed, I stayed up with the dogs, listening to the foghorns calling eerily from the Thames through the open patio doors and wondering what the next few years would bring.

The doctors still weren't sure what was wrong with Pamela and said it could have been Alzheimer's, dementia or Parkinson's, so they sent her to a hospital in central London for scan after scan. In the end they concluded that her condition was 'unusual' because she had a bit of everything. They put her on some medication that didn't help and her decline continued. Unbeknownst to me, she started to wander in the night and the first I knew about it was when the police came to investigate a report that she'd been seen walking down our road in her nightie. I was horrified because I didn't even know she'd been out. On other occasions, I'd discover her missing and have to go out in the car looking for her. Usually, I'd find her at the bus stop way down the road waiting for 'the man' to come and pick her up. It was all very upsetting.

After two years of struggling, I told my GP I was worried I'd soon be unable to look after her on my own. It wasn't that I was physically unable, and I was determined to stay fit and active for both our sakes, but she couldn't be left. In fact, I remained in rude health, apart from two arthritic knees that needed replacing whenever I could spare the time away from Pamela. I'd also inherited my father's curvature of the spine that was slowly starting to curl me over. Whenever I walked past a shop window and saw my own reflection, I'd think, 'Poor old fellow.' I stopped looking in the end because I didn't like the sight of my own profile. It would just have to be one of those things I had to put up with, but it didn't mean I had to look at it.

Neither of these problems prevented me from caring for Pamela physically, but I couldn't go shopping, visit the girls or go anywhere with the dogs. I was trapped. In 2002 the doctors agreed to admit Pamela into the dementia unit of a little hospital in Dartford. Ironically, it was exactly the same building where her father Reginald had been a patient until his death, although much improved from the mental hospital it had been then. She was taken in initially for six weeks to give me some respite and for them to carry out further tests, but I still visited her every day. Amazingly, she wasn't at all distressed about being there and had none of the outbursts I'd expected. They cared for her perfectly and she was kept tidy and clean.

At the end of the six weeks I thought I'd be bringing her home, with help, but she never came back. The staff told me that my dear wife had deteriorated to the point that she couldn't be left alone and that I wouldn't be able to manage. It was a tragedy that I couldn't look after her myself and I felt horrible about leaving her there but I was also thankful that she was safe and well looked after. And as much as it pained me to admit the truth, it was a relief for me to get her properly cared for at last. There was no other way to look at it and it helped me not to get distressed and depressed. Further anxieties lay ahead, though.

When the local authorities closed down the building, Pamela was transferred to a private home. I was so worried that I'd have to pay for her care, which I knew I couldn't afford. After a stressful period of uncertainty, the authorities agreed that I didn't have the means to pay, but we were scarcely out of the woods. Next time, though, it was Pamela herself, not money, that was the concern. The staff at the private home announced that she was too difficult to care for and said that they couldn't keep her. They moved her into a new specialist unit closer to Dartford Hospital and the NHS paid for her care – something for which I will be eternally grateful. She was so well looked after there and the nurses were wonderful; I couldn't fault them. But I could see they were very stretched so I went every day without fail to feed Pamela because she could no longer feed herself. I must say, the staff were pleased to see me because they were very short-handed and had too many patients to feed by hand. Several of our friends told me I was mad to go in every day when I didn't need to, and they asked me why I bothered.

I was indignant at that and told them, 'Why wouldn't I? I signed a contract when I married Pamela. I promised to care for her in sickness and in health, and I'm a man of my word.'

I'd always stay for two or three hours, holding Pamela's hand and sitting with her while she dozed, and it was funny because the nurses used to forget I was there. They'd chatter away to each other in what I call 'lady language' that I'm sure was never intended for my ears. After a while, I knew them all by name and heard all about their love lives, so we felt like a little family. Whenever the girls came with their families, I'd proudly introduce them all to my fellow carers. I was also a firm favourite with the nurses because I used to drive several of them home after their shifts, dropping them off on my way back to walk Harry. I didn't mind at all and it was my way of giving something back.

I also made friends with four or five of the women who visited their husbands in the unit, because I was the only husband. Some of these women were surprisingly young and some almost as old as me, but talking to them often helped because they were the few people who knew just what it felt like to be there. To cheer us all up, I had them all round for a few Sunday lunches, making a nice home-made soup, roast beef and Yorkshire pudding and then a sweet – usually a trifle just like my mother used to make, with lots of sherry and fresh whipped cream.

'Whenever did you learn to cook like this?' one of them asked and I told them, 'I can't remember a time when I couldn't,' telling them about Mother and her Victoria sponges and Granny Fanny and her rice puddings. They seemed surprised and a few of them asked if I'd consider cooking for them if they bought me the ingredients. I drew the line at that.

And there were some other happy events around this time, because Hannah was dating Colin, a finance director, and in 2004 they had a baby boy, Benjie – my third grandchild – and then they were married in Leatherhead, Surrey, the following year. As with Lucy's wedding, it was a lovely day, marred only by the sad fact that Pamela couldn't be there to share our joy and was instead sitting in the care unit waiting for me.

Once I knew Pamela was safe and well, I finally got around to seeing someone about my arthritic knees that had become increasingly painful in recent years and had started to affect my mobility. I then had two new replacement knees in two years, but was soon back on my feet each time thanks to cycling every day, which I found hurt less than walking. Rain or shine, I'd put my folding bike in the back of my car, drive out to the countryside with the dogs and cycle for about an hour as they followed on behind. It was the only way I could exercise all three of us together, it saved time, and helped my recovery because I didn't want to be away from my Pamela any longer than I had to be.

To watch someone you love decline through dementia is a kind of slow torture. You lose them before you lose them and that is what happened with my darling Pamela. It was such a lonely time for us both. I was home on my own with only Harry for company every night and for much of the day. She was sitting in a chair or in bed waiting for me to feed her. It was soul-destroying. One day, as I arrived with a bunch of her favourite freesias, she looked up at me, smiled and said, 'If you didn't come every day, Tom, I would be so lonely.' That really hit me hard as I knew what it felt like to be on your own, but I could only imagine how much worse it must be in a care home. I was painfully aware that there were many other old people there who had nobody to visit them at all – not a soul, year after year. That was terrible.

Towards the end Pamela couldn't really talk – maybe a little word here and there, but nothing more. On other occasions she'd have moments of sudden clarity that were lovely but cruel, as it gave us a glimpse of how she'd once been. We had to laugh on one occasion around her bedside, when I was chatting to the girls about our time in Spain and couldn't quite remember where something had happened. Halfway through our conversation, Pamela suddenly opened her eyes and said, 'It was Madrid.' She must have been listening and it was hilarious that she came out with the right answer. These vanishingly rare glimpses of the old Pamela came to mean so much to us all.

The 'two Jeans' continued to be very kind and arranged it so that once a month they'd go and feed her to give me a day off from visiting. I'd try to see the family on those days if I could, so I did one trip back to Bovington Camp with Lucy and her boys to revisit my time there and pose happily in front of a Churchill tank, which seemed much smaller than I remembered it. I also had days out with Hannah and Benjie to museums and parks – anything for a change of scene. And one day in May 2006 I travelled to see Lucy and the boys in

Bristol for a visit to the Haynes Motor Museum near Yeovil. Thomas, the eldest, has always been much more interested in World War II planes than cars and every year, for Christmas and his birthday, I sent him another metal replica for his collection. But despite his enthusiasm for things with wings, he found the red Ferraris as irresistible as I did. Our joy was short-lived, however.

We had just got back to their house and Lucy was pouring me a cold beer when the telephone rang. It was Pamela's care unit and they called to tell me that she had finally slipped away. She was seventy-one years old.

I think when you've been watching someone decline over a long period of time that you become numb to the idea of them not being there any more. I remember hearing the news, thanking them for letting me know, and replacing the receiver. Turning to Lucy, I said simply, 'Your mother is dead.' Neither of us broke down. We merely sat looking at each other as we gradually absorbed the information. I've never been laid aside by loss, and big shows of emotion are not the Moore way. Our lack of tears this time was also, I suppose, a result of the circumstances and Pamela's long, slow decline.

Grief affects people in many different ways. For all my apparent stoicism I was undoubtedly sorry that I wasn't with her at the end. It hurt, especially after so many years of being with her every day, but as one of the nurses told me, 'It happens all the time, Tom. People often wait until they have no one with them and then they slip away.' I refused to allow it to trouble me. I'd said my goodbyes long before and I knew it was a blessing for her – and for us – that it was finally over. Maybe I'm wrong, but I struggle to understand that some people have to say goodbye to those they loved. Perhaps I'm not sentimental enough, but I didn't believe that was necessary for us. Love is about being there over the years and caring for someone in all kinds of little ways. Death comes to us all and no amount of hand-wringing or crying by the bedside can change what happened in life. That's just me, though. And, as I say, grief comes all shapes and sizes.

It was when I went to collect Pamela's belongings and say my farewells at the home that the tears came. The nurses were all crying too and I told them that they weren't to be upset as she was at peace now. 'We know, Tom,' one of them said, wiping her eyes. 'But we're not crying for Pamela. We're crying because, after all these years, we're really going to miss you.' The feeling was mutual.

Pamela was cremated and her ashes scattered in Gravesend cemetery, so she was finally back home where she belonged. I agreed that a small piece of her brain could be taken for analysis, in the hope that scientists might find out more about her condition and help others. Sadly, they never came to any definitive conclusion.

There were about twenty-five of us at her funeral and Lucy and Hannah both read something lovely together. I couldn't bring myself to speak, but I asked the undertakers to play, 'We'll Meet Again' by Dame Vera Lynn, because I wanted to think that – one day – we might. After the service I had a rose bush planted in Pamela's memory and I put a bouquet of silk freesias on her marker that I hoped would last forever.

She was a wonderful wife and I was very lucky to have known her for as long as I did. She gave me two beloved daughters and more happiness than I ever thought possible in the second half of my life. For that I shall always be grateful.

20.

'People do not decide to become extraordinary.
They decide to accomplish extraordinary things.'

Sir Edmund Hillary (1919–2008)

Nelson Mandela was released from prison after
twenty-seven years behind bars in 1990.

It took me a long time to get used to the idea of being a widower, but it wasn't such a huge adjustment for me as it might have been for others. I'd been widowed physically and psychologically for four years.

And when I thought of all the problems I'd had beforehand, there was no reason to get low. Whenever I went into Pamela's dementia unit I used to look around and think, 'Why should I complain?' There were so many poor souls – and very often couples – demented in a home together. That hadn't happened to me. I was still there, physically and mentally. I'd survived, and I had my two girls. Although Betsy had died by then, I still had dear dog Harry.

Both daughters were happily settled with their families – Lucy in Caversham, near Reading (soon to become a successful homeopath), and Hannah half an hour from me in Epsom, Surrey, where she was working as a part-time consultant and no longer flying around the world at breakneck speed. Free of my obligations to Pamela for the first time in years, I decided that it would be nice to do something just for me. Ever since I'd returned from India sixty-one years earlier, I'd longed to go back, but I couldn't have done that with Pamela. She wouldn't have wanted to go in the first place and she hadn't the right temperament for India. She'd have found the crowds too oppressive and been frightened of her own shadow, convinced she was being watched all the time. This would only have made her anxious. Like Father with Freda, I thought of myself as her protector and it was my job to protect her from that kind of fear.

Once I was a free man, though, I contacted a travel agent and booked myself a trip back to several of the places that meant the most to me, although – confusingly – many of their names had since been altered from those given to them by the Raj. I travelled first to Bombay (now Mumbai), where I once again saw the Gateway to India that I'd seen in 1941 from the deck of SS *Duchess of York* when the heat and colour of the country had first assailed all my senses. I went on to New Delhi and the beautiful city of Jaipur with its stunning fort and painted elephants. I'd loved India the moment I set foot there and I loved it just as much on my return. I didn't travel alone; I went as part of an organized tour and made friends with several of my fellow travellers along the way, most of them delightful women – although none as old as me, at eighty-six. People often asked me why I never married again after Pamela, but it never occurred to me. Besides, I never found anybody suitable.

In what is known as the 'Golden Triangle' of New Delhi, Agra and Jaipur, we had our photographs taken at all the major tourist sites, including the breathtaking Taj Mahal. We also visited the fascinating lost city of Fatehpur Sikri, abandoned for a lack of water, and then I made my way to Poona (Pune) so that I could visit Kirkee (Khadki) and its war cemetery. The city – or cantonment – had changed almost beyond recognition but I was so impressed by the graveyard. One of more than 2,000 war cemeteries in over 150 countries

around the world that are managed by the Commonwealth
War Graves Commission, Kirkee holds the graves of more
than 1,600 service personnel from the Second World War
along with 600 from the Great War and several others who
served. In total there are 2,297 graves. As with all the CWGC
graves, the cemetery was manicured to perfection and the
white tombstones precisely spaced in a geometric grid. As I
walked up and down the rows in the intense dry heat that I'd
almost forgotten about, I wondered if I might recognize any
of the names engraved in Portland stone. Kirkee Camp had
been a hub for so many men before they were sent into
combat.

I spotted the names of a handful of Dukes, but I didn't
recall any of them personally. There was a twenty-year-old
second lieutenant called Harris who died in November 1944,
a Private Jones who was killed in 1942, and a Corporal Ryall
and a Lance Corporal Brewer, who died the same year. There
were undoubtedly more, but not Philip Thornton, sadly. He
was a long way away in Myanmar, formerly known as Burma.
Quietly, I saluted them all.

My return to India was certainly something to talk about at
our next regimental reunion, even though our numbers were
much reduced, year on year. So many of my old comrades
had died along the way and every year I'd write to members
only to hear back from their families that they were no
longer with us. My friend John 'Gog' Billham had died in his
sixties, and friends like Lieutenant Colonels Woods and
Agnew had both died in the late 1980s, as had 'Cocky'
Haslock and Major Bucknall. General Christison died in
1994 in his nineties, so there were only a few diehards left.
My decision to invite the wives years earlier really paid off

then, because several of the widows kept coming on their own and – latterly – with their children. Although the numbers had dwindled, it was still quite a big clerical task to arrange it each year, but I'd been fortunate to have the assistance of both helpful staff from the regiment who helped me with addresses and mailings, and Hannah whose organizational skills were second to none.

In 2007, the year after Pamela died, we marked the sixtieth anniversary of our reunions with just three of the original members left. I was thrilled to be presented with a beautiful statue of two 'Dukes', past and present, by none other than General Sir Evelyn Webb-Carter, the last colonel of the regiment before its 2002 amalgamation into the Prince of Wales's Own Regiment of Yorkshire and the Green Howards to form the Yorkshire Regiment. The inscription read:

> *Presented to Captain Tom Moore in appreciation of 60 years of organizing the annual reunion of the 9th Battalion, the Duke of Wellington's Regiment (West Riding) 2nd October 2007.*

This statue takes pride of place on my mantelpiece and is something that I hope will pass on through the generations.

Talking of which, at the end of that year, Hannah and Colin decided to set up and run their own business consultancy company and relocate both their home and business to a bigger premises in Bedfordshire. This would be much more central to their national operations and help with any travelling. I understood that need more than most, having moved many times for my job over the years, but I was a bit taken aback by the news at first because I knew I'd miss them being so close. Even though I'd only ever lived in Gravesend by default, I had no plans to move. Then Hannah told me,

'I'm not going unless you come with us. I won't leave you here on your own.'

Lucy also kindly offered to have me live with her family at their new home in Berkshire, and I was so touched that either of my girls would even consider having their old dad move in. To be honest, though, even at my age I didn't think it necessary. I drove every day and still did the gardening, shopping and chores without any assistance. Why would I put myself through the upheaval of a house move and leave the area that I'd come to call home? It was house hunting with Hannah and Colin that finally changed my mind. We'd looked at quite a few properties together and rejected them for all kinds of reasons, but I immediately liked the house we now live in, with its large garden, and lovely big rooms. An old rectory within sight of the church, it also had a separate two-storey coach house that seemed perfect for me (although I ended up living in the house anyway). Hannah was pregnant with my granddaughter Georgia, so the idea of living entirely independently, but close enough to watch the baby and Benjie grow up, seemed suddenly very appealing – especially after I'd missed much of that with Lucy's two boys, largely because of Pamela.

Without much ado, I sold my house and Hannah and Colin sold theirs, and we all moved to a pretty village called Marston Moretaine – a place I never now want to leave. I brought Harry the dog with me and Hannah and Colin had a rescue mastiff and a Rottweiler, so I had animals to walk and to play with. Although I've never claimed to be a gardener, I immediately volunteered for the role, operating a ride-on mower to cut all the grass each week. If the trees needed pruning, I'd cut them too, as I was the best chainsaw operator in the business – if a little more mindful of the nine and a half fingers I had left after my last sawing accident. I also looked after the greenhouse, where I grew mainly tomatoes that rarely came out as well as they should. They'd often go black and someone would tell me it was because they were overwatered and another said they weren't watered enough, so I came to the conclusion that people don't always know what they're talking about.

It's a shame I never mastered tomatoes, as I love to cook with them, and I'd told Hannah from the start that I would do all my own shopping and cooking. I still made the Sunday roast for the whole family every weekend and usually prepared the turkey at Christmas when Lucy and her family frequently joined us. I also made the Christmas cake (laced with brandy) every year, something I'd done for decades, and I always recreated my mother's sherry trifle. As she had once taught me how to cook, and as Granny Fanny taught her, so I passed on whatever knowledge I had to Benjie and Georgia as they were growing up. My granddaughter is a very good baker and Benjie is a good cook, and there is a difference. Not that Georgia – or anyone – can make a Victoria sponge as light as my mother, but then she didn't have anyone to whip the butter for her and modern-day food processors don't do anything like as good a job as whipping by hand. Instead, we make my famous oatmeal biscuits together and she turns out a lovely meringue, while Benjie is very capable with the oven and the barbecue. Cooking is such a great intergenerational thing to do with children and – drawn to the smell of food by their seemingly insatiable appetites – it is one of the few things that can lure them away from their phones.

Living with the family was a gradual adjustment, of course, as we each had to work out how to keep our independence, and maintain our sense of humour. We seemed to manage it all right and it was certainly a great comfort to have them there when sad things happened, like having to take Harry to the vet when his back legs finally went. I don't think I'm a hard person but I've probably cried more over the loss of my pets than I have over people. It's not that I'm any less sad when loved ones die, but – mostly – that's been half expected and feels like the natural order of things. Dogs become such dear and close companions and the creatures that get you through the darkest of days – and Harry had seen me through the last difficult years of Pamela's life – so the loss is torture, no matter how expected it might be. Everybody loved Harry, and Hannah had known him all his life, so I was surrounded by people who felt much as I did and we were all able to be sad together.

I can honestly say that my relationship with my youngest daughter has only got better and better by living under the same roof, especially once I stopped acting like a parent and scolding her or treating her as a child. I quickly realized this was fatal and not wise if we wanted to live together in peace. Not that I don't speak my mind. Her children are better behaved than she and Lucy were as teenagers, but if ever they do something I really don't approve of, I let them know. Interestingly, I also find it easier to talk about the past with Benjie and Georgia than with my own girls. I suppose when they were small I was busy working and helping to run the house so there wasn't much time to talk about my childhood or the war. That was all in the past and something we didn't discuss. But now I enjoy telling the next generation what it was like when I was a lad, and I'm happy to remind them how much things have changed, or to show them things like the large paper £1 note on linen paper that I still have, unwrap my old camera from its box, or show them my parents' prized coronation china. If I don't tell them they may never know, and then it will be too late.

I suppose I'm also ideally placed to give them whatever advice I might have about life in general, just as Granny Fanny and Grandfather Thomas did with me. My maternal grandmother taught me kindness, compassion and respect for others, and my grandfather showed me by his fine example that a man can come from nothing and grow to a position of great responsibility and public regard. Mostly, I want all my grandchildren to nurture their innate sense of curiosity and to expand their horizons, which they are already starting to do. Georgia has been going to summer school on her own in Spain since she was seven years old. Hannah just deposits her in the care of a flight attendant and our former au pair picks her up in Malaga. A keen golfer, she was invited to attend boarding school as a golf scholar. Benjie is also a keen sportsman who has been on cricket tours to South Africa and Sri Lanka as a twelve-year-old, as well as to France on his own, and Lucy's two boys, Thomas and Max, have been skiing since they were four and on rugby and golf tours in Canada and Europe. Having both done well at university in Bristol, they are about to fly. I tell them all to get outside as much as they can and to keep travelling widely and – if possible – independently, not following the crowds. From my first foreign trip to Switzerland with Uncle Arthur to my experiences in India and Burma, travel helped me to have a far better understanding of the world beyond mine and is something that I have not only always enjoyed but which has greatly enriched my life.

And even at ninety years of age, there were still plenty of places left that I wanted to visit.

In 2010 I flew all the way to Nepal so that I could finally see Mount Everest – one of the last items left on my 'bucket list'. Not that I really ever had a bucket list, as I'd done a fair bit of travelling and had quite an interesting life, and there wasn't really anything else I wanted to do, except perhaps meet Stirling Moss. Just as she did with Georgia, Hannah dropped me at the airport and I made my own way to Kathmandu, travelling the 4,500 miles to fulfil a dream. I'd seen glimpses of the Himalayas during my golden trip to Kashmir in the war, but to be in close proximity at last was almost heart-stopping.

I really loved the Nepalese people, too, who – like most of the Indians I have met – were joyful, friendly and positive. They were extremely poor with so little material reason to be happy and yet they seemed to be. Once I arrived and got settled, I booked a flight in a light aircraft to fly as high up the mountain as the pilot was allowed and, although I didn't quite make it to the top of Everest with a flag, I took lots of photos. In my mind I could almost see Sir Edmund Hillary and his trusty Sherpa Tenzing Norgay finally scaling the 29,028-feet summit fifty-seven years earlier, in 1953, when I was thirty-three and Hillary only a year older. I remember the news coming through on the morning of the Queen's coronation, which only made us all the more proud to be part of our great Commonwealth. Just as I had once rock-climbed in relatively ordinary clothes so did they largely, although Hillary added the concession of a woollen suit, long under-wear and a lightweight hooded jacket. If I didn't know better, I'd think he came from Yorkshire.

Having seen what I came to see, I sent the girls a postcard, and came home. But two years later I returned to India again, this time with Hannah and Lucy as my 'escorts'. Not that I needed escorting. If anything, it was the other way round as I knew more about the place than they did – even if I was ninety-two. I whizzed them round the place at breakneck speed on what they described afterwards as 'a gruelling but enjoyable schedule', which included stopping somewhere every morning to buy my copy of the *Daily Telegraph*. We visited the house of civil rights advocate Mahatma Gandhi, a man of great principle who died for his beliefs. He was assassinated in his own home, and the final steps he took before he was shot in 1948 were recreated in red stone, which I found very moving. We also went to the Red Fort and to India Gate, an impressive memorial designed by the British architect Sir Edwin Lutyens to commemorate the 70,000 soldiers of the British Indian Army who died in the Great War. This was commissioned by the predecessor to the Commonwealth War Graves Commission and stands not far from the vast and elegant government buildings, also designed by Lutyens, the place where the Partition that had such tragic consequences was decided.

Once again, I was entranced by the colour and chaos of India – a country where being in traffic is terrifying but everyone somehow manages to avoid each other. One of the things I especially love about India is that nothing is ever thrown away. Unlike most people in our throwaway world, they are fixers and keepers and if something is broken they'll mend it and keep it going for years. The taxis are old Austin Ambassadors from the days of the Raj and I kept my eyes peeled for any vintage motorbikes, wondering if I might even spot one of the old BSAs I'd trained dispatch riders on. All I saw were new bikes – which I'd expected to be Japanese, but were Indian made by a company called Hero. I promised to look them up when I got home.

The next year I was off again, this time to Italy on a WWI battlefield tour organized by the regiment and led by the officer who'd presented me with my statue, Major General Sir

Evelyn Webb-Carter. Hannah dropped me at the airport and I flew to Venice with a group of about twenty for a fascinating insight into a campaign against the Austrians that the Dukes took part in during the Great War on behalf of the Italians. It never once occurred to me that, in my nineties, it might be too much – and it wasn't. I wouldn't have missed it for the world. The year 2012 sadly marked the last of our regimental reunions. There were no 'Dukes' left alive but me. I was the last one standing. In the final years we'd still had one or two of the 'originals', but then I was the sole survivor.

I'm very proud of the fact that I'd managed to keep the reunions going since 1947. I'd even organized it from Spain and went back each year without fail. We'd held it in various places over the decades, some not as good as others, and finished at a nice hotel in Leeds. As everyone aged, it got to the stage where an evening event wasn't as easy for people to travel so we changed it to a lunchtime affair. I was sad to see it end, as I'd enjoyed catching up with everyone and talking about old times, as well as about new times. So much had happened in everybody's lives since it began. With everyone gone, there'd be no one to reminisce with about the cold nights in our tents in north Cornwall, the long voyage to India or the pet pig mascot that was cooked for supper. No one else would remember Philip Thornton and no one would ever again call me 'Tommy' Moore.

I have never lost my love of vehicles and was still driving up to the age of ninety-eight without any problems. I just had to get my eyesight tested every now and again and let the authorities know I was still alive. Other than that I was in fine fettle, apart from arthritic wrists that were so bad for a while that I couldn't manage buttons and had to wear jogging bottoms

– not my style at all. A couple of painkillers and some anti-inflammatory cream kept the worst of it at bay.

There was nothing wrong with my sight either, as long as I wore my spectacles, but I'd become so hard of hearing that if I didn't have my aids in I'd have been as deaf as my father. I sometimes wondered if my deafness was inherited, but more likely it was working with the crushers and explosives in the quarry that caused it. Being deaf made me much more sympathetic to what it must have been like for Father all those years, and how difficult it must have been to live in a near silent world. As he was, I am blessed by being surrounded by people who are patient and kind and who will take the time to speak loudly and clearly. Unlike him, I have access to the kinds of hearing aids and associated gizmos he could only dream of – all thanks to the wonderful NHS.

None of these minor health issues prevented me from driving, though, and I bought myself what I realized would probably be my last car – a Skoda Yeti (sadly, not in red) – and kept renewing my licence. I still have one to this day. I did think it a bit unfair when I was done for speeding twice – I was caught doing 38 mph in a 30 mph limit each time. I was tempted to plead that I should be exempt on the grounds that when I'd first learned to drive in the 1930s there was no driving test and no speed limits, but Hannah persuaded me otherwise. And quite right too. I took the medicine. I was given points on my licence the first time but opted for a speed-awareness course the second. You're never too old to learn.

I also went on a few holidays with the family, twice to Portugal with each of the girls, joining them for the second week of their two-week breaks and, in 2014, I took the girls to Cape Town, a place I'd always wanted to revisit after my happy days there in 1941. That wasn't the same at all, however, and the atmosphere of the city was changed. Despite the end of apartheid, it felt much more oppressive because of segregation of a different kind. The rich lived in compounds and the poor in shantytowns. Seventy-odd years after my first trip I spotted only a few vehicles of interest this time and the dear old Studebaker Champion was long gone. We visited the prison at Robben Island in Table Bay, a former leper colony and quarantine station where Nelson Mandela – a man I much admired and who later became president of South Africa – was imprisoned for eighteen of the twenty-seven years he spent behind bars. I also finally made it to the top of Table Mountain, which I'd imagined since seeing it in 1941 was as level as a tennis court, but which proved to be far from it. The rocky surface reminded me of the top of the Malham Cove escarpment not far from Keighley. I couldn't help but be a little disappointed. Sometimes, perhaps, a place is better left to the imagination.

More recently I went to Yorkshire with Hannah and her family to show the 'foreigners' where I grew up. It was the first time I'd been back in years. There were no friends or relatives left to visit as Brian Booth was dead and dear Charlie Dinsdale, of Laycock's tannery, had died in his sixties. I'd lost touch with Walter Mitchell from Cark Road years before and everyone else was gone. Club Nook was still there, although no longer called that, and the street was unrecognizable. My parents' bungalow in Carr Lane had also survived but around it had sprung up houses of every era since. The war memorial Grandfather Thomas built still sits proudly in the main square and many of the buildings he was responsible for bear enduring testament to the quality of his work. These include several mills, the Town Hall, the Jubilee Tower, several schools and the Star Hotel. They still form the fabric and history of the town but, all around them, Keighley has changed quite a bit since my day and I doubt my grandfather would recognize it.

Before we left, we visited the grave of my parents and grandparents where I quietly paid my respects, probably for the last time. The memorial to the German POW is still there, a few feet away, bearing testament to another time and a previous pandemic. The cemetery was just as I remembered it, but everything else felt different. I suppose after so many years, things do change, but I decided on my last visit that I didn't want to see it changed any more. I wanted to remember it just as it was.

21.

'I think one's feelings waste themselves in words;
they ought all to be distilled into actions which bring results.'

Florence Nightingale (1820–1910)

The normally teeming streets of London were empty
after the Covid-19 lockdown in March 2020.

LIKE ALL FAMILIES, over the years we have lived through several events that have required medical attention of some sort. There were the births of our girls, Lucy's childhood swimming accident, my temporal cellulitis, the arrival of all four grandchildren, my knee operations, Pamela's long-term care, and regular trips to A&E for Lucy's rugby-playing boys. It was all part and parcel of normal life and – every time we've needed it – the National Health Service that was born twenty-eight years after me was there to help us through.

The first two decades of the new millennium had seen a sharp rise in our various needs for care and in recent years we have called upon the emergency services more than ever before. The first major incident was with my granddaughter Georgia who, as a toddler, had a sudden seizure in which she stopped breathing. I was reading in my room and didn't hear a thing as Colin, who was home with Georgia while Hannah drove Benjie to a local tennis tournament, dialled 999. Hannah came rushing home, which is when I finally heard the commotion. I came out of my room to see Colin hurrying out of the house with my limp granddaughter in his arms, followed closely by a paramedic. She gave us all quite a scare. Fortunately, it was a one-off event and she made a full recovery but, for one terrible moment, I think we all feared the outcome.

CAPTAIN SIR TOM MOORE

Then in about 2017 I developed a dry, sore spot on the top of my head that wouldn't go away. I went to the GP who told me to put some Vaseline on it but it got worse and worse until I had quite a big lump there. It was one of those things that I meant to mention next time I went to the doctor but, as I rarely did and wasn't on any regular medication or in need of a check-up, I didn't get the chance.

A year later, it was Colin's turn to need an ambulance. It was the night before the village summer fête, which Hannah and Colin had agreed to hold in the grounds of the Old Rectory ever since we moved here. Hundreds of people were about to turn up on the doorstep and Hannah was in full organizational mode when Benjie came running to find her and tell her that Colin was in enormous pain and couldn't get out of bed. Hannah took one look at her husband and dialled 999 and the paramedics arrived very quickly. She quickly arranged for Georgia to stay with a friend before accompanying Colin to hospital, along with Benjie, leaving me home alone to greet the stalwart ladies of the village who were organizing the fête the following morning. There was never the suggestion that it should be cancelled. As I've said before, our word is our bond.

The doctors discovered that Colin had a gangrenous gall-bladder that needed to be removed, but he was too unwell for surgery so they had to stabilize him first. It was touch and go for a while and we genuinely thought we were going to lose him. He stopped breathing on several occasions and at one point – with Benjie and Hannah by his side – they thought he had died. He spent several weeks in hospital after his surgery while I held the fort at home and then he came home to recover. Incredibly, he appears to be none the worse for wear.

We'd only just recovered from that drama when I had the

silly fall that was to change my life. It was the winter of 2018 and I was in the kitchen emptying the dishwasher when I somehow got tangled up in my own size 11 feet. I fell over and crashed down on my right hip, hitting my head so hard on the dishwasher that I permanently dented the metal door. It was too painful to move and I couldn't get up. Nor could I breathe very well, which I put down to shock. Colin and Benjie were home, thankfully, but Hannah was in London on business. They sent for an ambulance as I lay there in excruciating pain and Benjie rang Hannah who dropped everything and came straight home.

By the time I reached Bedford Hospital all I wanted was something to ease the pain. As with every hospital, however, they first had to know my name, address and date of birth, bearing in mind that my date of birth always sparks a lengthy conversation in which people can't believe I was born in 1920. As is right and proper, nobody gets any treatment until they know those details, but it was frustrating to hear another astonished discussion about my age when I was in so much pain. The nurses kindly helped me into a hospital gown and I was sent for an X-ray to decide what the problem was, then they left me on my own for a bit while they decided how to treat the hip fracture that they'd discovered.

It soon became apparent that there was something wrong because I still couldn't catch my breath and the pain in my chest was intense. As I lay waiting for them to knock me out with some anaesthesia, I was told that they couldn't start dealing with my hip until my 'other problem' had been sorted. I wasn't aware of what the other problem was until two doctors came to stick a tube and a drain into my side, behind my ribs. Apparently I'd broken one of my ribs and it had punctured a lung. That procedure was, without doubt, the most painful thing I have ever had to endure, made worse by the fact that the first attempt wasn't successful so they had to do it again. I just wanted it to end.

I can't recall much after that but I felt poorly – probably the most poorly I have ever been in my life. I vaguely remember that Hannah arrived, took one look at me and immediately summoned the doctors. 'My father shouldn't look like this!' she told them, her voice shrill. 'He shouldn't be all puffed up. Something is very wrong.' It was a clever junior doctor who eventually diagnosed subcutaneous emphysema, which is what happens when the oxygen I was being pumped with somehow got into the cavities between my lung and my connective tissue and was filling my skin cells with air. I was blowing up like a balloon and the subsequent swelling had already closed my eyes and was slowly closing my throat. I have seen the photos Hannah took of me that day and I can't even recognize myself. I looked a mess. Without doubt, that doctor saved my life.

But I was to remain in hospital for over two months. My medical team had to stabilize me and wait for my lung to recover before they could risk operating on my hip. When I was finally well enough, they performed a part hip replacement and returned me to the ward where, once again, I couldn't fault the nurses. They were all fine, good girls who took care of me perfectly. I never once thought that I might not recover from my fall and I was very anxious to get home – the sooner the better – because my special airbed was horrid and uncomfortable and the nurses kept having to move and turn me every day, which was an extremely painful operation.

From the moment I arrived at the hospital on the night of my fall, I made it clear to the staff that I wanted a 'DNR' notice on my notes, which stands for Do Not Resuscitate. One of my doctors spotted this during my recovery and asked me, 'Why did you ask for this, Tom?'

It was kind of him to enquire but I told him, 'Why are you asking that? I am ninety-eight years old and I've had a good life. You should be agreeing with me! When you've gone, you've gone. I don't want to be resuscitated and end up in a worse state.' My philosophy is and always has been that one day my time will come – we all know that it's going to happen. Some people can't bear the thought of death, but I draw strength from it. It is the certainty of death that makes me so convinced that tomorrow will be a good day. Enjoy what you have today and don't be miserable about it.

After what felt like a very long time, I was finally released from hospital and sent to a recovery unit, where I was put on a ward with three other people. I wasn't unhappy about this and the staff were equally kind as they started my slow rehabilitation. To begin with, I could only take a few steps with a walker – just – and I couldn't climb stairs. They were very kind and helped me with walking, but it was their job to make me do my exercises every day even if I didn't feel like it. They also made me walk to another room for my meals, which often seemed a very long way and wasn't – if I'm honest – always worth it. I was in there for about a month and, with their patience and my diligence, everyone saw a big improvement. A team of occupational therapists visited our home in advance of me being discharged and, noting that my bedroom was upstairs and my lounge down-stairs, suggested I live downstairs permanently. Stubborn as a mule, and knowing what a palaver it would be to adapt a bathroom for me, I resisted, so we had stair lifts installed instead – temporarily, I hoped.

When all the necessary adaptions were completed, I was allowed home at last and back to my own big, comfy bed, which was such a delight. And it was there that I set myself the task of making a full and complete recovery. One of the first things I did was go online and order myself a little step machine that I could operate whilst sitting in my armchair. This promised to improve my muscle strength and boost my circulation, but I found it too hard for my leg, especially as I had a nasty bedsore on my heel from my time in hospital. Annoyingly, this became infected and gave me cellulitis, which only made my leg and hip very much weaker. Both have sadly never recovered and my mobility has been dramatically reduced. I was very frustrated and disappointed by this because there were so many things I used to do but could no longer accomplish. Even walking was still a struggle and could only be achieved painfully slowly and with a walker. Up until my fall, I'd been virtually running around the place and was fully occupied outside with the garden, in between driving to the shops, visiting the family or going on outings.

I had a perfectly good car that I couldn't now drive (and reluctantly had to sell). I had a ride-on mower that I knew more about than anyone else, and I couldn't even make it to the garage where it was parked. I hated being a burden on Hannah and Colin, so Sheila and Brian, a lovely couple from the village who help us out around the house, agreed to drive me to the doctors' surgery each time I needed to go, and a gardener was hired in my place, although Colin and the capable Benjie took on much of my outdoor workload. As time went on and I watched them from my room doing all the jobs that I used to do, I came to the unhappy realization that I could probably never do some of those things again. That was the hardest thing for me to accept after a lifetime of activity, but that was how it was. If I hadn't fallen I'd have been fine for much longer, but I did fall and that was that.

I refused to give up, however, and started thinking about buying a running machine. I also decided to make an appointment with a specialist to find out what they could do to improve my leg. It doesn't hurt me much in the day but when I roll over at night the pain keeps me awake. The physiotherapists gave me all sorts of exercises to do, along with tips about various sleeping positions and pillows between my knees, but nothing helped. I'm not done yet, though. I've got to learn to be persistent and do more jobs in the garden. I just can't manage it yet.

Because my bedsore was taking time to heal I had to visit the GP's surgery every week to have it looked at and get the dressing changed. That's where I became friendly with the nurses and used to take them my favourite Terry's Chocolate Oranges. It was Clare, one of the nurses, who spotted the sore lump on my head during one visit and asked a doctor to take a look at it. He seemed concerned and sent me to see a dermatologist who diagnosed skin cancer, probably triggered by my time in the tropics. I pointed out that sunscreen hadn't been invented when I was in the searing heat of India and Burma. I went to the hospital to have the cancerous lump removed, which was done while I was awake and under local anaesthetic. The doctor cut it out with something that sounded like a dentist's drill and then he scraped any remaining cancer from my skull. I can't say it was any more pleasant than it sounds. When they were done, the nurses put a huge dressing on it and sent me home.

I thought that would be the end of it, but the sore spot wouldn't heal. It was a bit of a mess. Once a month I had to go back to the hospital and twice weekly I had to return to the surgery and have the dressing changed, which I didn't mind so much because it meant I was able to see Clare and the other lovely nurses. Just as I had in Pamela's dementia unit, I found out all about their home lives and learned how busy they all were with husbands and children – so much so I couldn't imagine how they found the time to nurse. Still, my head wouldn't heal, and by then I had a huge medical file with all sorts of photographs and instructions from so many different people, all of them lovely, but none of them quite sure what to do. In the end they decided to operate on my head again and went to great lengths to tell me exactly what the surgery would involve. I went to hospital on the date I'd been given with my overnight bag but soon after the anaesthetist came to prepare me, a different surgeon came, looked at my head and said, 'We're going to leave it as it is, Mr Moore. Go home.' I think my age was a factor that time, although I have to say that – throughout my care – I never once got the sense that anyone was going to give up on me because I was so old. On the contrary. It was me, not them, who insisted on the Do Not Resuscitate sign.

Week on week, my head began to improve a little but it was a slow and frustrating process and meant that when I went outside I had to wear a hat. By the beginning of 2020, I was still seeing the nurses to have the dressing changed weekly and planning to write to the orthopaedic surgeon about further investigations on my hip. I'm not a medical man but I was convinced that there was something wrong – maybe new arthritis or the joint had slipped – because it was better in the beginning. Either way, I was determined to find out.

Then, something happened that none of us could have foreseen: the Covid-19 pandemic, better known as coronavirus.

*

Like my father before me, I read the newspaper from cover to cover every day. Unlike him, I also avidly watch the news on the big-screen television I treated myself to (with a special Bluetooth gizmo that beams the sound straight to my hearing aids so I don't blast out the whole house). Because of my addiction to the news, I was probably one of the first in the family to become aware of the coronavirus scare that had started in China. My immediate thought was that it was worrying but that we would get through this, as human beings always do.

The 1918 Spanish flu, the unusually deadly global influenza virus that lasted two years and only ended the year I was born, infected as many as 500 million people and killed up to 5 per cent of the world's population – most of them young adults. To have this tragedy so soon after the devastation of the First World War must have been especially cruel. Women who had lost their husbands in the trenches then lost some or all of their children soon afterwards. Almost an entire generation had been wiped out in a matter of years. It finally died away and scientists believe that it may have mutated to a less lethal strain. I was too small to remember any of this, although I do recall people in Keighley who'd been affected twice over, first by the war and then by the flu. There was still a workhouse when I was growing up and it housed many of those families who'd lost a breadwinner to war or disease.

During my long lifetime, the world has gone on to survive all kinds of diseases and epidemics – polio, tuberculosis, smallpox, HIV/AIDS, typhoid, Hong Kong flu, Ebola, bird flu, SARS. Then there were dreadful things like thalidomide, a drug given to pregnant women for morning sickness in the 1950s that ended up deforming their babies. That was terrible and I knew a lot of families who were affected in Keighley, and some in Manchester too. It was quite widespread and such a shame, because modern medicine is an incredible thing and these drugs are created to help people and they do, but sometimes they have devastating side effects.

Each time another epidemic happens, there's widespread panic, but when you've lived to 100 you come to appreciate that nothing is new. When people die it is all very worrying and sad, of course, but we do get through it and I sometimes think that the media could be a bit less pessimistic. I'm probably being too simplistic, but I believe there are always two ways of looking at things: they could draw us a graph of how bad things are, or they could draw us a graph of how things are improving. Instead of giving the percentage of people affected and dying, why not give the percentage of those who've had it and survived? And how many of those who did die would have died naturally anyway? As long as good old common sense is employed, then nobody needs to panic. As a race, we've gone through these kinds of scares before and lived through them all, and I've always believed that we'll get through this too.

Even though there were reports of people dying all around the world and the numbers were rising, I don't think any of us thought that it would get to the point where Boris Johnson (my twenty-fifth prime minister), would declare on 23 March that Britain was to go into a full lockdown, the strictest set of restrictions on British life in living memory. The government message was: *Stay at Home. Protect our NHS. Save Lives.* Declaring that the coronavirus was 'an invisible killer' and the 'biggest threat this country has faced for decades', Mr Johnson called for 'a huge national effort' to halt the virus because otherwise, 'no health service in the world could possibly cope.'

All except key workers were ordered to stay at home unless for extremely limited reasons, and all pubs, restaurants, churches and non-essential shops were ordered to close their doors. Only one hour of exercise a day was allowed beyond homes or gardens, and friends or residents of different households were forbidden from socializing, with a ban on more than two people meeting in public. Weddings and christenings were also banned, along with social gatherings of any description except for small groups at funerals that were, naturally, permitted. 'No prime minister wants to enact measures like this,' Boris concluded, looking genuinely contrite. 'I know the damage that this disruption will do to people's lives, businesses and jobs . . . The way ahead is hard and it is still true that many lives will sadly be lost.' He couldn't have known that, within weeks, he himself would be in intensive care fighting for his own life.

I knew that if Pamela had still been alive she would have been extremely frightened by this public announcement – as many were. It might even have tipped her over the edge. My worry was that healthy younger people were also very afraid, and I'm still concerned about how this surreal period might impact long-term on the next generation. Even before Covid-19 began I was already critical about teenagers not spending enough time outside in nature, looking up not down, and I feared that the after-effects of lockdown would only make them even more introspective. To my mind, children should be out of doors in the fresh air playing, walking, running about and keeping active – just as I was when I was walking the moors with Billy, cycling to Bradford, or going all the way to the Isle of Man as a lad. It didn't do me any harm.

And the older generation was also affected badly because so many, like me, fell into the 'shielded' category, which meant they were even more isolated and lonely than before. There would be no trips to the shops or a day centre, no cups of tea with friends or lunches out. Even if relatives visited only infrequently, as so often happens when lives are filled with work and children, a visit was still something to look forward to, as was social interaction of any kind. I realized to my eternal gratitude that if I'd remained in Gravesend, I would have been completely alone in the house, miles from my girls with no one to visit, do my shopping or keep my spirits up. That would have been a desperate situation.

One personal and rather selfish disappointment about the lockdown was that the party the family were planning for my 100th birthday on 30 April, five weeks after the national lockdown was put in place, would have to be cancelled. I felt sorry for the girls more than for me, as I knew they'd gone to a lot of trouble. I'd only wanted a small family party to begin with, but it grew like Topsy, and before we knew it there were going to be about sixty people attending, including fourteen members of the Duke of Wellington's Regiment – and they included Major General Sir Evelyn Webb-Carter who'd led us on the battlefield tour of Italy nine years previously. Bill Chandi, the postmaster, was coming with his wife, along with my helpers Sheila and Brian, my hairdresser, several neighbours, two former au pairs for the children who had become part of the family, including the one from Spain, our local nurses and, of course, Lucy and her family along with her parents-in-law Veronica and Chico Teixeira. There was to be champagne, a hog roast, a cake and all kinds of treats. One of these was to be a performance by a singer who specialized in singing songs from the Second World War and would undoubtedly sing me her version of Vera Lynn's 'We'll Meet Again'. It was a shame to be missing all that, but as I told Hannah, 'Don't worry, we'll celebrate it in our own small way.'

Lockdown also meant that I couldn't even go and see my smiling nurses any more. After the gates closed on our world, Hannah took frequent photographs of the top of my head on her phone instead and emailed them to the surgery via the magic of the internet. She then collected new dressings for me and dealt with the wound herself. These are the kinds of daughters I raised. Happily, Clare the nurse rang me once a week to check up on me and ask if I had any questions, and I always made a point of asking her how she and her family were coping and to make sure everyone else there was keeping safe.

What shone out for me with all of this right from the start – as it did for everyone else – is how incredibly selfless all the doctors and nurses, ambulance crews and care workers were being. At a time when 1,000 people a day were dying from the virus, they were putting themselves in danger every hour and in some extreme circumstances for the good of others. They were doing such a marvellous job. I thought the Thursday-night clapping for the carers was a really lovely, positive thing to have come out of the pandemic. Hannah and the children went to the gate every week to applaud the NHS heroes and all front-line workers along with the rest of the village, while I sat safely inside watching it on TV. It was so moving to see people singing from their balconies in Italy, applauding from candlelit rooms in France, or performing live music in Brazil. Then there were all the myriad and beautiful rainbows children and adults created, painted and hung up in windows and on buildings, all inspired by a nurse in east London who made an appeal for rainbow artwork to be shared digitally as a 'sign of hope' for patients and NHS staff across the country.

The spirit of what everyone was doing to pull together reminded me in so many ways of the war. Faced with a common enemy, we were all in this together – comrades in arms – only now the battle was against a virus. And just like the war, I knew that we would win. We always do in this country. It often takes time, but we win. That's what we do.

22.

'If to be feelingly alive to the sufferings
of my fellow creatures is to be a fanatic, I am one.'

William Wilberforce (1759–1833)

The conference centre in east London was converted into the Nightingale Hospital in response to Covid-19.

LOCKDOWN DID NOTHING to diminish my determination to get better, so at the beginning of April 2020 I decided to do some walking. I'd discovered that this was the best exercise because, although I was still constantly aware of my hip and leg and it was sometimes a struggle, it didn't seem to hurt too much when I walked.

I'd given away my little step-up gadget and bought myself a new walker to add to my growing collection. Each of them had pluses and minuses – good seat but too heavy, bad seat but lovely and light – so I gave away the one I liked least. One of these days I'll have to have a word with the designers, because they need to look more carefully at the relationship between the mechanics of these contraptions and the user's needs. If the seat is tilted and made of slippery material, then it tends to slide away from your bottom. And if the walker's too heavy then people with arthritic hands like me can't easily lift them when we turn. It's all a question of engineering, which I happen to know a little bit about. If I could lift one of my legs over it, I'd be sorely tempted to use a Scott Flying Squirrel instead.

All the nurses and physiotherapists who'd seen me since my fall eighteen months earlier had advised me to stay mobile and keep walking, but I didn't need to be told. I just knew; I've been walking all my life. I also stopped asking them how long it would be before my leg would get better because I realized I was never going to get a straight answer. They dared not say, because if they gave me a date and I wasn't better by then I'd be unhappy. No, it was down to me to do whatever I could for myself.

I started by taking my walker and moving up and down my room and then, bit by bit, along the corridor that leads from my room to the front of the house. This was relatively level and not too far, plus there was an alternative route for those who didn't want to get in my way. It wasn't easy to begin with, but I persisted. Then on Sunday, 5 April, less than two weeks after lockdown began, the sun shone beautifully – the first real sunny day of the year.

As I was no longer in charge of preparing the weekly Sunday roast and because the weather was nice, Hannah suggested we have a barbecue in the garden. 'Why don't you bring your walker outside today?' she said. 'I'll keep the dogs out of the way and you can walk up and down the driveway instead. Oh, and don't forget your hat.'

I hadn't been outside for weeks because of the wind and rain, so that sounded like a lovely idea. I put on my Panama hat, carefully shuffled with my walker out of my room, then along the corridor, past the kitchen and out into the sunshine. That was a good day.

Colin was at the table reading the financial pages on his telephone with all the Sunday newspapers spread out in front of him. Benjie was in charge of the barbecue, and Georgia, who was missing the golf for which she'd just won a scholarship to Millfield School, was enlisted to lay the table. It was a normal, happy family day and I was glad to be a part of it and once again so grateful not to be wasting away on my own in Kent.

Taking a pause, I looked along the full length of our 25-metre driveway and steeled myself. I hadn't walked that far since I came out of hospital. Colin looked up from his phone. 'Go on, Tom,' he encouraged. 'You can do it.' So, off I set. Stirling Moss wouldn't have been much impressed with my speed, or my style, but I plodded forward in my own steady way, one step at a time. The heat warmed my aching limbs and it was good to be outside for a change and to hear birdsong. I was really quite chuffed when I reached the end, but then I turned and saw how far it was to get back.

'Keep going, Granddad,' Benjie called as he flipped the burgers.

Colin added, 'Yes, don't stop. Let's see how many you can manage. I tell you what, Hannah and I will give you £1 per lap, so why not see if you can do a hundred by your hundredth birthday.' I laughed then at what I thought was all a bit of a joke. Everyone knew how much difficulty I'd had recently in getting around, and who on earth would give me £100 just for walking up and down my drive?

Nevertheless, on that that first Sunday, I managed one lap – down and back – and earned myself £1. I was tempted to try another lap, but I didn't want to overdo it and I still had to get myself back to my room.

Over a lunch of burgers and chicken, Hannah congratulated me on my effort and suggested that if the weather stayed nice I might try another lap the following day. 'I could ask around locally and see if family and friends might donate,' she said. 'Who knows, if you do enough you might even make £1,000 and give it to a local charity.'

It was a sound idea but as I'd only raised £1 at that point

and there were no guarantees that I'd get a penny more, I didn't think there was much point in discussing it further or considering which charity the money might go to. The main charities I'd supported over the years had been Guide Dogs for the Blind, St John's Ambulance, Battersea Dogs Home and various animal sanctuaries, but in the heat of the Covid-19 pandemic my thoughts naturally turned to the NHS. Privately, I thought that I'd like to give anything I made to them because I'd had such good service over the years and they'd done so well for me and my family recently.

I couldn't get the idea out of my head after that and later on, alone in my room, I decided to take Colin and Hannah up on the challenge. The following day I woke up even earlier than usual with a renewed sense of purpose. I'd figured out that there were twenty-five days to my birthday and thought that if I could manage ten laps a day, building up to it slowly, then I might be able to raise as much as £250. Then the nurses at the local surgery could maybe buy themselves something spoiling like chocolates or wine. Monday dawned fine, so I made my way out to the driveway and set off. To my amazement, and by taking it slowly with a few pit stops, I managed all ten laps. A huge fan of Formula 1, I thought a checkered flag was in order.

Hannah watched me plough up and down in my own slow way and knew me well enough to realize that I was now committed to the idea, so she swung into action. After her years in business and running a company of her own, she knew exactly what to do. She wrote a press release and it was sent out locally. The first to respond was our local MKFM Radio in Milton Keynes, who called us up for a live chat, followed swiftly by Three Counties Radio, who were equally excited.

Believing that people should be able to donate directly to whichever charity we eventually decided upon, Hannah quickly set up a Just Giving page for my efforts. This way, we wouldn't have to sift through any mail (if there was any) and it would take the money side completely out of our hands and deliver it straight to the charity in the simplest way. But now we had to say which charity the money would go to. Since lockdown we'd heard a lot about NHS Charities Together, an umbrella group of some 250 charitable organizations supporting NHS staff, patients and volunteers. They'd recently launched a Covid-19 Urgent Appeal so, together, we chose that because it seemed to fit best with my original intent. The page set up for me that day by one of Hannah's staff said: *Captain Tom Moore's 100th birthday walk for the NHS.* It added: 'Capt. Tom is walking 100 lengths of his garden for NHS Charities Together because our fantastic NHS workers are national heroes.'

Now all we had to do was persuade people to part with their hard-earned cash for a good cause. None of us could have imagined in a million years that Hannah's press release would set an unstoppable ball rolling. Even now, I am at a loss as to how it all happened and so quickly. Within twenty-four hours of my appeal being aired on the radio, we'd started to raise money towards the £1,000 that had seemed like an impossible dream – and I'd only done eleven laps. People told me that there was something about my little walk that captured the hearts of those still in shock at the crisis. With a rising number of deaths and the prospect of months of lockdown, everyone was desperate for good news. Apparently, a ninety-nine-year-old former Army captain who'd fought in Burma, was recovering from a broken hip, and doing his bit for the NHS was just what they needed.

I think if Hannah, especially, had known what the next few months held, she might have thought twice about writing that press release. Not that she regrets the success of what we did for one moment – none of us do – but she is essentially a very private person who already had a thriving business employing ten staff, as well as a house, husband and two children to organize, plus a live-in elderly father recovering from an injury. She had no idea that she was opening Pandora's box. Once the interview requests started to trickle in from other local media, it was Hannah who had to drop everything and answer the calls and emails, before setting a time for each one. The first television station to want to see me was ITV's *News Anglia* who sent a lovely reporter called Rebecca Haworth to chat from a safe distance while Johnny the cameraman filmed us.

That was all quite exciting and we managed all right, I think, and before we knew it the story was aired and we were well past the £1,000 target and heading to £2,000. Hannah was as astonished as I was and said, 'My goodness, do you think we might make £5,000 by the end of the month?' Everyone, including me, looked at her as if she were mad, but the donations and the interview requests kept coming in. One thing that was immediately clear to us all was that this wasn't something I could do alone. Because of my hearing difficulties and the distance reporters had to keep from me, I needed a member of my family to sit alongside and 'translate' each question. Colin was running the company and right in the middle of a major business deal, it wouldn't have been fair to ask the children who were home schooling, and Lucy and her family, self-isolating ninety miles away near Reading, were powerless to help and could only offer encouragement from afar. It could only be Hannah. Just as I had translated for my father at family gatherings nearly a century ago, so my daughter would now be doing the same for me. Still, we thought that there'd surely only be one or two more requests and then we could all get back to normal.

This was probably naive. The calls never stopped coming and the money never stopped rolling in. Within days it reached Hannah's hopes for £5,000, then £10,000, then £15,000. 'My goodness,' I thought, 'might we reach twenty-thousand?' Then it soared past that and kept going up. The kindness and generosity of those who'd donated money astounded me because, as well as giving to the charity, they started sending me birthday cards and gifts via the local post office, where poor Bill, our postmaster, was inundated. By the time I was invited to appear live on *BBC Breakfast* on the morning of Good Friday we'd raised an amazing £35,000. I simply couldn't believe it.

Nor could I believe that I was going to be interviewed by my favourite TV presenter Naga Munchetty, who with Charlie Stayt makes a delightful pair I watch every morning without fail before reading my newspaper. When Naga went on to social media to tell people that I'd be appearing the following morning, Benjie told me that the internet went into overdrive – I think he said 'viral' – so one of Hannah's team had to set me up with my own Twitter page, something I'd never imagined I'd need or want. I even had my very own hashtag: #WalkwithTom. Not that I really understood at the time what that meant, but it seemed to be important. Later that day Hannah told me, 'You're not going to believe this, but you have five thousand followers already!'

I frowned. 'What are they following?'

'You!' she replied, laughing.

'Why on earth would anyone follow me? And where are they?'

'Don't worry,' Hannah replied, 'they're not outside the gate. At least, not yet.'

My appearance on *Breakfast* via a video link seemed to go right enough, with Hannah's help. Naga was delightful and meeting her in person one day was something I decided to add to my bucket list. Kindly, she thanked me for bringing 'so much joy and positivity' to the nation and wanted to know my thoughts on the pandemic. In what was the beginning of a pattern, all those interviewing me seemed to assume that I was possessed with some sort of 100-year-old wisdom simply because I'd lived so long, which doesn't necessarily follow to my way of thinking, but I did my best. When asked if I had any advice for those in lockdown, I said that people should remember that: 'Tomorrow will be a good day. Tomorrow you will maybe find everything will be much better than today, even if today was all right. My today was all right and my tomorrow will certainly be better. That's the way I've always looked at life.'

Before I knew it, I had a new hashtag 'trending' on social media: #TomorrowWillBeAGoodDay, which seemed to spark a fresh feeding frenzy by journalists around the world who knew a good story when they saw one. Dame Kelly Holmes, honorary colonel of the Royal Armoured Corps, sent me a message calling me 'an amazing gentleman' and added, 'You have served your country and you are serving your country now by supporting the NHS.'

The total donated shot up to £50,000 and then – one day after my *Breakfast* appearance – it was £100,000 and before I knew it, £120,000. On Saturday, 13 April, I appeared on *Good Morning Britain* with Piers Morgan and Susanna Reid, where Piers generously announced that he'd donate £10,000 of his own money to my appeal. Within an hour of that interview, a further £60,000 had been pledged and more kept coming. That then doubled within three hours. I was speechless, but I managed to summon up a few words for national television by saying, 'You're all being so kind to give so much money to the NHS. If ever you've been in hospital you know that the staff all arrive bright-eyed and bushy-tailed, but they must be a little bit apprehensive now, entering the lion's den. They don't know what's going to happen but they know that they're in for a pretty tough day. By gum, they're brave.'

Ordinary life at the Old Rectory had changed beyond recognition in just over a week. My previously relaxed schedule of reading, watching TV, napping, eating and walking was largely forgotten, although Hannah was mindful of my age and made sure I always had time for my porridge in the mornings and there were regular breaks throughout the day. As well as all those who were already booked in to speak to me, random reporters and photographers started turning up uninvited at the gate. Some even pushed their way on to our land through the front hedge to take photographs of me walking up and down – something I was still trying to do every day to achieve my target. Desperate, Hannah put out an appeal to her friends in the village for help and before we knew it Nick Knowles of the TV programme *DIY SOS* volunteered a team who arrived to erect us a fence.

The dogs had to be kept in at all times and my daughter and son-in-law – whose business was run from the coach house – had to drop everything to deal with the furore. After talking to the beleaguered postmaster, Hannah released the address of the Marston Moretaine post office for the hundreds of cards and gifts that kept coming every day, so that another team of friends and neighbours who kindly volunteered could sort them there rather than sackloads arriving at the house.

Day after day, we were continually amazed and delighted by the warm response and the incredible generosity of everyone who made or sent cards, gifts or donated money to my page. In total I received more than 6,000 gifts including cakes and knitted goods, hampers of food, whisky, wine, some incredible artwork, poems, statues, teddy bears, handcrafted wooden signs and painted pebbles, a small selection of which was brought to the house every day before being distributed to local hospitals, hospices and care homes or put into storage to be dealt with later. The time, effort and care that people put in to choosing something to send me was incredibly touching. Even to get to the post office and mail something during lockdown was an effort and involved an element of risk.

And every time Hannah told me how much we'd raised I found it impossible to fathom. Only a week or so before, I'd been feeling a little bit sorry for myself sitting in my room looking out on to the lawn that I couldn't mow any more and the empty place in the drive for the perfectly good car I'd eventually had to sell. Now all of a sudden, and only because I'd decided to take a walk, people were reminding me in their thousands how remarkable human nature is and how well we all pull together in times of need. As I told anyone who asked, 'Let's keep it going and I'll keep on walking,' although this was becoming increasingly difficult to do with so many TV crews lined up to interview me on the driveway. Ten laps a day was still my target and about my limit before I needed a little rest. I did twenty in a day on a couple of the quieter days, but ten was better or I'd get too tired.

When it was too busy or raining I had to revert to the treadmill I'd bought so that I could still exercise indoors – something I forgot to tell Hannah about, so the first she knew was when a huge package was delivered. I never got as much pleasure out of the treadmill as through normal walking, however, and couldn't wait until the weather improved or everyone had gone home so I could get back outside. I preferred to be outside even if it was drizzling. Bad weather had never stopped me before.

Over the next few weeks Hannah put her entire life on hold to sit with me through every one of the many, many interviews we did – up to thirty a day – and with people from all around the world. Some were on the telephone to places as far away as Australia and America, all via Hannah's iPhone, and many with a live crew just outside the house, as no one was ever allowed in. Just like I'd had to do with Father, Hannah would lean over and speak loudly into my ear to tell me what each question was, so that I could give my response. The questions were often very similar so, after a while, I got a bit more accustomed to it and knew what to say, although I always tried to add something a little different for each one. What was lovely for me to see was how Hannah's children Benjie and Georgia embraced the whole experience, too, and if reporters ever asked them questions about what this meant to them, they always impressed me with their eloquent replies.

Whenever I was having a nap or didn't feel up to another interview so soon after the previous one, Hannah did them for me, but there were simply too many on several of the busiest days. At one point she burst into tears (which isn't like our Hannah at all) and she begged Colin, 'We need to allow me a few minutes each day to eat something and go to the toilet!' At that point, Colin the accountant immediately stepped in and created the ultimate media schedule on a spreadsheet that got us through the next few weeks. In the end, and again with the help of Nick Knowles, a PR company kindly volunteered to assist Hannah and Colin's own staff who'd had to stop work just to help deal with the onslaught. And thank goodness. I was worried that Hannah and Colin would be overwhelmed, although, at the same time, it was clear something very special was happening.

The phenomenon of 'Captain Tom' continued to grow and grow out of all proportion, and although the donations had started quite slowly, we were beginning to wonder when it would all stop and at what point. I also received so many lovely messages of support from the unlikeliest of people, including the Lord Lieutenant of Bedfordshire, Macmillan Support, and from doctors and nurses all over the world, including Pamela's great nephew – Adam Briki, a paediatrician with the NHS in Surrey. He recorded a short video from his A&E for the man he calls his 'Gruncle' in which he said: 'The nurses at my hospital are all falling for you, Tom, but then you're used to that. Your charm is enduring.' I also did an interview for British Forces Radio, and put out a statement that said: 'It is an honour to help all the NHS heroes who are working so very hard to ensure we stay safe or, if we are ill, to do everything they can to bring us back to full health.' I insisted that I would keep on walking as long as people kept contributing. This may have been a rather wild statement but I was from Yorkshire. I'd said I'd do it and I would. That was the intention anyway, so my legs would have to do the best they could. They were the only pair I'd got.

On Easter Sunday, a week to the day after I began my walk, we heard the sad news that Stirling Moss had died after a long illness. He was ninety years old. As I now had a social media presence (even if I didn't personally know how to use it), I was getting the hang of it and able to express my condolences to the team to put up online: 'I am so sad to hear of the death of Sir Stirling Moss,' I said. 'I followed him all my life – he is a true star and always will be.' And I meant it. That man was a legend and he achieved so much that made him truly worthy of his knighthood. The same day, I was asked to appear on *The Michael Ball Show* on BBC Radio 2. It was his first day back at work after he and his partner Cath had been affected by coronavirus and, as I liked him and the kind of music he played, I was pleased to accept. Michael was very kind and we had a great connection and it was he who said that I should be recognized in the next honours list, which made me laugh. 'I wouldn't hold your breath,' I told him.

Appearing on his popular show gave my appeal a massive boost, pushing it to a staggering £250,000. I was running out of words to express my gratitude on behalf of our NHS heroes, so my daughter Lucy kindly stepped in and said, 'I'm so proud of my father; he has inspired so many for such a great cause.' Hannah, who was as amazed as I was, added, 'Shall we raise the bar and try to get half a million pounds for NHS Charities? I think so – let's go!' Piers Morgan tweeted: '*Why stop at £500,000? Let's go for £1 million!*'

People were really getting behind my walk and me, and there was nothing I or anyone could do now but let the public decide where to take this and how far. Boris Johnson had recently come out of hospital after contracting Covid-19, and the comedian Tim Brooke-Taylor had just died of it. The virus and this incredible response to my appeal was far bigger than anything we could control. More and more celebrities and sporting heroes did their bit, too, by posting about me online and sending messages of support. I heard from so many legendary sportsmen and women, including Sir Alex Ferguson, Ian Poulter, Nobby Clarke, Rebecca Adlington and Will Greenwood – all people I'd watched and admired over the years. Then there were the good wishes from the Yorkshire

Regiment, the Armour Centre in Bovington and the British Army, all of which meant a lot to this old soldier. The Officers' Association tweeted: '*We are loving the fighting spirit from former British Army Captain Moore as he continues to raise money for our magnificent NHS.*' My goodness, this would have been something to have told the old boys at one of our regimental reunions, wouldn't it?

Within a day of appearing again on Michael Ball's show the total had risen to £750,000. I couldn't quite believe it and felt so proud and humbled. Back I went on to both breakfast shows on the fourteenth, this time with Louise Minchin and Dan Walker on the BBC, whereupon the Just Giving page crashed because it had too much traffic. And within hours the £1 million target was smashed and rose to £1.3 million as donations were increasing at the astonishing rate of £5,000 a minute.

'I may be walking in my garden to raise money,' I told everybody, feeling quite emotional. 'But this is the British public's contribution. You are all wonderful and what make Great Britain GREAT! Thanks to everyone. We stand united even during the most testing of times.' I meant every word because as I saw it, we had a war on our hands. In my day we service personnel were in khaki and navy, whereas those on the front line were wearing personal protection equipment in terrible circumstances. The money we were raising for them seemed out of this world, but I knew it would give hope to so many people who were finding it very difficult and I believed that this particular army deserved every penny.

With a new hashtag trending of #FeelGoodStory we soon reached £1.5 million and were told that over 100,000 people had donated from around the world. Some had given £1 and others several thousand pounds, but the average donation was

£15, which – at a time of such uncertainty with shops and businesses closed and people facing the possibility of losing their jobs – was all the more special. When we reached £2 million, then £3 million and then £4 million – all on 14 April – I was stunned. 'Never in my wildest imagination did I think this would be possible,' I said. 'The British public have been amazing and it shows how much they respect the NHS and all the NHS volunteer responders.' And to think I thought raising £1,000 would be a stretch. Hannah added: 'No words can express our gratitude to the British public for getting behind Tom and making this into a heartfelt story. And all we want to do is share this gentle man we know with the British nation.'

What I don't think I was ever able to fully express was how much this whole experience did for me, right from the earliest days. It gave me purpose at a time when I'd become a lot less independent than I had been for the preceding ninety-eight years. It also proved that age is no barrier to anything if you set your mind to something. Urged on by the goodwill of the country, I was determined to continue walking until somebody told me to stop.

As the donations poured in – £5 million by the sixteenth and a staggering £8 million two days later, it still felt so surreal. Where was all this money coming from? Why were people being so kind? The staff at Just Giving informed us that there were 90,000 people on my fundraising page at one time, and they were struggling to ensure the site didn't crash again. Dan Walker of *BBC Breakfast* told me: 'You'll be able to build your own hospital soon! This is truly amazing to watch. We may be pants at a few things in the UK, but we love a hero and a good cause.' Ridiculously, I thought, Piers Morgan started an online campaign to have me knighted, but his post with the hashtag #AriseSirTom received 65,000 likes within hours. There were also calls for me to receive 'an honorary upgrade' from Captain, all of which was kind and thoughtful, but I took it with a bucket full of salt. Personally, I still didn't think there was a ha'p'orth of chance of any of that happening, not least because I didn't feel as if I'd earned the right.

I received some more lovely messages from people like Bear Grylls, David Walliams, Tony Adams, Rio Ferdinand, Gary Lineker, Ant and Dec and Glenn Hoddle. One message that caused great excitement in our household was from Lewis Hamilton, my new no. 1 racer (and now Benjie's) since the loss of Stirling Moss, who said: 'What a legend! Captain Tom Moore is a total inspiration. I am blown away by his amazing achievement . . . We could all learn something from you.' High praise indeed from someone who is an even better driver than me. It was another very welcome name to add to my bucket list. As I said to him in reply: 'Thank you, Lewis. I love watching you do your laps. You are a hero of mine. It has been an amazing journey. I am not able to travel as fast as you but, like you, I am overwhelmed by the support of the British public.'

Health Secretary Matt Hancock, who I'm sure had far more important things on his mind, opened the next government Daily Briefing by hailing me as 'an inspiration' and thanking me for what I was doing for the NHS. And then there were all the wonderful spin-offs that we could never have foreseen. Children everywhere, most of them trapped in their own homes, started making birthday cards and sharing them digitally online using the hashtag, #MakeACardforTom. These were in addition to the more than 160,000 real cards sent to me in total, all of which had to be sifted through at the Northampton Sorting Office where I now had my own bay for mail and my own sorting machine. Once sorted the cards were delivered to Bedford School, where Benjie was in the fifth form, which had been closed since lockdown. There, they were displayed on the floor of the Great Hall after the headmaster not only agreed to host them but the school organized a scheme that enlisted children to remove the stamps from all the envelopes and donate them to the Sue Ryder and St John's Hospice charities. The family was also planning to incorporate the cards into a massive recycling effort that would raise money for a local good cause.

When Hannah showed me the photo of Benjie standing in the Great Hall surrounded by a sea of thousands and thousands of cards, I couldn't believe it. Many of them were home-made, and most were specifically designed for a 100-year-old. I couldn't imagine what that must have cost people in time and money – I mean, first of all, you think about buying the card at maybe £2, and then multiply that by 160,000 and then add the cost of the stamps, so when you add up what people have spent in just sending cards it must come to almost half a million pounds on cards alone. Then they have to put on a mask to queue at the post office or post it. We were also swamped with more thoughtful handmade items along with flowers, toys and even a door painted with my image. And I had so many kind offers of things to help me like new walkers, walking sticks and other health aids. I had to issue a statement thanking everyone but asking them to please donate these to a local care home in my name.

I was even more delighted that – inspired by my effort – an entire army of fundraisers sprouted up from nowhere. Many were disabled, on walkers like me, or doing sponsored events for those who were. There were also people in their nineties or even older than me stoically tottering around their gardens, climbing stairs, walking marathons, or doing laps of their local park. Between them they raised half a million pounds for hospices and some of the lesser-known charities that were struggling to cope with the pandemic. The ripple effect of my little walk went on and on and on.

The day before I was due to complete my 100th lap on 16 April we broke all previous fundraising efforts and I earned my first ever entry in the *Guinness World Records* as the biggest individual fundraiser of all time. I mean, imagine that? In the words of my granddaughter, it was 'awesome'! Even though I'd vowed to carry on walking as long as people kept giving, my milestone lap was now a cause for even more media interest, so back came the film crews cluttering up the drive and I completed the final lap of my garden marathon live on *BBC Breakfast* with an honour guard from the 1st Battalion Yorkshire Regiment saluting me as I toddled past. I was delighted to be surrounded by the right kind of people, but as I thanked them I remarked in all honesty that I didn't feel that I deserved all the fuss or was in any way special. I was just a part of everything that was going on.

Michael Ball was one of the many who took part in the live celebrations via the wonders of television and when he announced from his home that he wanted to sing me a song to mark the occasion, I was touched that he chose 'You'll Never Walk Alone', a perfect song for what had happened since I started my walk. Mouthing the words along with him as I watched on a monitor, I couldn't help but join in a bit – which everyone seemed to love – and Michael joked: 'It's a duet in the making!' The fresh publicity caused my Just Giving page to crash again and pushed the total to £12 million. It was all so unbelievable. How could this have snowballed from such a modest goal? The whole family watched the drama unfolding in a state of collective shock. Keeping us grounded, some funny chap at the television programme *Have I Got News For You* tweeted: '*As 99-year-old Captain Tom Moore raises over £12 million for the NHS, the government says if you could raise another £338 million by the end of the week that would be great.*'

I knew I had to keep walking and I did it with great pleasure and without any hardship because the funds just got better and better – £15 million, then £20 million and rising. I tried to imagine what that amount would look like in £1 coins, but I couldn't fathom it. The interest in what we were doing with my walk didn't just come from this country, but seemed to have an impact around the world. I had messages from all over and almost 200 reporters wanting a word with me. A grandmother called Granny Zina in Russia was knitting me some socks, a US veteran was walking miles for charity, and I was national news in New Zealand, Israel, Turkey, Argentina, Australia, Canada, Europe and Japan.

Wherever the story went it seemed to inspire good things and raise spirits, and that was perhaps the thing that delighted me the most. If I was able to brighten just one person's day then it was all worthwhile.

23.

*'May you live to be 100 and may the
last voice you hear be mine.'*

Frank Sinatra (1915–1998)

Six-times world champion, Lewis Hamilton,
made this lifetime Formula 1 fan very happy
when he wished me a happy 100th.

WITH OUR TOTAL A WHOPPING £28 million and the donations still pouring in at an extraordinary rate as my 100th
birthday approached – the one I'd said to Hannah that we'd
celebrate in our own quiet way – it was clear that it was going
to be far from that. Long forgotten was the hog roast and the
cake that someone in the village was going to make. There
would be no WWII sing-along with friends and family after all,
and the latterday members of the 'Dukes' were no longer
coming from far and wide. Instead, there was to be another day
of back-to-back interviews with a few surprises thrown in.

Before we even got to that special day, I had one of the
biggest surprises of all when not long after my 100th lap,
Michael Ball, whose BBC Radio 2 programme I'd appeared
on right at the start and a few times since, came up with a
crazy idea. After our little sing-song together on breakfast TV,
he couldn't stop thinking about the idea of us doing a duet.
Having spoken to his record company, Decca, and to his
producer, Nick Patrick, he asked me to collaborate with him
and the NHS Voices of Care choir on a rush release of 'You'll
Never Walk Alone'. I didn't need much persuading to record
a timely and poignant old Rodgers and Hammerstein showtime
number that had been written when I was still in my early
twenties. And the chance to sing alongside my new friend

Michael and some of our brave healthcare workers made it even more appealing, although I did point out that my ninety-nine-year old vocal cords weren't a patch on theirs. After all, it had been over ninety years since I'd been a soloist in the Keighley church choir.

My reprise as a songster, recorded by Hannah and Benjie on a smartphone as I sat in my armchair, didn't amount to much at all. In the final recording I really just half sang, half spoke the words in the background while the professionals – each of them recording their own individual part at home and with a bit of technical wizardry – mercifully drowned me out. As Michael said of my singing, 'I think some of that was in the key of Q!' In fact, I wasn't meant to sing at all, but – disobeying orders – I couldn't help myself. At one point an exasperated Hannah said, 'I can't stop him singing!' so, laughing, everyone decided to go with the flow.

What they managed to do with my little contribution was incredible and, when they'd finished, it sounded grand. How they managed to get all their parts recorded and across to Decca in fourteen hours in order to qualify for the midweek chart was even more amazing. They can't have slept. Zoe Ball, the Radio 1 DJ, played it first on her breakfast show early the following morning, 17 April, and by the time the song finished she was in tears. So, apparently, was the nation. It certainly seemed to strike a chord because within two days our 99p song had sold over 80,000 copies and gone straight to number one in the UK pop charts that Sunday. At the last count, sales were well over 100,000 copies. I'm not sure how much our record sales added to the NHS coffers, but it must have been something substantial as amazingly enough ours was the fastest selling single of 2020.

Interestingly, this wasn't the first time 'You'll Never Walk

Alone' topped the charts. This song had a great pedigree and continued to touch a nerve with people. Originally written for the musical *Carousel* in 1945, it was a number one hit in 1963 for Gerry and the Pacemakers and again in 1985 as a charity single for the victims of the Bradford City football stadium fire. Now it was our turn, which just went to show that you never do walk alone.

I have to say being number one really tickled me and made me think that even my old choirmaster might have been proud. Not to mention my grandchildren, who couldn't believe I was a chart-topper and had knocked a song they liked called 'Blinding Lights' by a Canadian singer called The Weeknd [sic] off the top spot. Since the charts first came into being I'd sometimes wondered what it must feel like to top them and to hear your own song on the wireless. Now I knew. I'm here to tell you that to follow in the footsteps of favourites of mine like Frank Sinatra feels marvellous. All this was lovely for the choir and for Michael, too, who'd never had a number one before, although he was at pains to say, 'This is one of the proudest moments of my career, but it's not about me, it's about Captain Tom.'

I had so many people all wishing me well that day, including Prime Minister Boris Johnson, who rang in the middle of all the fuss. Colin answered the phone and asked him to call back, which – astonishingly – he did. The one message that meant the most was from Prince William who, sitting next to Kate on a video call, told the BBC: 'He's been around a long time, knows everything, and it's wonderful that everyone's been inspired by his story and his determination. He's a one-man fundraising machine. God knows what the final total will be but good on him; I hope he keeps going.' With such a royal endorsement, how could I not?

Nothing surprised me any more, though, except perhaps the arrival of a chap from the *Guinness World Records* with not one but two framed certificates. I was now officially not only a record-breaking fundraiser, but also the oldest artist ever to have a UK number-one single. Sir Tom Jones, whose record I had beaten, graciously sent me a message of congratulations. What an adventure this was turning out to be. I don't think I'd ever felt more grateful, or more alive. And that was quite something to be able to say at my age.

My big day dawned and yet it felt like any other to begin with. I had never once considered that I would get to this age. Even though I've always been an optimist, I never imagined when Lucy was born that I was only halfway through my life. And by the time I was eighty I'd prepared myself mentally for the probability that I only had a few years left. Mother died at seventy-seven, Freda at eighty and my father at eighty-five, so I thought I'd do well if I lived any longer than that. I would never have believed that I'd still be around, and with most of my marbles, at 100.

And I had to keep going now. As Hannah kept telling me through all of this, 'You realize you are responsible for the happiness of the nation? You can't die yet. If anything happened to Captain Tom there would be a day of national mourning.' It was sweet of her to say so and I told her I planned to stick around for a bit longer.

In the quiet of my room that morning I got myself showered, shaved and dressed, putting on the tidy new regimental blazer that had been made for me by Souster & Hicks, our local tailors. I think that impressed Colin almost more than anything else I received, as the company had a branch in Savile Row. Above the gold-embroidered regimental crest sewn on to the pocket were pinned my three medals – the Burma Star, the 1939–45 Medal and the War Medal – nicely set off by my regimental tie. I'd never got around to applying for the Defence Medal I'd also qualified for, but I planned on doing that soon. Even without it, this was a day that required the lot.

Hannah, Colin, Benjie and Georgia were all waiting to greet me that morning when I shuffled into the kitchen for my porridge. 'How does it feel, Granddad?' Benjie asked.

'I don't know yet,' I replied, adding with a wry smile, 'but I suppose it's not everybody that makes it to a hundred.'

There were a few moments to open their cards and gifts and take congratulatory calls from Lucy and her family before I would play my part in a story that had become about so much more than just me. The now familiar and welcome media circus was waiting to share my day with those for whom my little walk had taken on great meaning. I took a deep breath and stepped outside into the chilly morning.

To describe all that happened over the next twelve or so hours would be impossible, but it was a wonderful day full of good wishes, kindness and plenty of cake, including a clever one with a tank and another with a Spitfire (though, sorry to say, neither was quite as good as Mother's Victoria sponge).

My first appointment was with *BBC Breakfast*, presented by the ever lovely Naga who asked me what it felt like to be 100. I said in all honesty that it hardly felt any different, adding, 'I don't know what you're meant to feel like when you get to be a hundred. I've never been a hundred before.' I was then shown footage of a whole host of people wishing me a happy day – everyone from local villagers to members of my own family. My neighbours put up banners and rang the church bells in my honour and our lady vicar thanked me for putting Marston Moretaine on the map and forever associating it with such a positive campaign. The children of key workers at schools all over the country made me cards and wrote poems, and one little lad at the local primary school said how 'cool' it was to live in the same village. Somebody else created an impressive sand sculpture on a beach in Jersey and there was a montage of the talented street art around the country in my honour.

My granddaughter Georgia, filmed standing in a sea of cards at Bedford School, said: 'I've lived with Captain Tom all my life and he's always been there for us. He's made us think that you can be whatever you want to be. It doesn't matter what other people think. It only matters what you think of yourself.' Now that is a dispatch I am proud to have passed on.

There were a hundred questions that day but the one I was probably asked most often was, 'What's the secret?' I usually responded with my little joke that you need to choose your parents and your grandparents. It was a bit of light-hearted nonsense because you obviously can't, and yet I did feel I'd been very fortunate with mine. Eventually, I said it was all about grounding in childhood and maybe inheriting good genes. 'If I knew the secret,' I added, 'I could make a lot of money!'

We were still live on air when the WWII Hurricane and a Spitfire from RAF Coningsby flew in low overhead for my honorary birthday fly-past, the throaty noise of their Rolls-Royce Merlin engines familiar to me from my youth. I was amazed how the pilots were able to pinpoint our house amongst all the others, although I expect they have all sorts of modern gizmos to help. These remarkable aircraft that symbolized so much about the resilience of this country, especially in the eightieth anniversary year of the Battle of Britain and the seventy-fifth of the end of the Second World

War, were a magnificent sight to see. My hand raised in a fist to punch the air as I sat wrapped in a blanket. I was really thrilled as the last time I'd seen those planes in the skies above me would have been in Burma, and in anger. It was so moving to think that they were now flying in peacetime and in honour of the brave pilots who saved us from Nazi rule.

Of the two planes that flew overhead in an echelon formation, dipping their wings in salute on not one but three passes, it was the Hurricane I favoured because they shouldered the greater burden in the early years of the war. It was the sight of three of them flying in low over Keighley just after war was declared in September 1939 that had first brought home the reality of that to me. The Spitfire was small and resilient, like a Jack Russell, and that was the beauty of it because it was fast and could nip in and out. It was a joy to see them both.

My next appointment was on *GMB* with Piers and Susannah, who – like all these lovely presenters I spoke to – were beginning to feel like old friends. They had lots of lovely tributes for me from people like David Jason, Julie Walters, Joanna Lumley and Bear Grylls, to name a few. Piers kindly said that while the country was going through such misery and loss I'd been 'a shining beacon of hope and inspiration' who'd raised morale. I thanked them for their support and said, 'It just shows what a marvellous country we are, made up of so many magnificent people keeping up their spirits however difficult it may be. Because at the end of the day we all know that we're going to win through. It may be difficult and it may take time but we will win through in the end.'

The day only got better. The Lord Lieutenant of Bedfordshire arrived in full regalia to present me with my official birthday card from the Queen, something I will always treasure and which I wasn't certain I'd receive during lockdown.

That really made my day, as I am such a huge fan of Her Majesty. An official spokesman for the royal family also issued a statement wishing me many happy returns. Prime Minister Boris Johnson sent a card and a video message, which was a lovely surprise and not necessary when he was still recovering from coronavirus and had so much to do. In his filmed message he said, 'Captain Tom, I know I speak for the whole country when I say we wish you a very happy one hundredth birthday. Your heroic efforts have lifted the spirits of the entire nation [...]

'You've created a channel to enable millions to say a heart-felt thank-you to the remarkable men and women in our NHS who are doing the most astounding job and whose courage and compassion will be why in the end we will defeat coronavirus. There is a tradition going back some years now where the Prime Minister takes a moment each day to thank someone for their service to others by recognizing them as a point of light. Captain Tom, that is exactly what you are – a point of light in all our lives. Thank you.'

I'd been born when David Lloyd George was the last Liberal Party prime minister of the country. The thought that, twenty-five prime ministers later, the present incumbent of No. 10 would wish me a happy birthday was astounding.

There were numerous other TV and radio interviews, including one with French TV who asked me if I had any special message for the French people. 'Oh yes,' I replied. 'If a *"rosbif"* can do it, then so can you!' Somebody else worked out that, for the distance I'd walked, I'd earned more money than Usain Bolt, which I thought was a hoot. The day went on with all sorts of lovely wishes and then another fly-past, this time by Apache and Wildcat helicopters from the Army Air Corps, so the past and the present was fully represented.

Then there were the phone calls and messages to get through, the first of which was from the United Nations Secretary General António Guterres wishing me happy birthday – now that's not something that happens every day. I also received a filmed message from Tedros Adhanom Ghebreyesus, the Director General of the World Health Organization, who awarded me the prestigious WHO 'Health for All' medal. Then I was shown photographs of a huge billboard at Piccadilly Circus, which read: 'Happy Birthday, Captain Tom Moore. The whole nation celebrates with you', and of the London Palladium where a similar message was put up on the marquee above the door.

This was no ordinary day.

I was truly delighted to be made an honorary member of the England cricket team and the MCC, the news of which was given to me with a special '100 not out' video the team members created, presented by former captain Michael Vaughan. I was also made an honorary member of the Lord's Taverners with a special commemorative bat and tie. Goodness, Father would have been tickled by all that. The McLaren Formula 1 team did much the same and sent me not only their good wishes but also a splendid signed helmet from driver Lando Norris. Then the band of the 1st Yorkshire Regiment put on their red dress uniforms to send me a Zoom rendition of 'Happy Birthday'. Someone else arrived with an Olympic torch for me as the whole family sang 'Happy Birthday Captain, Daddy, Grandpa', and my three-tier Spitfire cake was wheeled forward. The Swingle Singers performed a lockdown and rather jazzy version online, there was a moving video thanks from NHS staff presented by actor James Nesbitt, and so it went on. It was head-spinning stuff.

More locally, I was delighted that Bedford Hospital, where

my life had been saved, was visited by a company from Essex who gave them 100 food hampers to celebrate my birthday, and it was lovely to hear from the Bedford School Orchestra who performed 'The Wellesley', the regimental quick march of the Dukes. I was also thrilled to see the local fire brigade and several of the doctors and nurses from my local surgery standing two metres apart in the garden, including the lovely Clare. Several villagers were there also, including Bill the postmaster, who told me that the Royal Mail had issued a special postmark to pay tribute to my birthday, which would be stamped on all mail during my birthday week. It read: *'Happy Birthday Captain Thomas Moore NHS fundraising hero, 30th April, 2020'*. I was very touched.

It was a day of high emotion, even for me, and I only wished Lucy and her family, including my two clever grandsons, could have been there to celebrate with us. I was moved almost to the point of tears when the Yorkshire Regiment sent Lieutenant Colonel Thomas Miller, Commanding Officer of 1st Yorks, to present me with my missing Defence Medal. It was he who informed me that Sir Mark Carleton-Smith, Chief of the General Staff, had awarded me the title of honorary colonel of the Army Foundation College in Harrogate. That was marvellous as I had always been a proud member of the Duke of Wellington's Regiment, but this really was the icing on the cake. In a public announcement, Lieutenant Colonel Miller said: 'Captain Tom's mature wisdom, no-nonsense attitude and humour in adversity make him an inspirational role model to generations young and old.'

What is it they say – no pressure then? It was indeed a great honour, but 'Colonel' wasn't a title I'd use, unless I was trying to be a bit posh. Everyone knows I'm Captain Tom and I'm more than happy with that.

My final comment to the world that day was one of deep and sincere gratitude to everyone who had wished me well. 'Reaching a hundred is quite something,' I said. 'Reaching a hundred with such interest in me, and such huge generosity from the public is overwhelming. People keep saying what I have done is remarkable; however, it's actually what you have done for me which is remarkable.' Never a truer word was spoken.

When all the news crews had finally gone and I had the driveway back to myself, I took myself for a little walk for old times' sake. By then I was up to about 200 laps and determined to soldier on. Before I'd recorded 'You'll Never Walk Alone' with Michael and the choir I'd only known a few of the words, and never in the right order, but since I'd had to learn them, I took to singing it to myself as I walked up and down. And that's what I did that night, humming to myself and reflecting back on a wonderful day with so many memorable moments that the family and I would always cherish. When I began to tire, I went back to my room for a rest while the family strolled arm in arm to the gate to take part in the weekly and important Clap for Carers.

A little later Hannah woke me from a nap to bring me some momentous news. My Just Giving page, which was closing at midnight on my birthday, had just reached the biggest milestone of all. 'People have donated £30 million!' she said. 'In just twenty-six days.' I could hardly believe my ears. That really was an amount far beyond all our hopes or dreams when we'd started this for a bit of fun during a family barbecue.

It was the perfect end to a perfect day.

Tomorrow will be a good day.

Epilogue

I COULDN'T IMAGINE THAT anything could top my 100th birthday and the money we'd raised, but my country wasn't done with me yet. The campaign started by the media to award me a knighthood – and scoffed at by me – had attracted almost as much attention as my original appeal. A petition for me to be knighted received an astonishing 580,000 signatures, but still I couldn't believe it would ever happen, and nor did I believe I'd earned it.

When I think of all the knights and dames of the realm whom I admire and what they did to earn that highest of honours, there was no comparison: my childhood hero Winston Churchill, my commander-in-chief Bill Slim, Vera Lynn, who had a huge impact on me, as did Stirling Moss. The actress Maggie Smith, Edmund Hillary who climbed Everest, the writer Agatha Christie, the athlete Roger Bannister, and the wildlife campaigner Jane Goodall. These wonderful men and women were honoured for their long, varied and invaluable contributions to society, when all I'd done was walk around my garden. As I said to anyone who asked me if I thought I might be knighted, 'That'll be the day!'

In these extraordinary times I should have known better. The day I didn't believe would happen arrived on the evening of 18 May 2020, when a message from the Prime Minister was delivered. Somewhat ironically, it was a lovely sunny night and we were having another barbecue, just like the one on the day that had started it all. When Hannah opened the letter and told me the news, I shook my head and cried, 'No! That can't be true.' I simply couldn't believe it. How had this happened, when just six weeks earlier no one even knew who I was? Despite my incredulity, I was absolutely thrilled that Her Majesty has decided that poor little me should be knighted. It was the greatest honour and something I could never have anticipated. If only my dear father and mother, Freda, Granny Fanny, Billy and Arthur could have been alive to witness how 'our Tom' had done. I think that even Grandmother Hannah might have been impressed. By gum, the flag would have gone up at Club Nook and never come down.

The request for interviews rolled in again the following morning soon after the official announcement of my knighthood was made and I expressed repeatedly how overcome I was by everything that had happened and from something that had started so small. 'I've been overwhelmed by the gratitude and love from the British public and beyond,' I said. 'Never for one moment could I have imagined I would be awarded such a great honour. I'd like to think Her Majesty the Queen and the Prime Minister and the great British public. I will remain at your service.'

Hannah, who was as emotional as me, added, 'It is simply extraordinary. We never entered into the discussion and couldn't quite believe that it was even a possibility. We are in a golden bubble of joy and are simply thrilled for him. We shall now behave accordingly and call him Sir. We've been practising our curtsey but we're not doing very well, and my husband offered to polish his shoes this morning.'

As a small plane flew overhead and started to write my name in the sky, in one interview I joked that I hoped the Queen wasn't too heavy-handed with the sword as I'd be 'a weak old soul' by the time she got round to me after lockdown. When asked who I might take to the palace with me, I said, 'I suspect a lot of people will want to come. I might have to issue tickets.'

Everyone kept asking me what I'd be drinking to celebrate or what my favourite tipple was but – bearing in mind how many gifts I'd already received – I replied, 'I'm going to keep it a guarded secret or there will be a national shortage if everybody decides to do the same.' In the end, though, I couldn't resist mentioning my fondness for a John Collins back in my India days.

Piers Morgan asked me on live TV what I might say to the Queen but I told him quite bluntly, 'I don't believe you're meant to reveal what the Queen says, Piers, so I shall say thank you very much and the discussion between me and the Queen will have to be kept secret.' That told him.

Once again, all kinds of people lined up to wish me well, including Sir Andrew Strauss, the lovely Michael Ball, the fearless Lewis Hamilton and Sir Ian Botham. Lewis Hamilton told me, 'This is so well deserved for what you have done, bringing together a nation and inspiring so many and helping those that really need it most.' Andrew Strauss said, 'We are without doubt going through extraordinary times as a country and no one encapsulates that willingness to meet the challenge head-on and ensure that something good comes out of this period more than you.'

Sir Ian, who joked that he'd done 'a little bit of walking' since retirement (and raising more than £8 million for cancer charities himself) added, 'We've had a really hard time these last few months with maybe more to come yet, but the one thing that made us get up and turn on the television in the morning was to see how far you'd got and how much you raised. It was an amazing effort and in hard times the country needed somebody like you to inspire them.' Coming from the man who inspired the nation in the 1981 Ashes, that was really something.

Lieutenant Colonel Richard Hall of the Army Foundation College in Harrogate spoke of the inspiration of the older generation on the young and said that they had 1,300 trainees going through basic training who were currently stuck at home. 'Inspired by him, they are taking on all sorts of challenges such as half-marathons and burpee marathons. He's the new Joe Wickes of the nation.' That really chuffed me because I think it is essential that the young generation look ahead and realize that they have an enormous future, as does this country.

As if a knighthood wasn't enough, when my appeal finally closed the total amount that had been donated by 1,519,442 generous people was £32,796,436, which – with £6,173,773 in Gift Aid – came to a magnificent £38.9 million for NHS Charities Together. That floored me. This 100-year-old freshly minted knight of the realm had never been more humbled or more proud. It was incredible to think how my little walk would help transform people's lives and I only wished I could personally thank each and every one of those who gave money to the cause we all so passionately believed in. I couldn't even summon up an image of what that amount might look like in real terms, but I knew it would go to those who needed it most.

Millions had already been handed out to health trusts and hospitals around the country, giving Covid patients access to phones, tablets and Wi-Fi so that they could see and speak to their loved ones who weren't permitted to visit. Staff were provided with walkie-talkies, hydration stations and safe-space 'wobble rooms' for those who were exhausted and distressed to sit quietly and rest after long and difficult shifts. There were 'hero packs' and welfare hubs to provide food and necessary items for those unable to get to a supermarket or who – when they did – found the shelves stripped bare. More money was allocated to fund games, crafts and activities for young people struggling with anxiety, or those most likely to be emotionally and psychologically affected by the pandemic because of their increased isolation.

I was especially pleased about that, as I could only imagine how people like my Pamela – and even my first wife Billie – would have suffered faced with a national panic. One tranche of the money raised helped pay for a new befriending phone line for carers like me to help them feel less alone, which was a marvellous idea. I'd been lucky. I'd had my two girls, as well as friends and neighbours, but for those who had no one the burden of caring alone would have been intolerable. Funds had also been allocated to care homes, hospices and through-out the community for those recovering from the longer-term effects of the virus, and there was a huge sum of money set aside for the legacy of Covid-19 and its impact on the community.

And still the personal tributes never stopped coming. In the space of a few weeks I was awarded a gold Blue Peter badge from the television programme I used to love watching with the girls. I was proud to become the Imperial War Museum's first honorary patron, I was awarded the freedom of the city of Keighley and of the City of London, and received the latter at its first ever virtual ceremony. I had a bus and a train branded in my honour and I was made an honorary graduate of my local Cranfield University.

I wasn't done yet, though. Newly enthused by all these wonderful honours and accolades, I wanted to continue to do whatever I could to help people recover from this pandemic and to harness the wonderful kindness and goodwill of the nation in my name to do even more good.

It was Hannah who first came up with the idea of a Captain Tom Foundation, telling me, 'We want to carry your journey forward. We have a responsibility to create a legacy for all that has happened. We need to think of how you'd like any future money raised in your name to be spent.'

She was right. And it didn't take me long to come up with an answer: 'We need to give hope where it's needed most,' I told her. I was thinking of all the lonely people out there in the world, the residents of the care homes who never had anyone to visit them – like those in the unit where Pamela had lived and died. I was worried about all the anxious people confined to their homes by fear, disability or because they were shielding from the virus, thinking of how lucky I was to be with family, and how badly those with depression or mental health issues like Pamela would be suffering. I wanted to help those facing death, as well as all those who were caring for them, because I'd seen for myself how a little kindness and compassion makes all the difference to people at the end of their lives. It can be as simple as a squeeze of a hand, the patience of someone feeding you, the thoughtfulness of providing a hairbrush or a change of bedclothes. These were the causes closest to my heart, and – I realized – always had been.

I'd grown up witnessing first-hand the isolation my father had known because of his hearing disability. My Uncle Billy's wife Elsie had been crippled not only by her twisted body but also by the social anxiety that ultimately denied her the comfort of family. Billy himself must have suffered psychologically, to the point that he felt he had no option but to take his own life – as did my good friend Brian Booth. In the town where I grew up I knew of those like Emily Matchbox and Freddy Gramophone, constantly threatened with incarceration in a workhouse or lunatic asylum, who had to fend for themselves on the streets. The disabled and lonely of Keighley who'd been injured in the war or in the mills, or by birth defects, illness or old age, had little to look forward to until we set up the club for them. And my sister Freda, old and alone, had only admitted her loneliness and sought the solace of family in her final years.

The Covid-19 pandemic isolated people from every generation, cutting them off from the world and ordering them to remain alone in their homes for weeks and weeks without a soul to visit them. Young children accustomed to playing with their friends, teenagers in fledgling relationships or just starting out at university, the single, divorced and widowed, the reclusive and the elderly, were all trapped and helpless. That kind of forced isolation has a terrible impact on mental health and well-being and is something very close to our hearts. I feel so enormously privileged to have been given this opportunity to help people in the name of all we did together to look to the future and lift the spirits of the nation. And it would be truly amazing to help people who find themselves in a similar situation to my late wife and me.

If I have learned one thing from all that has happened it's that it is never too late to start something new and make a difference, especially if it brings light and life to people around the world. There is a future for everyone and there is always room for a global expansion in kindness. It's so important to have respect and compassion for others and to do the best you can for them, helping them in any way you can instead of trying to put them down. It doesn't take much. Even to give someone a little smile can brighten a day and the smile you get back will brighten yours. I'm sure it will be a challenge to set up and run the foundation, but I have the help and support of so many people, including my family, and I hope that my grandchildren will embrace its ethos and take it forward as part of their legacy too.

The secret to tackling any challenge is to treat it just like my walk. Start off with the first step, which might be a bit hard, but then take another one and another until you think, well, I can do more now, and that's how you keep going. Never give up. Try to build resilience through optimism. It is all in the mind. If you decide that you're going to have a terrible time and you're not going to get through something, then that's what will probably happen. We all go through bad patches, but we do get through them. I couldn't have got through my life if I didn't think things would get better, and they did.

Even now when I am old and my poorly legs don't work and almost everyone I know has died and I can no longer talk to them about so many things, I think of myself as so very fortunate. In fact, I've been fortunate all my life. Yes, there have been unhappy times, but I survived them and I'm still here and, generally speaking, my life has not been an unhappy one. Not many people can say that. The trick is to walk on with hope in your heart, just as the song says.

I've never been afraid of talking about dying, and I know I'm going to die so I feel no fear. It comes to us all. What I am afraid of is not having a good death. I want to drop like a stone and not linger on and on in some home. If ever it looks like I'm going down that path, I've told the girls that I'll do something to speed it up, like a quick nosedive into the moat. Most of all, I'll be very interested to find out if there is a Heaven after all. Granny Fanny certainly thought so and I'd like to believe there is one and that she's still up there, doing a grand job.

I have often thought that when I die all the people I loved the most will be waiting for me. Father will be first, and so proud of the fact that I made it to this age. I'd be very pleased to see him again and hope that he might finally be able to hear me when I tell him, 'It's good to be home.' Then my sweet mother, with Granny Fanny and Arthur, all smiles. And, of course, Pamela, who'd probably say, 'Where have you been, Tom? I've been waiting for you to take me to Marks and Spencer's!'

When I said tomorrow is a good day right at the beginning of this grand adventure, everybody really latched on to that, and that became the message of my walk and of my life. It is also the message of the Captain Tom Foundation, because it sums up what we all want to feel and hope for. If we make it until tomorrow, then that is a good day in itself. So, even if tomorrow is my last day, if all those I loved are waiting for me then that tomorrow will be a good day too.

Acknowledgements

THERE ARE FAR TOO MANY people to thank for making this whole experience possible and I know that I will accidentally leave people out if I attempt to list them all. I hope that this book fully acknowledges all those who donated to my appeal and the many people who have helped me in every possible way since I first set out on my walk.

A few names do deserve special mention, not least my wonderful family – the Ingram-Moores of Hannah, Colin, Benjie and Georgia, as well as the Teixeira family of Lucy, Tom, Thomas and Max, whose love and support have meant so much to me over the years. Hannah, especially, deserves a Distinguished Conduct Medal for sitting with me in interview after interview. I would also like to thank the O'Brien family, the villagers of Marston Moretaine, Carver PR, Gemma Courtney, Adam&EveDDB, the Maytrix team, and all at Bedford School.

My friend Scott Flaving, Volunteer Archivist and Honorary Secretary to the Duke of Wellington's Regiment Museum Trust, proved invaluable in helping me through the myriad military records of my time in the Army, and Eddie Kelly, keeper of the Keighley archives, has been a wealth of information that has corroborated so many of my memories dating back to 1920 and before. David Richardson at the

Commonwealth War Graves Commission, David Willie at the Armour Centre, Bovington, and Lois and Bruce Crompton of the Crompton Collection were also helpful.

Special thanks to My literary agent Bev James and to Rowland White and the team at Michael Joseph publishers for their belief in me and for making this book a reality. And to Wendy Holden, not just for helping me tell my story, but for making the process of doing so such a pleasure. Thank you all.

Picture Permissions

Every effort has been made to trace copyright holders and to obtain their permission for the use of copyright material. The publisher apologizes for any errors or omissions and would be grateful to be notified of any corrections that should be incorporated in future editions of this book.

Integrated pictures
Prologue: Emma Sohl - Capture The Light Photography (Courtesy Captain Sir Tom Moore). **Chapter 1:** Armed Forces Institute of Pathology/National Museum of Health and Medicine, distributed via the Associated Press (Public Domain). **Chapter 2:** Unsure of providence. **Chapter 3:** This image is available from the United States Library of Congress's Prints and Photographs division under the digital ID cph.3a23920. **Chapter 4:** Chronicle/Alamy Stock Photo. **Chapter 5:** Topical Press Agency/Hulton Archive/Getty Images. **Chapter 6:** Herbert Alexander Mason (1903–1964) (Public Domain). **Chapter 7:** This media is available in the holdings of the National Archives and Records Administration, catalogued under the National Archives Identifier (NAID) 306532. (Public Domain). **Chapter 8:** Public Domain. **Chapter 9:** Public Domain. **Chapter 10:** IMW (B5245). **Chapter 11:** This media is available in the holdings

of the National Archives and Records Administration, catalogued under the National Archives Identifier (NAID) 531340. (Public domain) **Chapter 12:** Picture Post/Hulton Archive/Getty Images. **Chapter 13:** This media is available in the holdings of the National Archives and Records Administration, catalogued under the National Archives Identifier (NAID) 535795. (Public Domain). **Chapter 14:** University of Liverpool Faculty of Health & Life Sciences from Liverpool, United Kingdom (Public Domain). **Chapter 15:** PA Images/Alamy Stock Photo. **Chapter 16:** Photo-Quest/Getty Images. **Chapter 17:** NASA (Public Domain). **Chapter 18:** Blank Archives/Getty Images. **Chapter 19:** Sue Ream, photographer (San Francisco, California). **Chapter 20:** Allan Tannenbaum/The LIFE Images Collection via Getty Images/Getty Images. **Chapter 21:** Paul Marriott/Alamy Stock Photo. **Chapter 22:** Reuters. **Chapter 23:** Dan Istitene/Getty Images. **Epilogue:** Pool/Max Mumby/Getty Images

Plate section pictures
Page 1: All courtesy of Captain Sir Tom Moore. **Page 2:** Top left: Providence unknown; top right: The Francis Frith Collection; bottom left: Courtesy of Captain Sir Tom Moore; bottom right: Mr Kevin Seaton, of Shann Lane, Keighley. **Page 3:** All courtesy of Captain Sir Tom Moore. **Page 4:** Top: Budapest Poster Gallery; middle right: Mr Kevin Seaton, of Shann Lane, Keighley; bottom: Tony Doyle image collection. **Page 5:** Top: Providence unknown; middle: Keig collection/Lily Publications & Manx National Heritage; bottom middle: Courtesy of Captain Sir Tom Moore; bottom right: Bradford Museums & Galleries. **Page 6:** all: Courtesy of Captain Sir Tom Moore. **Page 7:** Top left: providence

unknown; top right: IWM (A 6793); middle left: Courtesy of Captain Sir Tom Moore; middle right: Courtesy of Nick Chipchase; bottom left and bottom right: Courtesy of Captain Sir Tom Moore. **Page 8:** Top: Courtesy of the DWR Museum Trustees; middle and bottom: Courtesy of Captain Sir Tom Moore. **Page 9:** Top: providence unknown; middle and bottom: Courtesy of Captain Sir Tom Moore. **Page 10:** Top: IWM (IND 3285); middle right: Courtesy of Captain Sir Tom Moore; bottom left: IWM (IND 3409); bottom right: Australian War Memorial SUK 13085 (Public Domain). **Page 11:** top: IWM (H 16962); middle right: Courtesy of Captain Sir Tom Moore; bottom left; Morgan Sports Car Club. **Page 12:** Top left, top right, bottom left: Courtesy of Captain Sir Tom Moore; bottom right: Courtesy of Rowland White. **Page 13:** top left, top right, middle left, middle right, bottom right: Courtesy of Captain Sir Tom Moore; bottom left: BBC. **Page 14:** top: IWM (OMD 2878); middle, bottom left, bottom right: Courtesy of Captain Sir Tom Moore. **Page 15:** top, middle, bottom left: courtesy of Captain Sir Tom Moore; bottom right: /Emma Sohl - Capture The Light Photography (Courtesy Captain Sir Tom Moore). **Page 16:** Emma Sohl - Capture The Light Photography (Courtesy Captain Sir Tom Moore).

End Paper pictures
Front: Courtesy of Captain Sir Tom Moore; Back: Justin Tallis/AFP/Getty Images

Waterstones End Paper pictures
Page 1: First three courtesy of Captain Sir Tom Moore, bottom image The Francis Frith Collection. Page 2: First three Courtesy Captain Sir Tom Moore, bottom left Bill

Lovelace/Daily Mail/Shutterstock, bottom right: providence uknown. Page 3: All courtesy of Captain Sir Tom Moore. Page 4: First three courtesy of Captain Sir Tom Moore, middle right: Michael Ball/Emma Sohl – Capture The Light Photography (Courtesy Captain Sir Tom Moore); bottom: Chris Jackson/Getty Images.

Index